Highland Homecomings

Family history research, or genealogy, has become one of the world's most popular pastimes. The migratory experience of modernity has spurred a contemporary quest to discover our roots and origins. Meanwhile, the associated practice of 'roots tourism' has become a burgeoning phenomenon.

Highland Homecomings examines the role of place, ancestry and territorial attachment in the context of a modern age characterised by mobility and rootlessness. People of Scottish descent are dispersed throughout the world: Paul Basu explores the journeys they make to the Scottish Highlands and Islands to undertake genealogical research and seek out sites associated with their ancestors. He argues that through these genealogical journeys, individuals are able to construct meaningful self-narratives from the ambiguities of their diasporic migrant histories, and so recover a more secure sense of home and self-identity.

Paul Basu is Lecturer in Anthropology at Sussex University, specialising in cultural heritage, landscape and memory. In addition to numerous articles, his previous publications include *Exhibition Experiments*, edited with Sharon Macdonald.

Highland Homecomings

Genealogy and heritage tourism in the Scottish diaspora

Paul Basu

 Routledge
Taylor & Francis Group

LONDON AND NEW YORK

First published 2007
by Routledge
2 Park Square, Milton Park, Abingdon, Oxon OX14 4RN

Simultaneously published in the USA and Canada
by Routledge
711 Third Avenue, New York, NY 10017

*Routledge is an imprint of the Taylor & Francis Group, an informa
business*

Typeset in Sabon by
Taylor & Francis Books

British Library Cataloguing in Publication Data
A catalogue record for this book is available from the British Library

Library of Congress Cataloging in Publication Data
A catalog record for this book has been requested

ISBN13: 978-1-84472-128-3 (hbk)
ISBN13: 978-1-84472-127-6 (pbk)

Contents

Illustrations

Figures

Tables

Prologue
Other landscapes

> But what of *our own* journeys, the travelings of our (so-called 'ordinary')
> selves . . . ?
>
> Edward S. Casey, *Getting Back into Place*

Diasporic identity is defined by its relationship with a landscape other than
that in which 'it' resides. It is defined by an 'other landscape', an 'elsewhere', which is as much a symbol as a physical territory.

Neil M. Gunn, one of the key figures of the Scottish literary renaissance of
the 1930s and 1940s, whose last novel was entitled *The Other Landscape*,
had a remarkable and subtle understanding of the place-world, its capacity
for holding meaning. In his novels, person and place are intrinsic to one
another, but not in any simplistic conflation of blood and soil. Rather, Gunn
uses his characters to demonstrate how different sensibilities, knowledges and
understandings converge on the same landscape – which implies that, experi-
entially, there in fact is no 'same' landscape. Indeed, apparently conflicting
perspectives exist within single characters such that the experience of place
becomes complicated, plural and prone to constant renegotiation: an ambivalent and sometimes perplexing state approximating reality.

Many of Gunn's novels are set in and around Dunbeath, the crofting
and fishing village where he was born and grew up on the grey coast of
Caithness in the Northern Highlands of Scotland. His books are full of
departures from and returns to place, and there is no doubt that this
reflects his own experience, first, as a child living in a community in which
emigration was almost inevitable for young men and women who wished
to 'make something' of themselves – 'there's nothing for a young fellow
here; nothing at all', counsels a father in one novel to his son who has been
offered an opportunity to go 'out into the world' (Gunn 1976: 221). And,
second, since Gunn himself was sent away from home to live with an elder
sister in Kirkcudbrightshire, in the far south-west of Scotland, aged thir-
teen, returning, it might be argued, only as a kind of tourist in later life.
Actually, it could equally be argued that Gunn never really left Dunbeath:
he certainly dwelt *on* – if not *in* – that place throughout his career. Much

of this book is concerned with such a distinction between dwelling on and in place, between the *idea* of a place and its materiality.

Like most towns and villages in the United Kingdom, Dunbeath has its war memorial. But Dunbeath's memorial brings to mind not only those who lost their lives fighting in the wars of the twentieth century, but also the impact that emigration must have had on this tiny community: both were to sap its vitality and steal away its young. On two sides of the small granite obelisk, of the nineteen young men of Dunbeath listed as having been killed in the First World War, over half belong to Canadian regiments: Neil Gunn's brother, Ben, amongst them. Leaving home for the 'New World', few emigrants expected to return. It is sadly ironic that, in this instance, their expectations were confounded. The village has claimed back its own.

The cry of the curlew and the peewit

Into his 1937 novel, *Highland River*, Gunn weaves an account of a reunion between his brothers, Ben and John, that took place in the trenches of northern France shortly before Ben's death. In the novel, the character, Angus, is based on Ben, and the character, Kenn, is based on John. In the fictionalised account of the meeting, a third character is also present: a second-generation, 'full-bred Canadian' named Gus, a comrade of Angus. Although Canadian-born, Gus is of Scottish Highland descent, his ancestors being natives of Strathnaver in Sutherland, the county bordering Caithness. Whilst Gus has never visited 'the old country', he is nevertheless steeped in its history and lore:

> 'I am a Mackay out of the Mackay country – Strathnaver. I have an ancestor who fought with all the other Mackays – and a few of you – out of the Province of Cat, in the wars of Gustavus Adolphus [his namesake]. Do you know', he said, turning to Kenn, 'that Angus here didn't know what the Province of Cat meant!'
> For an instant the eyes held Kenn, and then the Canadian-born clansman laughed. 'Say, you're not too sure yourself! And you call yourselves Highlanders!' (Gunn 1991: 155)[1]

Gus goes on to say how, after the war, he and Angus intend to visit Scotland, and it will be the Canadian who is going to teach the Highlander about the Highlands: 'When this little affair is over, I'm going back with Angus and, from the highest of the granite peaks of Ben Laoghal, I'm going to show him our ancient heritage' (ibid.). Incognisant of the fact that Angus will be dead within a week, it is Kenn who suggests that there are other kinds of knowledge.

> 'I'll tell you what we'll do', said Kenn quickly. 'I'll make an offer. We may not know much about the history, but we know a lot about the

ground itself. We'll take you up our river and we'll show you all its pools, and we'll poach salmon, and we'll watch the sun rise behind the Orkneys from the top of Morven or Ben Laoghal. How's that?'

'That would be wonderful! Absolutely wonderful! Is it a promise?'

'Yes', said Kenn.

'Why you smiling?' asked Gustavus.

'I was thinking', said Kenn, 'about the first time I ever saw Angus land a salmon. It was at a pool called Achglas'.

'Ach-glas – the grey field', said Gustavus.

'Yes, there is a field below it', Kenn nodded. 'It was once cultivated, too. You can see the broad swathes still. All that's on it now is the cry of the curlew and the peewit'.

'The curlew and the peewit! The words used to make my grand-mother homesick. Hear that, Angus? The cry of the curlew and the peewit. Incantation of the old Druids!' (1991: 156)

For Gus, the old country has become aestheticised and peopled with figures from history books and clan lore, it has become a 'heritage land-scape'. Whereas, for Kenn, the 'ground' is known through direct, phenomenological experience, its human and natural history untaught in the schoolroom, yet encountered and intuited in the landscape itself. But the outsider/insider distinction is also complicated, since it is the Canadian who retains some knowledge of Gaelic and who is thus able to 'read' the placenames in a way that has become obscure to the native. Contrary to the perception which still dominates in the Scottish Highlands and Islands, the perspective of the returning migrant is not necessarily less valid or authentic than local perspectives, it is simply different.

Returning to the source

Christopher Tilley has recently foregrounded the relationship between metaphor, material culture and anthropological discourse (Tilley 1999). Metaphor, he stresses, is fundamental to human comprehension and expression: at its simplest, it is the understanding of one thing in terms of another, a transference of meaning (ibid.: 4–5). Lest this 'metaphorical logic' seem a self-evident characteristic of human cognition, it is worth recalling that it has not always been so apparent – even (or perhaps espe-cially) to anthropologists. Lévi-Strauss's famous dictum that totemic animals might be selected for their metaphorical qualities rather than their culinary ones (1964: 89) only highlights the ethnocentrism of earlier anthropological ideologies which grappled with the 'primitive mind' and deemed it unlikely to engage in such complex thought processes. After all, the notion that certain animals and other components of the phenomenal world (features of the landscape, for instance) might be 'good to think', is something to which we in the 'West' have long put our own primitive minds: we progress, we hope, like pilgrims along life's course, hunters of the elusive salmon of knowledge.

The popular practice of genealogy or family history research, a central theme of this book, is dominated by arboreal metaphors: we speak of the 'family tree' and of having 'roots' (Bouquet 1996; Malkki 1992). The tree has been used as a regenerative symbol and symbol of cosmic order across many cultures for thousands of years and continues to have relevance in our own time (Eliade 1958: 265–330). To be rootless or uprooted is to be unanchored in time and space, to have no purchase on the ground, no way of drawing sustenance from the place in which one finds oneself. The contemporary quest for roots, argues David Lowenthal, is a response to the trauma of displacement associated with migration which has become a 'global commonplace' (1998: 9). 'So many Jews today seek memories of *shtetl* forebears', he writes, 'that East Europeans call them "roots people"' (ibid.: 10). There are, of course, other metaphors through which one might apprehend the connection between person, place and past: fluvial metaphors, for example. Seen from the air, river systems resemble root systems or the branches of trees, and, like trees, they have long been prominent cosmological symbols. But, in the context of genealogy, whereas our familiarity with arboreal metaphors has perhaps dulled their power to 'evoke', the symbol of the river remains alive and provocative.

The quest for roots is a quest for origins: a journey to the 'source'. This book is concerned with journeys made by people of Scottish descent dispersed throughout the world to such sources in the Scottish Highlands and Islands. The individuals who undertake these journeys are often fully aware of the symbolism inherent in their ventures, consciously employing a metaphorical logic to impress upon the enquirer the seriousness of their endeavour. One North American informant, born in Scotland, writes, 'I am not a salmon but like a salmon long at sea I am drawn to where I was born or from whence my kind come'.

Gunn, an adept angler who, no doubt, also found salmon 'good to eat', drew upon the Celtic legend of 'Fionn and the Salmon' to add yet another metaphorical layer to *Highland River*. According to the fable – which invokes both fluvial and arboreal metaphors – it was Fionn who was given the wisdom of all ages when he inadvertently tasted the flesh of the salmon that had fed on the hazel nuts of wisdom, which had fallen from the hazel tree into the pool where for so long the salmon had evaded capture. As a child, the unsuspecting Kenn (he who, years later, will meet his brother Angus on the cratered banks of the Somme) comes face to face with such a salmon as he moodily goes about his chores, fetching water from the village well beside the river. Kenn's hunting instincts are immediately aroused and the boy goes plunging in after it. It is a life-changing moment, a moment, in the words of one commentator, in which Kenn is 'shocked into an awareness of things beyond himself, of things *in* himself which he cannot consciously control' (Burns 1988: 46).

The salmon is a resonant 'root metaphor' in *Highland River*. It fulfils both the 'summarizing' and 'elaborating' characteristics of Sherry Ortner's nomenclature, working both to condense meaning and to expound and explain through analogy (Ortner 1973). Daydreaming at school, Kenn imagines the mysterious migration his salmon has made from the dark depths of some Atlantic abyss to the light and aerated waters of the very river in which it was spawned. 'The salmon', Gunn writes, 'is swimming back to the source of its life' (1991: 30). It provides a model for the older Kenn, who, having survived the abyss of trench warfare (in which, significantly, he is temporarily blinded and therefore also plunged into an abysmal darkness), resolves to make a journey to the source of that same river.

> The simple fact that he had never actually gone to the source of his childhood's river had quietly taken possession of his mind, and by a slowly growing impulsive need had started it on this long, intricate quest of lost times and places, but not for the mere sake of evoking them, or of indulging pleasant or sentimental memories, but of capturing, of isolating, a quality of awareness and delight in order to provide the core of life with warmth and light. (ibid.: 222)

Writing in his autobiographical work, *The Atom of Delight*, it is clear that, for Gunn, both journey and place are more than merely literary devices:

> Our Strath we knew throughout its length – or very nearly. To walk its full length to the river source – always called the Waterhead – was the ultimate adventure and the thought of it inhabited the mind with a peculiar strangeness. Unlike the old lady who did not believe that Jerusalem was on this earth, we believed the Waterhead was – but only just. (Gunn 1993: 15)

It is interesting to note that whereas Gunn does not identify Dunbeath or the Dunbeath Water explicitly in *Highland River*, he does refer to the river's source, Loch Braighe na h'Aibhne, by its real name, suggesting that it is already adequately fabulous. The Holy Land allusion in the above quote is also made in the novel, as is a parallel with the Hindu/Buddhist pilgrimage to the source of the River Ganges: Loch Braighe na h'Aibhne is thus symbolic of the Tibetan Lake Manasarovar, the sacred 'lake of the mind' (Gunn 1991: 210; Snelling 1990). Comparing aqueous cosmogonical symbols in different cultures, Eliade explains that, in their respective traditions, such sites represent the 'world navel' or 'centre' from which the 'tree of life' arises (1958: *passim*). Through a process of metaphorical transference Gunn thus imbues the 'ordinary' landscape at the source of a small Caithness river with such transcendent qualities.

Pilgrimage has been described as combining 'an outward physical journey through concrete space to a geographically-defined centre, with a concomitant inward spiritual quest' (Snelling 1990: 393). Similarly, Kenn's 'intricate quest' to the source of the river occurs at multiple levels and is, among other things, also a psychological journey 'into the source of himself' (Gunn 1991: 52) and a cultural journey 'into the source of his forebears back beyond the dawn of history' (ibid.). These disparate journeys converge on a single source as Kenn discovers both his own continuity with the 'vanished races', whose presence is tangible in the archaeological remains of their settlements and burials along the river's banks, and the apparent emergence of their ancient culture – *his* ancient culture – like the river from the land itself. 'Pict, and Viking too, and Gael; the folk, through immense eras of time; sea and river, moor and loch; the abiding land: of which the departing figure [Kenn] was a silent emanation' (1991: 241). Thus, as Kenn ventures for the first time to the higher reaches of the river – 'the spawning land' (ibid.: 228) – he finds it strangely familiar, 'For he was at home here. He was drawing back into his own. He could feel the pull – as the salmon felt it' (ibid.: 229).

The river of time

Whilst *Highland River* may be read as allegory, it is also a subtly constructed discourse on the mnemonics of landscape. In 1972, shortly before his death, Gunn again wrote of the unedifying nature of the educational system in which he had been raised. In school history lessons the children learnt to devalue their own heritage as they were taught the grand, Anglocentric narratives of British national history. Meanwhile Gunn describes how Dunbeath's past came to impress itself upon his imagination through his experience of the landscape itself.

> Let me stick to Dunbeath and its river which rises near mountains and winds through miles of moorlands; a real Highland river with its salmon and spawning beds, on the way to that spot marked on the map as Picts' Houses. Many a night have I camped amid their ruins and had long thoughts about my ancestors as they came up from the river, moved around the ancient foundations and passed on to the endless moor. To listen to the near silence and then to the silence beyond the distant cry of a curlew . . . to far standing stones or stones in a sun circle. Then in the morning light back to the river, the Falls Pool, the endless variety of pools, with their known spots where the salmon lie, down to the Tulach, the green eminence on which the ancient broch stands. The guard chamber in the wall; which, as a boy, I never failed to scan carefully before entering the courtyard and crossing over to the small entrance in the high wall and coming erect again in the inside chamber, shaped like a slightly crushed beeskep, with a high corbelled roof that made us wonder what 'kept up' the stones, for the chamber in my boyhood was as perfect as when it had first been built. (1972: xiii–xiv)

Mémoire and *histoire* merge as Gunn evokes the same scene in *Highland River*:

> The great wall had tumbled into ruins, but this little room was as it
> had been in the days of Christ. The stone shelving still stuck outward
> and deep in the earth sea shells could be found.
>
> When Kenn and Beel crept in through the little door and stood in
> the gloom, they were vaguely disturbed as if the little door telescoped
> backward into a remoteness that at any moment might come up at
> their elbow.
>
> Neither would care to enter the place alone nor to linger there. The
> stones were so near, the entrance so small. From two thousand years back
> time's fingers could touch them in less than an instant. (1991: 118–19)

The river (and, by extension, the wider landscape) becomes quite literally a
'river of time', a medium in which past and present become interfused,
and, as Kenn ventures along Dunbeath Strath, he therefore ventures 'down
the straths of the past' (ibid.: 158). But neither is this half-intuited, half-
fantasised past restricted to the distant times of the Picts and Vikings. It is
there in the remains of more recent structures, in the scattered ruins of
croft houses in the remote 'far country', and in the placenames of that
country: names which seem to arise in legends, but which are 'more intimate and thrilling' because Kenn has heard them used by older members
of the community who knew the places as children and who would occasionally tell stories of them (ibid.: 127).

In his literature, and particularly in *Highland River*, Gunn demonstrates
how the past may become present through the phenomenological
encounter with landscape, how personal memories and cultural histories
become sedimented in place, how such layers of meaning may be
'retrieved' through a 'close reading' (an intimate, embodied reading) of its
palimpsest of topographic and toponymic signs (Tilley 1994).

There is, however, a final significance I'd like to draw from *Highland
River*, one which makes this novel a particularly appropriate place to begin
thinking about what I want to go on to discuss. For it was along the banks
of this river, the Dunbeath Water, that I first became aware of the profundity of the 'homecoming' journeys which are the subject of this book. While
conducting fieldwork for an earlier research project in which I was
exploring the mnemonic role of ruins in the Scottish Highland landscape
(Basu 1997, 2000), I met a middle-aged couple from Arizona, USA. They
had come in search of his Ross ancestors who, in the eighteenth century,
were recorded as being millers at Milton, a small 'mill town' across the
river from Dunbeath broch. I was invited to accompany them when they
were taken around the ruins of the long-deserted settlement by a number of
local people. The Arizonans were regaled with stories of the place and
details of its history – *their* history – before standing to have their photograph taken beside a large broken millstone that had been built into a

nineteenth-century wall. Finally, the couple were shown the old, overgrown well that had once served Milton's community. With tears in their eyes, they knelt first to cup the still-clear water in their hands to drink, and then to fill their emptied flasks so they could carry the spring water back to Arizona with them. I was immediately struck by the symbolism of what I observed and the powerful emotions it seemed to engender. The significance of this site . . . this source . . . this shrine . . . became unequivocal, and I realised then that there was manifestly nothing 'ordinary' about their journey.

Acknowledgements

This book has a genealogy of its own of course. Although its roots reach much deeper, it is based on doctoral research conducted whilst a graduate student in the Department of Anthropology, University College London. The research was funded by an Economic and Social Research Council studentship for which I am extremely grateful. My sincere thanks go to my academic supervisors, Barbara Bender and Christopher Tilley, my examiners, Sharon Macdonald and Catherine Nash, and many others in the wider academic community who enthused and encouraged me throughout my research and writing up. I am also particularly appreciative of Ross Noble and his staff at the Highland Folk Museum for providing such a stimulating home for my project. My greatest thanks, however, go to the many informants who took me into their confidence and shared with me their family histories, their stories, reflections, emotions and journeys. I hope I have not misused their trust.

Earlier versions of parts of the book have previously appeared in the following publications: 'Hunting down home: reflections on homeland and identity in the Scottish diaspora', in B. Bender and M. Winer, eds, *Contested Landscapes: Movement, Exile and Place* (Oxford: Berg, 2001); 'Route metaphors of "roots-tourism" in the Scottish Highland diaspora', in S. Coleman and J. Eade, eds, *Reframing Pilgrimage: Cultures in Motion* (London: Routledge, 2004); 'Macpherson Country: genealogical identities, spatial histories and the Scottish diasporic clanscape', *Cultural Geographies* 12 (2005): 123–50; 'Roots tourism as return movement: semantics and the Scottish diaspora', in M. Harper, ed., *Emigrant Homecomings: The Return Movement of Emigrants, 1600–2000* (Manchester: Manchester University Press, 2005); and 'Pilgrims to the far country: North-American "roots-tourists" in the Scottish Highlands and Islands', in C. Ray, ed., *Transatlantic Scots* (Tuscaloosa: Alabama University Press, 2005).

1   Introduction

Early morning, Morag looks out the train window. Small rocky hillsides are
sliding past, and fir trees, and white birches. Brown creeks (here called
burns?) tumble along over stony riverbeds. A station flashes by. The train
does not stop, but Morag reads the sign.
                    CULLODEN
     There is such a place. It really exists, in the external world. Morag feels
like crying.

Margaret Laurence, The Diviners

The above quote is taken from *The Diviners* (1989), a novel by the
Canadian writer of Scots-Irish descent, Margaret Laurence, in which
Morag, the heroine of the book, makes a journey from Manitoba to the
Scottish Highlands, the old country from which her ancestors had
emigrated. Laurence describes a quest to a place that had been imagined
long before even the possibility of visiting it could be conceived of. The
shock of discovering that that iconic site of Highland identity, Culloden,
actually exists, 'in the external world', outside of Morag's personal imaginings and the cultural narratives which give rise to them, is a profound one;
equivalent, perhaps, to the 'peak experience' described by Alex Haley in
his seminal family saga, *Roots*, after journeying to his ancestral home in
the 'back country of black West Africa' – 'that which emotionally, nothing
in your life ever transcends' (Haley 1991: 676).[1]

   This short excerpt from Laurence's novel introduces an essential aspect
of the nature of the Scottish homeland for people of Scottish descent
dispersed throughout the world. Scotland is at once a notional and a material reality, an imagined place as much as a geographical territory, a
symbol, even a sacred one, that may yet be seen, touched, photographed,
driven across, walked upon (Tilley 1994: 33). This book is concerned with
the relationship between Scotland as homeland ('home-land' embodying
this notional-material duality) and what may be construed as the Scottish
diaspora. More particularly it is concerned with examining the
phenomenon of 'roots tourism' in the Scottish Highlands and Islands: journeys, such as that described by Laurence, made by people of Scottish

descent ordinarily living in the United States of America, Canada, Australia, New Zealand and other regions where Scots have historically settled to the Scottish Highlands and Islands to search for and visit places associated with their ancestors.

Genealogy, or family history research, is often cited as being one of the most popular leisure pursuits worldwide and is reckoned to be the second most common use of the internet (after pornography) (Warren 1999). 'Ancestor hunting has been very much a growth industry in recent years', writes the Scottish historian Gordon Donaldson in the foreword to one family history how-to guide, 'part of the package for visitors from overseas' (in Cory 1996: ix–x). Indeed, so popular has roots tourism become that in 1999 the newly reconstituted Scottish parliament identified it as one of three key niche markets to be targeted in its *New Strategy for Scottish Tourism* and commissioned the Scottish Tourist Board (STB) to research and develop a plan with which to encourage it further (Scottish Executive 2000) (Figure 1.1).[2] Tourism, it should be remembered, remains one of Scotland's principal industries and is particularly important in the rural and sparsely-populated Highlands and Islands where it provides employment for 15 per cent of the workforce and accounts for 20 per cent of gross domestic product (R. Smith 1998: 55). Of course, what the STB's visitor profiles and market-research statistics fail to answer are those most fundamental questions: Why do people make these genealogical journeys? What is it that they find among the ruins and graveyards of their family histories? And, perhaps most importantly for an agency concerned with promoting tourism, its research fails to ask why it is that these visitors rarely consider themselves to be tourists at all and may even be offended at being identified as such. 'My Scotland feelings are very personal to me', explains an informant from Ontario,

> I am not, and never will be, a tourist in Scotland. I felt Scotland many years before I was there. I paid tribute to Scotland on purpose and continue through my quest to learn all that I can about it and how Scotland, and especially the Highlander, evolved. It's only through their world, through their eyes, and through their pains and joys that I want to understand Scotland. I owe Scotland that, because I feel that Scotland invites me home, to be me.

Such homecomings take on many forms. They may involve journeys to those sites which recall the grand narratives of Highland history (places such as Culloden, Glencoe and Glenfinnan with their 'intentional monuments'), but also to sites which figure in the more intimate histories of the family: the graves of relatives never known, the ruins of deserted croft houses or other settlements, places which, in Alois Riegl's terminology, function as 'unintentional monuments' (Riegl 1982; see Chapter 7). Some are highly organised, packaged events such as the 'Orkney Homecoming'

Figure 1.1 'Come home to Scotland'. A Scottish Tourist Board advertisement of 2002 targeting the 'genealogy' niche market (VisitScotland).

of 1999, in which over 150 Canadians of Orcadian descent travelled together to their ancestral islands for a week of tours and lectures, concerts and a special homecoming service held at St Magnus's Cathedral (Basu 2004a) (Figure 1.2). Others are organised by the clan associations and societies which proliferate in the USA and Canada. These typically involve

Figure 1.2 Arrival of the St Ola ferry at Stromness during the Orkney
    Homecoming of 1999, which saw over 150 Canadians of Orcadian descent
    'returning' to their ancestral islands (Paul Basu).

visits to places associated with clan history and lore and often culminate in
a march through the clan's historical territory behind the clan insignia: a
parading of identity and affiliation at once local and transnational (Figure
1.3). Some journeys take the form of family reunions, more private events,
in which ordinarily dispersed family members gather together at a significant place in the old country to reaffirm their connections with each other.
Such reunions may involve *céilidhs* with local performers, dinners and
excursions to places associated with the family history (Figure 1.4). But
many of these homecomings are very much more personal events undertaken by individuals or couples, small sibling or parent-children groups
(Figure 1.5). It is these more personal journeys that provide the particular
focus of the book.

In an era of academic eclecticism and the proliferation of sub-
disciplines, it is impossible to situate these 'acts of meaning' (J. Bruner
1990) within a particular theoretical or disciplinary context. My approach
is thus equally eclectic and does not force interpretation in response to a
single body of work – for example, that which constitutes an anthropology
of tourism. Instead, I navigate a course through a variety of discourses,
encompassing heritage tourism, pilgrimage, globalisation and localisation,
landscape and memory, historical and autobiographical narrative, social
and personal identity, and so forth. I choose, after Marcus (1995), to
follow the people, the story, the metaphor . . .

Figure 1.3 A parading of identity. Members of the International Clan Grant Society marching behind the Saltire, Stars and Stripes, Maple Leaf and clan insignia at Nethy Bridge, Strathspey during their gathering of 2000 (Paul Basu).

Figure 1.4 Four generations of a single Canadian and Australian Mackay family visiting the 'Mackay country' of Strathnaver. Eliot Rudie of the Strathnaver Museum guides them around the deserted settlement site of Achanlochy (Paul Basu).

Figure 1.5 Sisters, Janet and Elspeth, from Victoria, Australia visiting Teampull Mhoire on their ancestral island of Pabbay in the Sound of Harris (Paul Basu).

Hunting down home – (re)locating identity

Recent collections of essays such as those edited by Olwig and Hastrup (1997), Lovell (1998), and Rapport and Dawson (1998) demonstrate a desire to explore ethnographically what has hitherto been a somewhat theoretical discourse on the nature of identity, belonging and territorial rootedness within the complex contexts of globalisation. 'An examination of these concepts', writes Lovell, 'appears especially topical since displacement, dislocation and dispossession have become such common themes in contemporary political experiences and debates' (1998: 1).

One of the dominant tropes to emerge in this anthropological project to relocate identity is the notion of 'home'. Home is, of course, a most capacious concept. Indeed, as Edward Casey argues, 'part of the very meaning of "home" is that it is able to give rise to quite divergent perceptions and significations' (1993: 294). Much recent academic discourse concerned with modern Western identity has sought to demonstrate that individuals are quite 'at home' in a world of movement, that they are quite adept at negotiating the flux of multiple and mobile attachments. Quoting Iain Chambers, Rapport and Dawson are, for example, convinced that 'one's identity is "formed on the move": a "migrant's tale" of "stuttering transitions and heterogeneities"' (1998: 27). In our understanding of the contemporary world, 'metaphors and motifs of movement' have, it is argued, displaced earlier models of stasis and boundedness, and must now be considered 'of the quintessence in the conceptualization of identity' (Rapport and Dawson 1998: 26).

Despite the cosmopolitanism of academia, there is, however, an alternative view of home, which clings to the commonplaces of dictionary definitions: home as 'a dwelling place'; 'an environment offering security and happiness'; 'a valued place regarded as a refuge or place of origin'; 'a source'; 'an abiding place of the affections'; 'one's native land'; and even 'the native and eternal dwelling place of the soul' (*American Heritage Dictionary* 2000; *Webster's Revised Unabridged Dictionary* 1998). Thus conceived, home remains the physical, social and cognitive place 'in which one best knows oneself, where one's self-identity is best grounded' (Rapport and Dawson 1998: 21). However, if this proverbial home may be understood as a *place* where one belongs in some profound sense, to be in a position to make a homecoming suggests that one is not in such a place already: that this home exists elsewhere, somewhere and/or sometime other than the here and now. To contemplate making a homecoming is therefore to recognise that one is living in exile from this longed-for state. Indeed, there is much to justify the view that this seemingly most commonplace of locations has, in an age characterised by movement, also become one of the most elusive. As society becomes increasingly mobile and fragmented, there is thus a corresponding nostalgia for the (imagined) stability and coherence of past times and places. As Morley and Robins write,

> there is an increasingly felt need for 'some expressive relationship to the past' and for attachment to particular territorial locations as 'nodes of association and continuity, bounding cultures and communities'. There is a desire to be 'at home' in the new and disorientating global space (1995: 87, citing Michael Rustin).

Perhaps the most detailed exposition of this contemporary nostalgia is provided by Berger, Berger and Kellner in the classic sociological text *The Homeless Mind*. Berger *et al.* argue that the 'correlate of the migratory character of [the modern individual's] experience of society and of self has been what might be called a metaphysical loss of "home"' (1973: 82). As the familiarly Durkheimian argument goes, with modernity comes not only dislocation from a physical home-place (migration to cities or across other borders), but also a movement away from the cohesiveness of a social home or milieu represented by 'traditional society' and bound by the normalising *conscience collective* of shared beliefs, values and experiences. Thus, the experience of 'external mobility' has an impact 'at the level of consciousness' (ibid.: 184), with the consequence that 'modern man is afflicted with a *permanent identity crisis*' (ibid.: 78; italics in original). Alienated from the place and corresponding social structures which hitherto conferred an externally determined and 'given' identity, the individual is forced to search inwardly for some coherent sense of self in a life-world which is increasingly fragmented, plural and shifting. The consequent sense of disorientation – physical, social, psychological – is perplexing and 'engenders its own nostalgias . . . for a condition of "being at home" in society, with oneself and, ultimately, in the universe' (Berger *et al.* 1973: 82).

Of course, it is possible that Berger *et al.*'s analysis of modern identity is itself susceptible to this nostalgia, and this is the crux of Rapport and Dawson's critique of their argument. 'While *The Homeless Mind* remains a challenging thesis', they write, 'it is steeped in a communitarian ideology that can decry modern "ills" (individualism and pluralisation, alienation and anomy) only to the extent that it posits an idyllic past of unified tradition, certainty, stasis, and cognitive and behavioural commonality' (1998: 32). Rapport and Dawson discard such a postulated past on the grounds that it is 'mythic', and they believe that the whole theory 'remains ethnographically ungrounded in the present' (ibid.). Rapport and Dawson are being intentionally provocative here. Their polemic is directed to a specific goal: to weaken the close association of identity and territory, 'to disarm the genealogical rhetoric of blood, property and frontiers' (ibid.: v and 22, citing Paul Carter). Their objective may be laudable, but does the ethnographic evidence really support their argument? Are they correct in stating that home *versus* movement is an outmoded paradigm that has now been superseded by home *as* movement (ibid.: 30)? It is a contention of this book that Rapport and Dawson undermine the strength of their argument by dichotomising the debate. Home, I suggest, is not to be found *either* in movement *or* in stasis, but in the articulation of both. To demonstrate quite how modern, mobile individuals negotiate these apparent opposites, thus keeping the augured identity crisis at arm's length, will be one of my objectives.

Individuals, Rapport and Dawson insist, are 'at home in personal narratives that move away from any notion of fixity within a common idiom, and their identities derive from telling moving stories of themselves and their world views' (ibid.). In discussing narrative as a mobile resource, however, they seem to discount the possibility that narrative may also be used by individuals as a way of rooting themselves in particular places. Rapport and Dawson may be correct in doubting the *objective* reality of lost edenic homes evoked in migrant tales, but surely they underestimate the significance of the *subjective* reality of such myths for the individuals who live by them and for whom they provide some sense of ontological security in a world often perceived to be moving 'too fast' (Samuel and Thompson 1990).

The imperative to 'hunt down' a more authentic sense of home is vividly expressed in the contemporary search for roots (Basu 2001), and this widespread practice would seem to betray a more pessimistic view of modernity in which the individual evidently does not celebrate his or her liberation from the 'genealogical rhetoric' of blood and territorial attachment, but on the contrary seeks to re-assert it. The process, as evinced in the following comments, offers the dislocated self an opportunity to relocate itself both spatially and temporally.

> I want to be able to tell my children where their ancestors came from. I think it gives them a sense of belonging in a world that sometimes moves too fast (i.e. everything is always changing). (EL, New South Wales, Australia)

> I have found, after being in the States for a few months that there is an opinion that the reason a number of people here feel lost and hopeless is the loss of roots. I have found a great deal of people are realizing this. I have always felt that it is important to know these things and have passed many of the family stories on to my children and plan to write a family history for the benefit of the whole family. I consider myself very lucky in knowing where my roots are. (CW, Alberta, Canada – working in California, USA)

> How can I, a USA national, get a passport and/or some form of citizenship with the homeland of my heritage? I shall never feel like a whole being until I can feel and be part of Scotland. Please Scotland give to me some form of simple citizenship, for then I may no longer have to suffer the slings and arrows of mental and physical separation from my true homeland. (AB, Louisiana, USA)

> Walking through Cawdor village and castle knowing my ancestors also walked there. I felt like I came home after several generations' journey. (BC, Texas, USA)

The often strenuous efforts of individuals to reconnect with a past from which they feel separated and recover a 'sense of belonging' in a particular place, culture and family – the desire to 'come home' after generations of movement – may be seen in the context of what Berger *et al.* characterise as the 'demodernizing impulse'. This impulse, which Berger *et al.* suggest may account for various kinds of ethnic and religious revivals, 'seeks a reversal of the modern trends that have left the individual "alienated" and beset with the threats of meaninglessness' (1973: 196).

> The liberation of modernity has been, above all, that of the individual. ... Indeed, it has been suggested that the theme of individual autonomy is perhaps the most important theme in the world view of modernity. The experience of 'alienation' is the price of individuation. Quite logically, therefore, an important theme in demodernizing movements today is the protest against the allegedly excessive individualism of modern society. The individual is to be

liberated *from* this individualism *to* the solidarity of either old or new collective structures. (ibid., italics in original)

It is tempting to understand the homecoming journeys with which this book is concerned – including their idealisations of past times, places and communities – as an exemplar of this demodernising impulse. But, again, the reality is more complex. The modern individual wants it both ways: the self is therefore both 'at home' in a world of movement and 'at sea'; celebrating the freedom and creativity of self-determination on the one hand, whilst, on the other, craving a 'return' to the security of an externally-determined 'collective' identity. Modern identity is thus, above all, *ambivalent*, suspended in a kind of 'dialectical tension' between the order of stasis and the disorder of movement (Benjamin 1992: 62). Thus, rather than arguing narrowly for the location of home and identity either in stasis or in movement, we should therefore concentrate on exploring how these two postulated opposites apparently coexist within the same individual.

Homeland and diaspora

This brings us to a second metaphor of modern identity, one which embraces the 'dual consciousness' of stasis/movement, past/present, home/away: the notion of 'diaspora'. 'Diaspora cultures', suggests James Clifford, 'mediate, in a lived tension, the experiences of separation and entanglement, of living here and remembering/desiring another place' (1997: 255). Indeed, I would argue that diaspora should be considered as only one half of a twin trope with that 'other landscape', the 'homeland'. Like the global and the local, these are relative terms, each constituted in the other, such that there can be no diaspora without an implied place of origin (real or imagined), no homeland without an implied sense of displacement.

In recent years, diaspora has become something of a buzzword across the social sciences, used to describe almost any dispersed population regardless of the circumstances of its dispersal: 'where once were dispersions', bemoans Khachig Tölölyan, 'there now is diaspora' (1996: 30). Tölölyan maintains that, despite its more neutral etymological roots, a semantic stability had prevailed around the term from the second century CE until the late 1960s, based on what he describes as the 'Jewish paradigm' (1996: 13). This 'paradigmatic diaspora' is characterised primarily by the coercive nature of the forces resulting in the uprooting and resettlement of a population outside the boundaries of its established homeland. Diaspora, thus defined, may therefore be 'juxtaposed to the voluntary and cumulative emigration of individuals or small groups, which can also result in the formation of dispersion and enclaves in host countries' (ibid.: 12). Accordingly, Tölölyan argues, as well as the Jewish Diaspora, one can legitimately identify, for example, African and Armenian diasporas by the unequivocality of their respective cultural traumas, whereas to contemplate an Indian diaspora, for instance, formed by the migration of indentured labourers, or a British diaspora, formed by colonisation and voluntary emigration, requires a fundamental semantic shift – a problematic shift in which the meaning and power of the word itself becomes diffuse.

Despite Tölölyan's protestations, it appears that diaspora has indeed become a 'promiscuously capacious category' (1996: 8). 'For better or worse', writes Clifford, 'diaspora discourse is being widely appropriated' and 'is loose in the world' (1997: 249), where it joins an 'unruly crowd of descriptive/interpretive terms [that] now jostle and converse in an effort to characterize the contact zones of nations, cultures and regions' (ibid.: 245). It is, of course, no coincidence that the decline in the prominence of the Jewish paradigm in diaspora studies over the last thirty years corresponds with an increasingly global outlook in the social sciences and a concordant shift in attention (and therefore vocabulary) from the nation-state to various supranational categories of identification. Indeed, in an earlier, less critical, article Tölölyan himself describes diasporas as 'the exemplary communities of the transnational moment' (1991: 4). Rather than those of nations, it is the 'chronicles of diasporas', suggests Chambers, which 'constitute the ground swell of modernity' (1994: 16).

Whilst Tölölyan resists this expansive interpretation of the notion of diaspora, other theorists are keen to push its boundaries further. William Safran, for instance, recognises that diaspora may be used as a *metaphorical* designation to encompass the disparate experiences of several categories of people including 'expatriates, expellees, political refugees, alien residents, immigrants, and ethnic and racial minorities *tout court*' (1991: 83). He draws a parallel with the use of terms such as 'ghetto' and 'holocaust', which are also widely appropriated and employed (sometimes contentiously) in non-Jewish contexts. Perhaps the most thorough revision of the notion of diaspora to date, however, comes from the sociologist Robin Cohen (1997). Cohen argues that there is a need to 'transcend the Jewish tradition' (1997: 21) and return to the etymological origins of the word, the Greek to *sow over* or *scatter*, and its earliest usage in relation to human dispersion, referring to the Greek *colonisation* of Asia Minor and the Mediterranean. Such a tactic permits Cohen to develop a nine-point summary of common features of diasporas (Table 1.1) and to assemble a typology which includes 'labour', 'trade', 'imperial' and 'cultural' diasporas as well as the more conventional 'victim' type.

Such sub-categories resemble Weberian 'ideal types' since diasporas rarely occur in any 'pure' form. Indeed, it is the inexact match between linguistic categories and socio-spatial phenomena which allows this loaded term to be deployed strategically in both academic and popular discourses. Thus it is that members of an 'imperial diaspora' – descendants of nineteenth-century settlers in the British colonies, for example – may identify themselves as 'victims' of displacement, emphasising the so-called 'push' factors of migra-

Table 1.1 Common features of a diaspora

1	Dispersal from an original homeland, often traumatically, to two or more foreign regions
2	Alternatively, the expansion from a homeland in search of work, in pursuit of trade or to further colonial ambitions
3	A collective memory and myth about the homeland, including its location, history and achievements
4	An idealization of the putative ancestral home and a collective commitment to its maintenance, restoration, safety and prosperity, even to its creation
5	The development of a return movement that gains collective approbation
6	A strong ethnic group consciousness sustained over a long time and based on a sense of distinctiveness, a common history and the belief in a common fate
7	A troubled relationship with host societies, suggesting a lack of acceptance at the least or the possibility that another calamity might befall the group
8	A sense of empathy and solidarity with co-ethnic members in other countries of settlement; and
9	The possibility of a distinctive creative, enriching life in host countries with a tolerance for pluralism.

Source: R. Cohen 1997: 26

tion studies literature (poverty, famine, avaricious landlords, etc.) rather than the 'pull' factors (employment opportunities, land grants, assisted passage, etc.), choosing to ignore their ancestors' own agency.

Positing a Scottish diaspora

My argument in this book is predicated on an assumption that it is possible to recognise such a thing as a *Scottish* diaspora. Without such recognition, the range of meanings and inferences articulated in diasporic discourse would have no relevance in the Scottish context and therefore no particular influence on those individuals and groups throughout the world who claim a Scottish heritage. This is by no means incontrovertible and it would be true to say that, until recently, there has been no popular recognition of such a diaspora: the authors of *The Penguin Atlas of Diasporas*, for example, include only 'Jews, Armenians, Gypsies, blacks, Chinese, Indians, Irish, Greeks, Lebanese, Palestinians, Vietnamese, and Koreans' in their survey (Chaliand and Regeau 1997: xix). Cohen's more inclusive approach, however, allows us to go beyond the narrower definitions which usually dictate such lists. Indeed, an elaboration of his nine-point summary in specifically Scottish contexts is implicit throughout the book, and I address the two key interpretative points (1 and 2 – 'victim' diaspora *versus* 'trade/imperial/colonial' diaspora) in detail in Chapter 9. The following brief statements, addressing each of Cohen's points in turn, are therefore intended merely as introductory 'scene-setting' remarks. [3]

(1a) Dispersal from an original homeland, often traumatically . . .

It is estimated that between 1815 and 1914 over 50 million emigrants left Europe for North America, Australasia and other destinations. In absolute numerical terms, Scotland's 2 million share of this seems almost insignificant. Relative to its population size, however, the impact of this emigration was immense and constitutes, for the Scottish historian, T. M. Devine, the *haemorrhaging* of a population from a small country (1999: 469) – a provocative image, knowingly employed. Although all regions of Scotland were affected by this 'great exodus', emigration from the Scottish Highlands and Islands was especially severe, particularly in the aftermath of the subsistence crises of the 1830s and 1840s. In the period 1841 to 1861, for instance, the western Highlands lost up to a third of its population either overseas or to the industrial towns of the Scottish Central Belt and northern England (ibid.: 468–9). The Highlands remain one of the least densely populated regions in Europe.

This mass emigration from the Highlands is often conflated with what has been described as 'one of the sorest, most painful, themes in modern Scottish history' (Richards 2000: 3): the Highland Clearances. Occurring approximately in the period 1790 to 1855, and driven by the economic ideology of 'Improvement', the Clearances involved the removal of the small tenantry from their traditional land holdings on many estates throughout the Highlands and Islands so that the land could be opened up for large-scale sheep farming. This process speeded the demise of a system of joint-tenancy farming that was already well in decline and entailed the resettlement of tenants on individual small-holdings (crofts), often on relatively poor land, incapable of producing an adequate yield for a family to subsist on, and thereby forcing the tenants into more 'industrious' labour such as kelp burning, fishing or trade to provide a supplementary cash income. 'Although', as Eric Richards states, 'there were several episodes in which people were cleared and directly embarked for overseas, it has yet to be demonstrated that, in general, the Clearances accelerated either migration or emigration' (2000: 324). Yet, despite this, as Devine notes, in the popular mind, the Highland Clearances and Highland emigration have become inextricably linked and 'the depopulation of northern Scotland is seen as the direct result of the expropriation of the traditional peasantry and their forced removal from their homeland' (1992: 84).

The Clearances are not only one of the sorest of themes in Scottish history, they are also one of the most densely mythologised and deeply contentious, and arguments continue to rage in popular and academic histories, in newspaper letters pages and on the internet regarding what exactly happened and why. Two interpretations of these huge population displacements dominate the literature. These may be characterised as, first, the academic historians' view, which emphasises the complexity of causal factors (for instance, a massive increase in the rural population without a corresponding expansion in economic capacity to accommodate the growth; the relative isolation of the area from earlier agricultural modernisation; the expansion of *laissez-faire* capitalism and the corresponding decline in traditional social and economic structures; the demand for domestically produced mutton and wool during the Napoleonic Wars; the aestheticisation of the Highlands and development of sporting estates, etc.) (e.g. Mitchison 1981; Richards 1982, 1985a, 2000; Devine 1988); and, second, the popular historians' view, which argues that the Clearances were the continuation of a malicious process begun in the aftermath of Culloden – namely, the genocidal destruction of a distinctive tribal society which was perceived as a hindrance to the development of the modern British state (e.g. Mackenzie 1883; Grimble 1962; Prebble 1969).

Regardless of motive and, therefore, meaning (it is enough, in the present context, to state that both are equivocal), the 'removals' were sometimes carried out with a callous indifference to the welfare of those affected and have become forever associated in the popular imagination with scenes of rural poverty, destitution and famine: consequences of the Malthusian trap which the 'improvements' arguably sought to relieve. Thus, Richards describes how, as with the contemporaneous Irish Famine narrative, 'vivid simplicities' have come to displace the opacity of historical 'truth' (Gass 1982: 131):

> A large, but unknown, proportion of the population of the Highlands departed the region in the age of the clearances. As always, the popular recollection of the story is dominated by dramatic images: the ragged remnants of a once-proud peasantry hounded from the hills by the factors and police were driven aboard disease-ridden ships bound for outlandish colonies, their families broken, their ministers compliant, and the collective agony sounded by the pibroch and the wailing of pathetic humanity. It is a tale of 'inconsolable anguish' which parallels the Irish orthodoxy identified and criticised by Patrick O'Farrell [1976]; it depicts emigration as draining the life blood of the country, inflicting heartbreak and misery on those who left and on those who stayed, a monstrous continuing eviction contrived by the English. (Richards 1985a: 179)[4]

(1b) . . . to two or more foreign regions

The popularity of different overseas destinations for Scottish emigrants varied over time. Until the 1840s, British North America (the Dominion of Canada after 1867) was particularly popular and many distinctively Highland communities became established in the maritime provinces and Upper Canada (Ontario) at this time (Bumsted 1982; Bennett 1989, 1998;

Table 1.2 The Scottish diaspora, population distribution

Region	Estimated population of Scottish descent
United States of America	12,190,000
Canada	3,782,520
England and Wales	3,650,000
Australia	2,061,420
New Zealand	475,200
Northern Ireland	414,260
South Africa	285,558

Source: D. A. Bruce 1997: 280

Devine 1999: 470; M. Harper and Vance 1999). Later in the nineteenth century, Australia and New Zealand also began attracting large numbers, particularly during the Victorian gold rush of the early 1850s (D. Watson 1984; Brooking 1985; Richards 1985b; Prentis 1987); around the turn of the nineteenth/twentieth century there was also a flurry of emigration to South Africa. The United States of America, however, was by far the most popular destination with more than half of all emigrating Scots going there between 1853 and 1914 – even more were to head to the States after initially emigrating to Canada (Aspinwall 1985; Hewitson 1993; Devine 1999: 471).

Although some sources claim there are as many as 40 and even 90 million people of Scottish descent dispersed around the world today (Cromarty 2001: 4; Conroy 1996; Gerber 1997: xv), a more realistic estimate is put at around 28 million (D. A. Bruce 1997: 280). Of these, only 4.6 million are to be found in Scotland itself, with the largest populations of this posited diaspora residing in the USA, Canada, Australia, and elsewhere in the United Kingdom (see Table 1.2).

(2) Expansion from a homeland in search of work, in pursuit of trade or to further colonial ambitions

Mass emigration from Scotland began before the period of the Highland Clearances and continued long after, and although it is the trauma of forced eviction and exile that is often articulated in emigrant stories and songs (see Thomson 1989; Meek 1995; Newton 2001), it is clear that in the vast majority of cases, emigration was driven by a more complex set of co-existent 'push and pull' forces: most notably the 'pull' of the prospect of work, land and economic security. The reasons most frequently recorded for emigration from the Highlands in the late eighteenth century include 'racking rents', 'in hopes of good employment', 'to push his fortune', 'for wealth', 'want of employment', 'to provide for his family a better livelihood', 'to get a place' and to 'better their fortune' (Cameron 1930).[5] Whilst there is no denying the trauma of even economic migration, there is, as Cohen points out, a qualitative difference between this and migration forced by the threat of violence. In their desire to better their fortune in the colonies, many Highlanders exerted their own agency and thus, ultimately, emigrated voluntarily. Perhaps, considering the lack of viable alternatives, we could say that, in the majority of cases, whilst the Highlanders were not forced by physical coercion to emigrate, they were nevertheless *forced to choose* emigration as the lesser of evils – the victims of circumstance at the most.

Devine argues that, whilst some Scottish migrants were indeed destitute, many also 'came with considerable advantages which allowed them to exploit the opportunities of the New World and influence its development out of all proportion to their numbers', and that, 'unlike the Irish Catholic emigration to the Americas, the Scottish diaspora was not mainly the flight of the poor' (1999: 471–2). Indeed, many of the great empire builders of the United States, Canada, Australia and New Zealand were Scots or of Scottish descent: a fact attested to in such hubristic volumes as *The Mark of the Scots*, which proudly catalogue the many Scottish statesmen, explorers, missionaries, military commanders, scholars, inventors, engineers, and so forth who have shaped these settler societies (D. A. Bruce 1997; see also Herman 2002; Fry 2002 and 2004). We are here concerned with that alternative national stereotype: the 'Enterprising Scot' who, in an emigrant context, successfully deployed skills, and sometimes capital, acquired at home 'to build a new life (and for the lucky few, a fortune) in the colonies' (Donnachie 1992: 102). Even those who were not rewarded with such immediate bounties generally became established within the space of a generation or two and attained a much improved standard of living compared with those who remained in the old country. Success in the colonies was, however, won at the expense of those whose land was colonised, and even the poor rural migrants of the Highlands of Scotland, dispossessed of their own lands, cannot be exempted from responsibility for the often more bloody dispossession of others in their encounters with native populations. Devine is therefore obliged to include that darker side of the often celebratory narrative of the Scots abroad:

> Scots pioneers in Victoria were often land-grabbers and squatters who were notorious for their ruthlessness, and the Scots, like the English, Welsh and Irish, played a full part in the harsh treatment of the Aboriginal peoples. It was ironic that some of those most notoriously involved were Highlanders who themselves had suffered clearance and privation in the old country before receiving emigration assistance under the auspices of the Highland and Island Emigration Society. (1999: 474)

Whilst Cohen's list suggests *either* involuntary dispersal (resulting in a victim diaspora) *or* voluntary expansion (resulting in a trade or colonial diaspora), it is evident that the two are not necessarily mutually exclusive. The history of the Scottish Highland diaspora is an exemplary case in so far as it can be interpreted in different ways according to the meanings one wishes to invoke: Scots as exiles banished from ancient homelands, as pioneer settlers civilising savage places, as agents of British imperialism, as perpetrators of displacement in the homelands of others. Such are the apparent incompatibilities which yet seem to cohere in Scottish diasporic identity. (Or, indeed, perhaps it is that they do not cohere so easily that provokes the restless search for home that characterises this particular kind of belonging.)

(3 and 4) A collective memory and myth about the homeland, including its location, history and achievements, and an idealization of the putative ancestral home and a collective commitment to its maintenance, restoration, safety and prosperity, even to its creation

'The myth of a common origin', writes Cohen, 'serves to "root" a diasporic consciousness and give it legitimacy' (1997: 184). Such origin myths are typically territorialised and may constitute 'highly romanticised fantasies of the "old country"' (ibid.: 185). Cohen reminds us that, for the Jews, the '"promised land" flowed with milk and honey' (ibid.), so it is with the Scottish homeland, that 'promised land of modern romance' (Marx 1970: 728): *the Highlands.*

It will already be apparent that I refer to Scotland and the Scottish Highlands (and Islands)[6] – and therefore the Scottish diaspora and the Scottish Highland diaspora – somewhat imprecisely. This imprecision is, actually, fundamental to Scottish national and, particularly, Scottish diasporic identity. Generally-speaking, when 'Scotland' is imagined outside Scotland, it is *Highland* Scotland that is imagined. As Devine points out,

> To the rest of the world in the late twentieth century Scotland seems a Highland country. The 'land of mountain and flood' adorns countless tourist posters and those familiar and distinctive symbols of Scottish identity, the kilt, the tartan and the bagpipes, are all of Highland origin. (1999: 231, citing Scott)

This is certainly borne out in Celeste Ray's study of the Scottish heritage revival in North Carolina where, she reports, 'The identity embraced as "Scottish" by the Scottish-American community is a Highland identity', though not necessarily one which is recognisable as such by Highlanders in Scotland (2001: 17 and xiii).

The emergence of this (trans)national iconography has a particular genealogy of its own and has been the subject of much scholarship in recent years (e.g. Withers 1988 and 1992; Womack 1989; Pittock 1991). The region has repeatedly been constructed as the primitive/peripheral/exotic 'other' to the hegemonically dominant Scottish Lowlands, England and/or the anglophone British state. This external construction and representation, at once ideological and aesthetic, may be seen in the light of Said's discussion of Orientalism (1978) and gives rise to a parallel discourse which has been labelled 'Highlandism'. This discourse has its roots in the fourteenth century when, with the increasing Anglicisation of the Lowlands and the retreat of Gaelic-speaking society to the mountainous north and west, the Highlands emerged as a distinct 'culture region'. However, it was in the period 1746–1822, in the aftermath of the Jacobite Uprisings,[7] that the discursive construction of the Highlands as we know it today took place.

> The creation of the Highlands is the result of several agencies in combination: the geographical 'discovery' of the region; the idea of the Highlander as 'noble savage' in the context of enlightenment theories on the stages of societal development; and a Romantic interest in primitive virtue alongside interests in the aesthetic pleasures to be gained in contemplation of picturesque scenery. (Withers 1992: 145)

In his Barthesian analysis of the 'myth' of the Highlands, Peter Womack describes the region as being colonised by 'the empire of signs' (1989: 1) and reminds us that this 'colonisation' occurred at a particular time 'in response to specific ideological requirements and contradictions which are both exhibited and disguised by its eventual form' (ibid.: 2). Central to this movement was the Lowland appropriation of Jacobitism. As Devine argues, it was the very decisiveness of the Hanoverian military victory at Culloden that made possible the 'sentimentalisation' of the Jacobite cause (1999: 236–7). By the end of the eighteenth century Jacobite rebelliousness had been so thoroughly tamed and metamorphosed that it provided the key iconography for a new unified, assimilationist, Protestant 'North British' identity – one of the very things it had rebelled against. The Jacobite myth, with its motifs of love, loyalty, exile and loss, and its close association with Highland tradition entered national and international consciousness, becoming further aestheticised in music and literature – not least in the work of those great proponents of Highlandism: Burns, Hogg and Sir Walter Scott. This transformation reached its zenith in George IV's visit to Edinburgh in 1822, which saw the Hanoverian monarch 'clad in kilt, plaid, bonnet and tartan coat' and presented as 'The Chief of Chiefs' and a Stuart to boot (ibid.: 235). The 'King's Jaunt' was famously stage-managed by Scott, who is generally credited with finally marginalising Lowland culture (though not its political and economic dominance) and replacing it with a 'Celtic fantasy', one far removed from the realities of the Highland past or present (ibid. 236). Thus Scottish culture became, in Prebble's words, 'a bogus tartan caricature of itself' (1988: 361), and a classic exemplar of the 'invention of tradition' (Trevor-Roper 1983).

Receiving further royal patronage when Victoria began her summer residencies at Balmoral in 1848, the cult of the Highlands gained momentum throughout the nineteenth century, particularly with the expansion of tourism (first elite tours and field sports, later, in the wake of the railways, mass tourism to resorts – see Andrews 1990; Gold and Gold 1995). This period saw a great deal of cultural 'inventiveness', including the establishment of a proliferation of Highland games and gatherings, the emergence of clan and Celtic societies, the erection of monuments at iconic sites such as Glenfinnan, Glencoe and Culloden, and the landscaping of estates so that they might accord more faithfully to the picturesque aesthetic (a process that has become known as the 'Balmoralisation' of estates). Indeed, this 'ideoscape' of the tragic-heroic past remains the dominant image in Scottish tourist promotions to this day. As Gold and Gold note in their analysis of tradition, representation and promotion in Scottish tourism since 1750,

> It was Scott who conflated the highland identity with Scottish identity, peopled the landscape with characters from a mythical past and ensured that visitors would feel that they needed to visit the Highlands to see the 'authentic' Scotland. In a very real sense it was Scott who wrote the script for the promotion of Scottish tourism in the years to come. (1995: 83)

There is much more to be said about the rise of Highlandism, but my concern here, and in my discussion in Chapter 4, is to explore this phenomenon in the context of the Scottish diaspora. For diasporic Scots, the myth of the Highlands is, of course, also the myth of the homeland, and, indeed, it is in the diaspora – particularly in North America – that this mythic idealisation is most forcefully invoked and where it continues to expand and transmogrify. This extends far beyond the wearing of tartan and participation in the Highland games and gatherings that abound across the continent. As Ray observes, 'the Highlandist perspective of Scottish heritage has acquired many new dimensions and celebratory rituals in the last few decades of Scottish heritage revival' (2001: 39). Witness, for example, the invention of new traditions such as the 'Kirking of the Tartan', the enthusiasm for re-enactment groups which stage mock battles in Highland dress, and the establishment of an annual National Tartan Day in the USA on the anniversary of the signing of the Declaration of Arbroath (Hague 2002). Perhaps, however, the most powerful expression of this diasporic idealisation of the Scottish homeland is the 1995 feature film, *Braveheart*, a classic example of romantic nationalist obfuscation that must be understood as both product and partial cause of the Scottish heritage revival.

Having characterised the idealisation of the Scottish (Highland) homeland thus, it is important to add that this 'caricature' is not viewed uncritically by all members of the diaspora. Many diasporic Scots start their journeys of discovery with such stereotypical images in mind, but in the course of their research and exploration become fully acquainted with the complexities of Scottish historiography and eventually regard such 'tartan tomfoolery' with derision. Therefore, despite the mass appeal of this dominant discourse, the homeland becomes imagined in multiple ways and the contestation of authenticity forms a significant counter-discourse.

(5) The development of a return movement that gains collective approbation

'Return migration' is a largely overlooked aspect of international migration studies, but, as Mark Wyman has demonstrated in *Round Trip to America* (1993), historically this was an extremely significant phenomenon.[8] Wyman states that, in the late nineteenth and early twentieth centuries, no less than a third of European mass migrants to the USA returned permanently to their original countries. These return statistics vary across different European nationality groups, between rural and urban populations, and at different periods of time, and reasons for return include both success and failure in the New World, changed circumstances in the old country (the inheritance of land or family responsibilities, for example), an inability to adapt to the American way of life and, indeed, plain homesickness.

Although the terms 'return migration' and 'return movement' are sometimes used interchangeably in migration studies literature, the connotations of each are actually quite different. Whilst migration is undoubtedly movement, a movement is, of course, more than migration: it can be a collective project, a cause or campaign. There are religious movements, political movements, aesthetic movements: in diasporic contexts there are *return* movements such as Zionism and Rastafarianism, movements which are at once religious, political and aesthetic. With the exception of Zionism, the role of the homeland for most such movements has remained largely symbolic. It is the argument of this book that the two- or three-week homecomings made by Scottish roots tourists may also legitimately be understood as instances of a diasporic return movement (see Chapter 9). Such symbolic returns are not a new phenomenon – note that planned by Gus and Angus in Neil Gunn's *Highland River*; and, indeed, not far from Gunn's native Dunbeath, at Badbae, stands a monument erected in 1911 by a New Zealander from the stones of the cottage in which his father had been raised prior to emigrating (Basu 1997: 48–9). It is true to say, however, that this movement has gained momentum in the late twentieth century such that it may now be described as a *mass* movement and therefore one that has gained collective approbation.

(6 and 8) A strong ethnic group consciousness sustained over a long time and based on a sense of distinctiveness, a common history and the belief in a common fate, and a sense of empathy and solidarity with co-ethnic members in other countries of settlement

A sense of 'Scottishness', of belonging to a distinctively Scottish community, transcends national boundaries and is articulated in many ways:

through the activities of international clan societies; the celebration of calendrical events such as Burns' Night, St Andrew's Day and now Tartan Day; the cultivation of tastes in identifiably Scottish food and drink (e.g. haggis, game, shortbread, oatcakes, Scotch whisky); the wearing of kilt, tartan and associated paraphernalia; the appreciation of Scottish music and literature; the learning of Scottish languages; and, not least, through acquiring a knowledge of Scottish history and taking an interest in Scottish current affairs. In *The Mark of the Scots*, Duncan Bruce, an office holder of the St Andrew's Society of New York, summarises this diasporic 'ethnic group consciousness' as follows:

> Somewhere within the depths of all of us who are of Scottish blood, there is a knowledge that despite our dispersion throughout the continents and our constantly increasing assimilation into other nations, we are still somehow one people, held together by fragments of a common culture and genes inherited of ancient kings. And because of this awareness we perceive with pride that our nation, though one of the smallest and poorest in origin, is nonetheless one of the most successful. (Bruce 1997: xiii)

As I shall argue in Chapters 4 and 5, the internet is playing an increasingly important role in enabling and sustaining this sense of distinctiveness in otherwise assimilative national contexts. However, the internet has not wholly displaced other forms of media. There are, for example, a large number of Scottish-interest print periodicals that are published in diasporic countries and distributed internationally; examples include:

Am Braighe (published in Nova Scotia, quarterly)
Celtic Heritage (published in Nova Scotia, bi-monthly)
The Highlander (published in Illinois, bi-monthly)
SCOTS (published in New South Wales, quarterly)
The Scottish Banner (editions published in Florida, Ontario and New South Wales, monthly)
The Scots Link (published in Victoria, quarterly)

SCOTS, for example, is a high-quality, 218-page glossy magazine with, according to its editor, 'a global readership of 150,000 per quarter', split more or less equally between Australia and New Zealand, the USA and Canada, and Europe (Bruce Stannard pers. comm.). In a subscription promotion, the publishers claim that *SCOTS* is 'more than a magazine' and that it 'Bring[s] Scotland Home' to its subscribers, 'no matter where in the world' they live (*SCOTS* 2001 #12: 126). In Chapter 4 I include some analysis of the representation of the Scottish homeland in its articles, illustrations and advertisements.

Although diasporic orthodoxy posits 'ethnic group consciousness' as being *continuous* with the past (rhetorically, a *survival* in the face of oppression, and a failure of coercive forces to destroy the spirit and identity of an oppressed people), it may be argued that such assertions of distinctiveness may also emerge or re-emerge in response to wider socio-cultural dynamics in the host society. Whilst Cohen does not state in his nine-point summary that a group consciousness may form where none had previously existed or where it had become dissipated, he does seem to acknowledge this possibility when he writes, 'a strong attachment to the past, or a block to assimilation in the present and future, must exist in order to permit a diasporic consciousness to emerge or be retained' (1997: 186). I suggest, however, that, in certain circumstances, diasporic consciousness may itself be constructed and deployed as a means to blocking or reversing assimilation: the emergence of Scottish diasporic consciousness is, I argue, a case in point.

(7 and 9) A troubled relationship with host societies, suggesting a lack of acceptance at the least or the possibility that another calamity might befall the group, or the possibility of a distinctive creative, enriching life in host countries with a tolerance for pluralism

These definitional points present the greatest challenge if we are to imagine a Scottish diaspora. Using examples as diverse as the Chinese in Malaya, Kurds in Turkey and Sikhs in Britain, Cohen argues that diasporic populations generally experience antagonism and legal or illegal discrimination in the host countries in which they have settled, and may even become the objects of violent hatred (ibid.). Indeed, it is this alienation from the dominant society which, it is suggested, leads to diasporic communities retaining primary allegiance to their original homeland and thus failing to assimilate as other immigrant groups supposedly do.

> What makes this form of inter-ethnic tension different from the general case is that in some measure these groups can look outside their immediate communities (for comfort, comparison and identification) to co-ethnic communities elsewhere. (Ibid.)

It would, however, be difficult to describe people of Scottish descent in the USA, for instance, as either an ethnic minority or victims of ethnic discrimination. As has already been noted in response to Cohen's second point, Scottish migrants were influential in shaping those societies in which they settled, and thus form part of the dominant cultures of the host countries which they are, as a diaspora, supposedly to be defined against. As I shall argue in Chapter 9, however, in choosing to identify with their Highland roots, many diasporic Scots are implicitly rejecting their positions of relative power and privilege and are instead identifying themselves as members of a victimised minority group. This phenomenon may be seen in the context of what Peter Novick describes as a more general 'culture of victimization' that, he claims, is sweeping through America (1999: 190). In Australia, in the wake of the Aboriginal rights movement, a so-called 'black arm band' interpretation of colonial history has become prominent among cosmopolitan white populations, in which the descendants of pioneer settlers are negotiating senses of guilt and responsibility for injustices meted out on indigenous populations in the colonial encounter (Curthoys 1999). This may entail either a denial of the agency of one's own ancestors (e.g. by asserting that they, too, were victims) or the desire to find one's own 'aboriginal' landscape – a place to which one can legitimately belong without implying the displacement of others.

A less contentious claim (Cohen's ninth point) is that the migrant Scots, by virtue of their relative dominance, have enjoyed the freedom of celebrating their distinctive heritage in creative and life-enriching ways, for instance, as members of clan and St Andrew's societies, participants in Highland games and gatherings, pipers in marching bands, and in countless other ways. Indeed, many Scottish-Americans are particularly proud of the fact that the American Declaration of Independence and the American Constitution were both influenced by Scottish precedents (the Arbroath Declaration of 1320 and National Covenant of 1638 – see D. A. Bruce 1997: 38–43 for textual comparisons), thus contributing to the creation of a 'tolerance for pluralism' in their host country. We should not forget, however, that the Ku Klux Klan was founded in the aftermath of the American Civil War by Scottish-American ex-Confederate soldiers who drew inspiration from the secret societies of rural Aberdeenshire in their invention of Klan traditions (Hewitson 1993: 107–9).[9] Euan Hague records that the Ku Klux Klan purportedly recommend the film *Braveheart* to its members, and that other right-wing organisations such as the Council for Conservative Citizens have targeted Highland Games in the USA for the distribution of literature 'outlining how "Third World" immigration will make "American Scots" an "endangered species"' (Hague 2002: 155n13 quoting from *The Herald* and *Citizens' Informer*). Researching among the North Carolinian Scottish-American community, however, Ray stresses that the vast majority of her informants explicitly distinguished their clan from *the* Klan and distanced themselves from any racist agenda (2001: 191).

The point of including mention of such minority interests in the present discussion is simply to further demonstrate that Scottish diasporic consciousness is fraught with complexities and contradictions. This capacity for equivocation, together with the definitional mutability of the term 'diaspora' itself, enables the notion of diaspora to be articulated in the arena of global identity politics by individuals and groups of Scottish descent who may have very different ideas about what a Scottish heritage means.

Reinforcing my argument that diaspora and homeland should be understood as correlative concepts, it will be noted that of the nine characteristics Cohen identifies as being common to all diasporas, the first five relate directly to the putative homelands from which the migrant populations were dispersed. The homeland is both literally and metaphorically at the centre of diasporic consciousness, an observation which underlies the methodological approach I have adopted to investigate Scottish diasporic consciousness in this book: that is, by situating the research from which it is drawn in the homeland rather than in the host countries of the diaspora as convention would perhaps dictate.

Before going on to describe my research methodology in greater detail, I should like to conclude this introduction with an extended quote from the editorial from the first issue of the aforementioned *SCOTS* magazine. Under the title of '*Ceud Mile Failte*: A Hundred Thousand Welcomes' and accompanied by a photograph of Eilean Donan Castle (captioned 'home of Clan MacRae'), the fifth-generation Australian editor with roots 'deeply embedded in the rich soil of the Black Isle', provides a typical example of how a specifically Scottish diasporic identity is asserted in popular culture. In brackets, I cross-reference the editor's comments with Cohen's check-list of common features of diasporas.

> Throughout Scotland's long and turbulent history, her greatest export has been her proud, patriotic and independent people. In one of the great mass migrations in human history, many hundreds of thousands of Scots, in some cases entire villages, packed up and left for the New World. While some went willingly [2], untold numbers of others suffered the pain and ignominy of dispossession and exile that started with the Highland Clearances, the cruel and long drawn out process in which sheep replaced people following the final, disastrous Jacobite rising of 1745 [1a].
>
> From the icy wastes of Patagonia, to the soft green hills of New Zealand, the vast open spaces of Australia, Canada and the United States [1b], Scots men and women settled and left an indelible mark. Few other emigrant groups can claim to have had such a pervasive influence on the politics, commerce, banking, medicine, engineering, literature and philanthropy of the New World as have the Scots [2, 6, 9].
>
> We're a clannish, loyal people. The Gaelic word, *Clann*, literally means children. And it's that bond of loyalty to our Scottish heritage that sets us apart [6, 8]. In today's swiftly changing world, we can take inspiration from the courage and determination of our ancestors. In this part of the world we are but 200 years young, and yet our Scottish ancestry stretches back to the beginnings of human history. Our people have run a proud and colourful race through the centuries, and in linking ourselves to that history we make ourselves more complete human beings [3, 4, 6]. (Cromarty 1998: 4)

2 An itinerant anthropology

> Because post-modern ethnography privileges 'discourse' over 'text', it fore-grounds dialogue as opposed to monologue, and emphasizes the cooperative and collaborative nature of the ethnographic situation in contrast to the ideology of the transcendental observer. In fact, it rejects the ideology of 'observer-observed', there being nothing observed and no one who is observer. There is instead the mutual, dialogical production of a discourse, of a story of sorts.
>
> Stephen A. Tyler, 'Post-Modern Ethnography'

This book is forced to confront two tenacious anthropological prejudices: one which continues to prioritise the exotic at the expense of the suppos-edly familiar, the other which continues to be suspicious of research data produced outside the classic ethnographic fieldwork method of sustained participant-observation within a spatially-bounded, preferably small-scale 'culture region'. Despite decades of reflexivity and auto-criticism, the disci-pline remains reluctant to abandon what are, after all, still perceived to be its defining characteristics. Is an anthropology such as I present here – one concerned with Western, cosmopolitan conceptions of identity and belonging in mobile and fragmented contexts that provide little opportu-nity for long-term 'dwelling' with informants – still anthropology? Certainly Malinowski would have difficulty recognising it as such since it evidently does not conform to the 'proper conditions for ethnographic work' he took such pains to delineate and which remain defiantly canon-ical: living 'among the natives', 'camping right in their villages' (1953: 6; cf. Geertz 1988: 78–101). The real issue is, of course, whether anthro-pology is more concerned with preserving its distinctive identity within the academy, securing its own particular claim on professional authority, or whether the discipline takes seriously its own critique and attempts to adapt to a world (and worldview) very different from that from which it emerged. Perhaps, ultimately, the discipline will have no choice. As Vered Amit argues, a greater threat is posed to the discipline's credibility if it does not succeed in becoming more heterodox in its methodological approach and therefore able to engage with a broader, more complex, range of social and cultural phenomena.

If in cleaving to a methodological orthodoxy, anthropologists a priori limit rather than leave open the scope of circumstances to be studied, they will be operating at epistemological cross purposes with their own disciplinary objectives. Thus the answer to what happens to anthropology if its practitioners adapt their fieldwork practices to the exigencies of new circumstances is that it wouldn't remain as anthropology if they didn't. (Amit 2000: 17)

Arjun Appadurai urges that, if the discipline is to retain its relevance, anthropology must confront some 'brute facts' about the contemporary world, even if, in doing so, it is forced to depart from the research techniques on which its authority conventionally rests. 'Central among these facts', he writes, 'is the changing social, territorial, and cultural reproduction of group identity' (1991: 191).

As groups migrate, regroup in new locations, reconstruct their histories, and reconfigure their ethnic 'projects', the *ethno* in ethnography takes on a slippery, nonlocalized quality, to which the descriptive practices of anthropology will have to respond. (Ibid.)

Whilst we might conceive of new hypertextual ways of *describing* this slippery new world, Appadurai does not, alas, detail exactly how anthropologists might respond to this world in their methodological practices. What techniques might anthropologists employ to research groups which are 'no longer tightly territorialized, spatially bounded, historically unselfconscious, or culturally homogenous' (ibid.)? Just where is 'the field' when one's research subjects are mobile individuals, connected through dispersed or discontinuous social networks, whose social interaction may be 'episodic, occasional, partial and ephemeral' (Amit 2000: 14)? Amit asks rhetorically,

How do we observe interactions that happen sometimes but not necessarily when we are around? How do we participate in social relations that are not continuous, that are experienced most viscerally in their absence? How do we participate in or observe practices that are enacted here and there, by one or a few? How do we take into account unique events that may not be recurring but may still have irrevocable consequences? (Ibid.: 14–15)

It may be argued that all anthropologists, including those working in small-scale, spatially-bounded communities, are confronted with such 'disorder' in their fieldwork experiences and that the 'order' apparent in their subsequent ethnographies is an imposed one, a product of the cognitive and descriptive practices of writing (Clifford and Marcus 1986; Geertz 1988). However, these challenges are surely compounded in a milieu such as that with which I am concerned: a definitionally-dispersed group, which is bound not by any social network but by a mutual interest in a particular place and its past. The majority of my informants do not know or meet each other, or exist in relationships of exchange with each other, but they share a 'discursive space' and participate in cultural practices which are ostensibly similar. If they inhabit a village, it is manifestly a global one.

Amit's response is that anthropologists must become as mobile as the contexts they are studying. They must accept that their interaction with informants may also have to be episodic, occasional, partial and ephemeral, and may have to 'purposively create the occasions' for that interaction (2000: 15). Such a creative, opportunistic approach is, as George Marcus argues, largely unproblematic in other disciplines. Considering the fragmentary nature of the evidence they deal with, the projects of cultural history and archaeology, for example, are essentially 'reconstructive' and concerned with 'the composition and probing of the relationships of dispersed materials' (Marcus 1995: 100). We are beginning to understand that the study of contemporary social and cultural phenomena is equally reconstructive and that there is no privileged, omniscient position from which to perceive 'the whole'. Anthropology, too, must dwell in the 'contact zones' traversed by things, people, ideas, narratives, symbols and so forth (Clifford 1997). Indeed, Clifford suggests that, in this new 'world (dis)order', culture itself must be understood as 'traveling culture', and the 'location' of that culture is marked by such 'translation terms' as 'diaspora', 'borderland', 'immigration', 'migrancy', 'tourism', 'pilgrimage', and 'exile' (1997: 11). If culture is thus to be found in 'a series of encounters and translations', in an 'itinerary rather than a bounded site' (ibid.), then surely anthropology – the reconstruction, (re)interpretation, (trans)translation of culture – is called upon to be itinerant too? A deterritorialised, itinerant anthropology for a deterritorialised, itinerant world:

> What a new style of ethnography can do is to capture the impact of deterritorialization on the imaginative resources of lived, local experiences. Put another way, the task of ethnography now becomes the unravelling of a conundrum: what is the nature of locality, as a lived experience, in a globalized, deterritorialized world? (Appadurai 1991: 196)

Dynamism and depth – multi-sited ethnography

It is not, of course, only in the moment of migration and its immediate aftermath that people are compelled to reconstruct their histories and reconfigure their ethnic projects. This book is concerned with a 'group' (the category is itself problematic and may be employed aspirationally, part of the 'project') for whom migration is an historical fact rather than something experienced directly. Indeed, I am concerned with even more unfamiliar anthropological objects: people who are not only deterritorialised, spatially unbounded, historically self-conscious and culturally diverse, but also largely middle-class, cosmopolitan and white. At first sight, such people seem quite 'settled' in their relatively affluent and mobile lifestyles, but it is apparent that they are also using the opportunities afforded by their disposable incomes and increased leisure time, as well as the technologies of globalisation – cheap air travel, ease of global communication via the internet, and so forth – to pursue a project that would appear to indicate the opposite. Through the practices of family history research and roots tourism such people are apparently seeking to reterritorialise their identity, become more bound by place, develop more authentic senses of continuity with their ancestral past, and recover a degree of cultural distinctiveness. It is the objective of this study, the purpose to which its methodology is directed, to examine whether this assessment withstands serious scrutiny.

In designing a research methodology that would provide both the dynamism to engage with informants who are literally 'on the move' and the depth to ensure the disciplinary rigour of the scrutiny levelled, Marcus's discussion of the emergence of multi-sited ethnography has been particularly useful (1995). Accepting that 'there are many more concepts and visions for doing multi-sited ethnography than there are achieved exemplars' (ibid.: 103), the potential of this approach 'moves out from the single sites and local situations of conventional ethnographic designs to examine the circulation of cultural meanings, objects and identities in diffuse time-space' (ibid.: 95). Thus Marcus proposes a framework which acknowledges that the posited 'object[s] of study' may themselves be 'emergent' and underdefined, and which shifts the anthropologist's role to one of discerning the 'logics of relationship, translation, and association' among these 'mobile and multiply-situated' objects (ibid. 102). He summarises this inevitably constructivist approach as follows:

> Multi-sited research is designed around chains, paths, threads, conjunctions, or juxtapositions of locations in which the ethnographer establishes some form of literal, physical presence, with an explicit, posited logic of association or connection among sites that in fact defines the argument of the ethnography. (Ibid.: 105)

To such ends, Marcus recommends a series of techniques in which the ethnographer is called upon to 'trace' the movement of identified cultural phenomena across different contexts: to be *led by* the phenomena (and to be amenable to being led along unanticipated paths) (ibid.: 106). Again, proponents of conventional ethnography, informed by their own practical experiences in the field, will legitimately claim that there is nothing novel in Marcus's schema, but this does not diminish the value of his endeavour to make explicit and formalise what has hitherto been implicit, informal and, in Malinowskian terms, 'improper' – something to be relegated to the anthropologist's 'diary' (Geertz 1988: 73–101). Multi-sited ethnographers are thus encouraged, as appropriate, to 'follow the people', 'follow the thing', 'follow the metaphor', 'follow the plot, story or allegory', 'follow the life or biography' or 'follow the conflict' (Marcus 1995: 106–10). Applying this conceptual framework to the specific contexts of Scottish diasporic roots tourism, a number of possible methodological strategies emerge:

Follow the people – to join people of Scottish descent, ordinarily residing in the USA, Canada, Australia, New Zealand, etc., on their journeys in the Scottish Highlands. To participate as much as possible in these journeys and to observe. This might include participation in larger group events such as organised homecoming tours or international clan gatherings, but also more personal journeys made by individuals and small family groups. Who are these people? What kinds of places do they visit? What do they do at these places? What do they say they are doing?

Follow the thing – to examine the material culture of Scottish diasporic consciousness, particularly objects associated with and acquired during visits to the Scottish Highlands. This might include souvenirs either purchased or collected during visits, objects that roots tourists bring with them on their journeys (old photographs, heirlooms that migrated with their ancestors, personal possessions left as 'ex votos' at ancestral sites, etc.), photographs, diaries and so forth. How do people use these objects to tell stories about themselves and their heritage?

Follow the metaphor – to explore how the Scottish Highlands are consti-tuted as a symbolic and metaphorical homeland as well as a physical place in Scottish diasporic consciousness. What is the relationship between this 'imagined' homeland and its material counterpart? How do people negotiate inconsistencies that become apparent in their jour-neys from the 'discursive realm' to the 'real'? How does this affect their identification with the region?

Follow the plot, story, or allegory – to investigate the narrative processes that accompany these journeys. The journey itself may be narrativised in different ways (emplotted as a homecoming, a pilgrimage, a quest, or a vacation, for instance). This might be examined through infor-mants' stories of their journeys, through their use of photography and video, and in other narrative practices such as the writing of diaries and journals. But the narratives of these journeys are also rooted in the narratives of the family history, which in turn are related to wider cultural narratives (the myths and histories of clans, regions, nations and the diaspora itself). How are these different narratives articulated within roots tourism and other genealogical practices?

Follow the life or biography – to consider the ways in which journeys to the Scottish Highlands are constituted as meaningful within the individual life stories or biographies of the diasporic Scots who undertake them. Might we understand these journeys in terms of what Giddens (1991) describes as the 'reflexive project of the self'? In this respect, what is the relationship between an individual's self-identity and their social identity? Is it possible to suggest that these somehow converge on the 'sites of memory' visited in the Highlands, and, if so, what are the implications for how we might understand the relationship between people and place more generally – particularly considering the supposedly deterritorialised nature of modern identity?

I approached the task of tracing these intersecting trajectories through a variety of means which, nevertheless, fell into two broad categories. These, in turn, mirror the two realms through which the homeland is experienced: the discursive realm of the global media (and, especially, the internet), and the material realm of the physical homeland: the Scottish Highlands.

'Homepages' – global media and communications

Studies of 'virtual communities' have tended to reify the internet as a discrete world – an inhabitable cyberspace, separate from the 'real' world and its unmediated communities. Jonathan Sterne, for example, suggests that studies of 'cybersociety' have typically been tainted by the 'rhetoric of millennial transformation' and he argues that,

> Only by treating the Internet as one site among many in the flow of economics, ideology, everyday life, and experience can Internet research become a vital intellectual and political component of media and cultural studies. Only by recognizing the Internet's banality can Internet research move beyond the clichés of the millennial imagination. (1999: 282)

Agreeing with Sterne, my objective has been to examine the 'interconnectedness' between the representation of Scotland in global media and communications systems and the actual place/country/nation: indeed, I believe it is impossible to even consider one without the other. The internet is only one facet of this, but whereas the 'creation' of Scotland in art, literature and cinema (e.g. Hart 1978; Macmillan 1992; Nicholson 1992; Petrie 2000), or in tourist promotions (e.g. Gold and Gold 1995; McCrone *et al.* 1995), has been well-researched, its representation on the internet, with its spatial and navigational metaphors, has not. There are hundreds of thousands of Scottish-interest web sites and hundreds, if not thousands, of related email discussion lists, newsgroups and chat rooms. It is also true to say that the internet has revolutionised the process of family history research and has become an indispensable tool for genealogists. Many people of Scottish descent dispersed throughout the world spend a great deal of time on the internet reading online versions of Scottish newspapers, pursuing their family history research, planning and organising their journeys, and participating in networked communities with others who share similar interests. These discursive realms play a crucial role in the creation and maintenance of Scottish diasporic consciousness.

My methodological approach to exploring these realms was a simple one, which ironically is actually more analogous to single-sited ethnography, and this was to regard these various sites of discursive production and consumption as the 'online habitus' of my informants. Over the course of a two-year period, I therefore spent an appreciable amount of time 'dwelling' in that same habitus, visiting Scottish-interest web sites, participating in and observing Scottish-interest and genealogy email discussion lists, subscribing to and reading online Scottish newspapers and Scottish genealogy journals, and so forth. The number of web sites I visited and monitored – including the personal web sites of diasporic Scots, clan society sites, genealogy sites, official tourism sites, etc. – was vast and, mirroring the practices of my informants, followed no particular logic beyond 'surfing' (discovering sites via search engines, recommendations and following hyperlinks). My subscriptions to email discussion lists were more quantifiable, however, and included:

Scottish general interest lists:

celtic_cultures@onelist.com
clans@rootsweb.com
fuadach-nan-gaidheal@list.sirius.com
jacobites@rootsweb.com
scotland@onelist.com
scotsusa@onelist.com
scottish_cultures@onelist.com

Scottish genealogy lists:

gen-trivia-scotland@rootsweb.com
scotland-genweb@rootsweb.com
scots-origins@egroups.com
sct-inverness@rootsweb.com

I also subscribed to a popular online weekly newsletter called 'Scottish Snippets' and to the online genealogy journals 'Rootsweb Review' and 'Missing Links'. I generally did not participate in discussions in these online fora but rather observed the interaction between active members. Although I maintained a low profile on these lists, I also established a list dedicated to the research project itself – homecomings@onelist.com – on which, as 'list owner', I was an active member.

The approach I have so far outlined to 'virtual ethnography', one which has become widely practised, is essentially textual. Discussion lists are literally text-based, and it is simple enough to observe and participate in various lists dealing with one's theme – one can either be explicit about one's objectives or 'lurk' and catalogue the various textual expressions and interactions anonymously. With the growing sophistication of internet technologies the analysis of web site content might also include less literal texts such as photographs, graphics, animations, sound clips, movie clips, live web cams, etc. – all of which may be found on Scottish-interest web sites. However, I also wanted to use the internet as a way of effectively 'conversing' with the diaspora, of eliciting the views and opinions of informants dispersed throughout the world, and, pragmatically, as a way of contacting roots tourists prior to their visits to Scotland. This necessitated a different kind of approach. Thus I decided to establish a research web site for the project itself and to promote this through existing Scottish-interest online networks.

The 'Homecomings' web site included a description of the project's research interests and objectives, an online questionnaire, a subscription page for the aforementioned discussion list, a clickable map of heritage centres and groups throughout the Highlands and Islands, links to other related web sites, my ESRC research proposal and a growing number of articles that I had written as the project progressed. The site and associated discussion list proved to be extremely successful and as well as generating a vast amount of comment on issues pertinent to the research – the discussion list, for instance, functioned as a kind of 100–150 person-strong 'focus group' for the duration of the project – the site enabled me to make contact and develop relationships of trust with those whom I would later join on their journeys. Given the relative brevity of the time spent touring with individual informants in the Highlands (two weeks at most), this prior correspondence meant that when we eventually met 'in person', we were not entirely strangers to each other.

The web site was also used as a way of feeding back research findings to those who had contributed to the project. This culminated in providing an online version of a touring exhibition that I curated in association with the National Museums of Scotland, which addressed the themes of the research.[1] This fostered a sense of collaboration and shared 'ownership' of the research project among informants, which, in turn, had a positive effect upon the time and effort informants were prepared to spend contributing to the project and thus enhanced the quality of the research data.

'Homelands' – the Scottish Highlands and Islands

In the non-mediated – or, at least, less obviously mediated – material world, my core objective was to spend as much time as possible actually travelling with roots tourists as they made their journeys. As already stated, the internet was an especially important tool in making this possible: first to make initial contact with potential informants and then to develop a relationship of trust with them through email correspondence about their forthcoming journeys (thereby acquiring a knowledge of their aspirations and expectations of their journeys). In many cases it was then possible to arrange to accompany informants on all or part of their journey in the Scottish Highlands and Islands, and then, again through email correspondence, to learn of their experiences and more distanced reflections after their return home. It was thus possible, over two years or so of fieldwork on- and offline, to track their homecomings from vague aspirations, through planning stages, to the physical journey itself, and then back again and the reintegration into ordinary life. When making journeys with informants, I would usually offer to drive: my informants and I would stay in the same accommodation,[2] we would eat together, visit people and places together and, in between, spend a good deal of time talking. At some stage in the journey I would usually conduct an informal recorded interview.

Although much of my research involved travelling with informants to locations throughout the Highlands and Islands, I felt it was also important to have a formal base for the project at an appropriate and recognised institution. Thus, after consultation with various heritage and local authority bodies, a research 'headquarters' was established at the Highland Folk Museum in Kingussie, Inverness-shire. The Highland Folk Museum was chosen for a number of pragmatic reasons: it is a relatively large, long-established, local authority-run museum which could offer me my own office/meeting room along with other office facilities; it has its own excellent research library and archive covering the whole of the Highlands and Islands region; and is both a heritage attraction and academic institution. Most importantly, Kingussie is situated on the main north–south, east–west communications routes, literally in the heart of the Central Highlands, and it therefore provided a convenient base for travel to all areas of the Highlands and was also easily accessible for potential informants. Situated on the River Spey, with the Cairngorm mountains to the south-east and the Monadhliath range to the north-west, Kingussie is a small town at the centre of an area renowned for its scenic beauty and is therefore a popular tourist destination itself. It was also the home of James Macpherson, 'translator' of *The Works of Ossian* and one of the great romanticisers of the Scottish Highland landscape. In the neighbouring village of Newtonmore is the Clan Macpherson Museum – established in 1952, the first such clan museum in Scotland – which forms a focus for the activities of the international Clan Macpherson Association.

For the period of my fieldwork during which I was based in Kingussie (from April 1999 to October 2000), and when I was not travelling, I kept regular office hours at the Highland Folk Museum and encouraged potential informants to pop in to see me if they were in the area. The Highland Folk Museum had recently undertaken an ambitious expansion of its 'open air' site which included the reconstruction of a *c.*1700 Highland township based on the archaeological excavation of nearby Easter Raitts (Lelong and Wood 2000) and a *c.*1920 working croft. This proved useful in attracting more casually interested roots tourists to travel some distance to see me and effectively add the research project to their existing tour itineraries. Contact with such informants was naturally more superficial and typically involved an informal two-hour recorded interview. At the start of the spring/summer tourist season I was able to brief the seasonal museum staff about my research and encourage them to recommend the project to potential informants whom they might identify in their day to day interaction with visitors (diasporic visitors are often keen to identify themselves as having Scottish roots in their interactions with museum staff, bed and breakfast operators, etc.). When I was away travelling, a questionnaire and contact sheet were left at the Museum for staff to hand out to potential informants.

At one level my informants undeniably *were* tourists. Their journeys typically lasted between two and four weeks, they would travel by air, rail, ferry and hire car, they would use hotel and bed and breakfast accommodation, and they would visit general heritage attractions as well as more personally meaningful sites. If I was to gain access to those visitors who had no previous knowledge of my research project while they were touring around the Highlands and Islands, I realised I would have to promote the project as if it were a tourist attraction itself. Thus, as well as meeting informants with whom I had already established contact, much of the first phase of my fieldwork was spent advertising the project in one way or another. A key tool in accomplishing this was the production of an eye-catching leaflet which could be distributed throughout the Highlands and Islands as well as in key locations outside the region. Ten thousand copies of the leaflet were thus printed and distributed to tourist attractions, museums, heritage centres, libraries, archive offices, local and family history societies, hotels, B&Bs, etc. Using graphics and text, the leaflet introduced the themes of the research and encouraged visitors to participate in the project, either by making contact while they were travelling in the area or, if this was not possible, to make contact by email or ordinary post or to complete the project's online questionnaire once they had returned to their ordinary place of residence.

The project was promoted in other ways too. For instance, I frequently presented talks to local history groups and at heritage or family history events in the Highlands. This provided interaction with people who shared an interest in the themes of the research and who had regular contact with diasporic visitors (such groups had many insights of their own to share and would often mention my work to potential informants). I also issued press releases to local newspapers and tourism agencies; these were received enthusiastically and resulted in numerous more extended newspaper articles and radio interviews about the project. These efforts at promoting the research ensured that the project maintained a high profile and thus attracted diasporic visitors who might otherwise have been unaware of its existence or not considered it worthwhile taking time out of their hectic tour schedules to participate.

My fieldwork additionally included participation in packaged events such as the 'Orkney Homecoming' of 1999 and 'Gordon 2000' (also promoted as 'The Highland Homecoming'), in a number of international clan gatherings (most notably the Clan Macpherson gatherings of 1999 and 2000, and the Clan Grant gathering of 2000), and in numerous more general events such as Highland games, folk festivals, heritage walks and exhibitions. As well as roots tourists, I conducted interviews with organisers of such events and with other individuals concerned with roots tourism: heritage managers, professional genealogists, policy-makers, and so forth.

In 2001, after the main phase of my fieldwork was completed, I spent nine months working in a small community-run heritage centre in Dunbeath, Caithness. Through the efforts of its volunteer staff, the centre boasts a superb genealogical database of Dunbeath families past and present. I was amazed that during the summer months, in this tiny village in the far north of Scotland, a week did not pass without at least one overseas visitor announcing that she or he had ancestral connections in the area. Such announcements would be met by a flurry of activity as box files, photographs, maps and family-tree charts would be produced and, over countless cups of tea, excursions to long-deserted crofts or settlements in the area would be arranged. The scenario is a familiar one to heritage centre and museum staff throughout the Highlands and Islands, and demonstrates the key role such venues have not only as repositories of documents, artefacts and memories, but also as the 'contact zones' between roots tourists and the communities among which their ancestors once lived (Clifford 1997). Although not planned as such, the experience of working with a small community heritage initiative proved an essential component of the research.

The focus of these journeys was, of course, the ancestral home itself. As we shall see in Chapter 3, this can be manifested in different ways: for some it is Scotland as a whole, for others a particular house in a particular village or settlement (and including every increment between). Thus, time was also spent exploring different aspects of this heritage landscape: analysing the displays of clan museums and heritage centres; visiting the iconic sites of Highland history (examining how these histories had been commemorated in their monuments and interpretive signage); visiting less obvious sites which nevertheless figure in the region's cultural narratives (most notably settlements deserted during the Highland Clearances or in subsequent times, investigating the alternative ways in which local populations used the sites to tell stories of the past). I was also keen to situate the journeys I was researching within wider contexts. With this in mind, I made a tour of museums and heritage sites in Ireland, investigating the validity of parallels drawn between the Highland Clearances – the cultural trauma which, in Scottish diasporic consciousness, is often used to explain the dispersal of the Highlanders – and its posited equivalent in Irish diasporic consciousness: the Famine.

Such a range of qualitatively different experiences and interactions with informants – from two-hour recorded interviews, to two-week journeys in their company, to two-year email correspondences – clearly produces an equal variation in the nature of the data collected. These 'encounters' do not constitute the 'total experience' espoused by anthropologists working in more bounded contexts (Okley quoted by Amit 2000: 15), but, as I have argued, such holism is not possible in the study of the journeys with which I am concerned. Believing this should not render them inappropriate objects for anthropological research, I therefore adopted the pluralistic strategy outlined above, an approach which exemplifies that described by Amit in which researchers must 'purposively create the occasions for contacts that might well be as mobile, diffuse and episodic as the processes they are studying' (2000: 15). Amassed, the resultant data forms a collage – of glimpses and fragments, but also of more substantial, nuanced impressions. The task of the ethnographer thus remains to posit what 'logics of association and connection' he or she discerns in the collage, and hence, as Marcus suggests, to construct the argument of his or her ethnography (1995: 105).[3]

3 Genealogy and heritage tourism in the Scottish diaspora: an overview

In this chapter I present an overview of the roots tourism phenomenon with which the book is concerned through the analysis of material collected via the questionnaire that featured on my research project's web site. During the fieldwork phase of the research, I received 244 completed questionnaires, totalling some 80,000 words of comment from visitors and would-be visitors to Scotland on issues relating to genealogy, heritage tourism and Scottish diasporic consciousness. Although providing some additional commentary, my intention here is to resist interpretation and permit the 'voices' of the roots tourists themselves to be heard. Their insightful comments anticipate many of the themes around which subsequent, more analytical, chapters will revolve.

Although the questionnaire was designed to elicit qualitative data, basic quantitative data was also sought for contextual purposes. Whilst this was an online questionnaire and access to the internet is not evenly distributed across all ages, occupation groups and nationalities, a particularly high level of internet usage has been identified among this interest-group, the internet having become an indispensable tool for conducting family history research. Fifty-four per cent of my questionnaire respondents were female, 46 per cent male. Approximately two-thirds had visited Scotland in the past, the remaining third hadn't visited at the time of completing the questionnaire but, almost without exception, were either planning a visit or expressed a desire to visit in the future. The following further inferences may be drawn from the statistical data.

'That mid-life thing' – age range and interest in family history

Figure 3.1 shows the age spread of questionnaire respondents. Peaking at the age range of 50–54 years, this demonstrates that an interest in family history research and roots tourism is not limited to individuals of retirement age as is often assumed. Although this spread may be influenced by a lower level of internet usage in older age groups, it also reflects a greater propensity for younger middle-aged people, whose children have typically

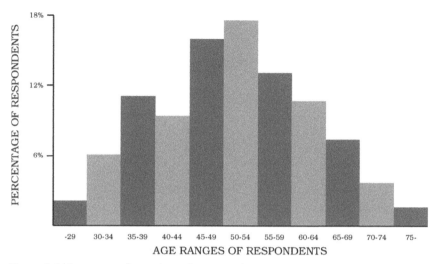

Figure 3.1 Age range of questionnaire respondents

left home and who have relatively high disposable incomes, to travel over-seas to pursue such interests.

Many respondents, particularly those who grew up hearing stories from grandparents, indicated that they had been interested in their family history since childhood, but that this interest often lay dormant until later life. A renewed enthusiasm for family history in middle age was provoked by a number of factors, including having children of their own, caring for elderly parents, the death of parents or grandparents, regret at taking family history knowledge for granted, a sense of responsibility concerning the transmission of this knowledge to future generations, vaguer senses of entering a more 'reflective' time of life ('that mid-life thing' (JS, Victoria, Australia)), and more pragmatic factors such as increased leisure time in retirement or part-retirement. Many of these themes are conveyed in the following selection of responses to a question enquiring whether family history had always been an active interest:

> As a child and young adult I had the vague notion I was 'British' in origins but had nothing to verify it and didn't care too much anyway. In rare moments I would wonder about it, especially if I had Scottish ancestry. In my middle age, I found myself seriously questioning the whole ancestry thing and decided to do something about it. Ancestral connections are now very important to me. (AS, Auckland, New Zealand – age 66)

> After both my parents died I realized that I couldn't ask them any more questions, so to help my children I want to find out everything I can now. (AS, Illinois, USA – age 47)

I heard many stories of my paternal grandmother's family but it wasn't until she died that I realized how much I lost and promised myself that I would not take it for granted again and have been working on it ever since. (KC, Ontario, Canada – age 37)

Always somewhat important, but as my own children grew and are on the verge of moving away, I am aware of their connectedness to the past. My family history research validates the values I have sought to teach them, and gives me a chance to preserve their history for them before my mother's generation are all gone. (DB, British Columbia, Canada – age 51)

Like most people, I found it mildly interesting when I was a child, and more so as I got older. The older you get the more your life becomes an extension of the past. (BM, Western Australia, Australia – age 62)

'White collar affluents' – a middle-class milieu

The vast majority of respondents worked in the 'white collar' sector, with notably high numbers engaged in secretarial or administrative work (8 per cent), education (11 per cent), health care (15 per cent), business management, finance and other professions (29 per cent). Approximately 20 per cent indicated that they were retired. Accepting the limitations of the online methodology and the self-selection of respondents, the serious pursuit of family history research thus appears to be an overwhelmingly middle-class activity. A mere 2.5 per cent of respondents were engaged in manual labour. This demographic is also reflected in Scottish Tourist Board (STB) market research, where the genealogy niche market is described as including 'US Seniors' ('travellers, aged 55–75, with an income over £35,000 a year') and 'Australian White Collar Affluents' ('sophisticated "baby boomers" aged between 45 and 70 from urban, East Coast or Western Australia ... "empty nesters", travelling in couples, whose children have left home') (www.scotexchange.net).

Indices of identity

One of the objectives of the questionnaire was to analyse the correlation between notions of self-defined 'cultural identity' and other indicators of identity such as country of birth, country of residence and passport nationality. In round figures, 47 per cent of respondents lived in the USA, 23 per cent in Canada, 13 per cent in Australia, 6 per cent in New Zealand, 6 per cent in England, 2 per cent in Scotland (the remaining respondents were spread between South Africa, Ireland, Wales, France, Denmark and the Netherlands). The full data is presented in Table 3.1.

It is interesting to note that a significant minority of respondents were born in Scotland but now reside overseas. Many of these people emigrated as children with their families, sometimes reluctantly: the issue of 'belonging' to Scotland for this group is clearly highly charged:

> I have never gotten over leaving Scotland. My heart is there every day of my life. (MR, Ontario, Canada – emigrated aged 9)

> Scotland has and always will be a very big part of my life. Although I am very comfortable and happy in Canada, the fact is that I felt that I was wrenched away from Scotland at an early age. (RD, Ontario, Canada – emigrated aged 10)

> I believe because I did not choose to leave my homeland it will always remain in my heart as my home. It is important to me to know that I can always return to my country and feel at home. (BK, Ontario, Canada – emigrated aged 15)

The most fascinating observation to be drawn from Table 3.1 is, however, the disparity between a person's own descriptions of their identity and the bureaucratic equation of identity with the nation in which a person was born, resides or holds citizenship. Although only four of the respondents actually lived in Scotland, 39 defined their cultural identity as 'Scottish' (with a further 11 describing themselves as 'Highlanders' and 19 in terms of the clan with which they identified). This varied in different regions of the diaspora. Thus, averaging the three indices of 'bureaucratised' identity (birth, residence and citizenship), whereas nearly two-thirds of Australian informants described their cultural identities as 'Australian', under a third of American, Canadian and New Zealander respondents described themselves respectively as 'Americans', 'Canadians' and 'New Zealanders' (with noteworthy differences between American and Canadian respondents).

Table 3.1 Indices of identity

Country	Residence	Birth	Passport	Cultural ID	Disparity
USA	47.1	40.8	44.0	13.3	30.2
Canada	23.3	17.9	19.3	4.6	22.8
Australia	12.5	11.7	11.5	7.5	63.0
New Zealand	6.3	4.2	4.5	1.7	34.0
Scotland	1.7	12.9	n/a	16.3	223.3
England	6.3	7.5	n/a	0.4	5.8

Note: figures in first four columns are percentages of total number of respondents, figures in the last column represent the disparity between cultural identity and an average of country of residence, country of birth and passport nationality (e.g. 4.6% of respondents identified their cultural identity as being Canadian, this is only 22.8% of those who might be identified as Canadian through birth, residence and citizenship).

Although my focus was on the Scottish diaspora outside the UK, the percentage of English respondents describing their cultural identity as 'English' was even smaller.

Considering the multicultural nature of contemporary New World societies, particularly in the USA, Canada and Australia, it is not surprising to note that nearly half of all respondents used a more complex description of their cultural identity: sometimes these were familiar compounds such as 'Scottish-American', or other terms indicating ancestry such as 'Canadian of Scottish descent', but there were also many more elaborate descriptions: 'American Scotch-Irish with Highlander roots', 'Heinz 57 – colloquial for American – but strongly feel the need to be rooted in Scotland and Ireland', 'MacKinnon Clan and Highlander Descent born in Canada', 'South African but would love to be Scottish', 'American of basically Celtic (Scots, Irish and Welsh), German and Native American (Indian) descent'. For those descriptions, such as the last, which really demonstrate what the 'Heinz 57' colloquialism means, the key question ought perhaps to be what draws an individual to identify with one possible identity rather than another. For example, a respondent living in Virginia described her cultural identity as 'Half Swedish, Half Scottish-Irish-English' and explained that she was planning to visit her ancestral homes in Scotland, Ireland and Sweden, but that she had no interest in visiting England: 'I feel absolutely no affinity for England at this time' (CFM, Virginia, USA). Another, from Australia, writes, 'Although I also have English and Irish ancestry, I've always felt a strong association with all things Scottish, particularly Highland. I can't explain why' (LH, ACT, Australia).

I have observed this 'selectiveness' when it comes to choosing which part of one's heritage to pursue on many occasions. If a person has Polish, English, Lowland Scot and Highland Scot ancestors, for instance, it is quite typical for the person to choose to pursue an interest in her Scottish heritage above her Polish or English heritage, and her Highland heritage above her Lowland heritage. In her study of the 'ethnic options' available to white populations in the USA, Mary Waters observes a similar ranking of different ethnicities. Interestingly, Waters' research was carried out among Catholic populations in California and Pennsylvania, and Scots – identified as staunchly Protestant – featured as the most unpopular of possible ethnicities with which to identify (1990: 82–3). Since Waters' work in the mid-1980s, and thanks to films such as *Braveheart* and the broader 'Celtic revival', Scottish (particularly Highland) identity has, however, been rehabilitated and is no longer so closely associated with the negative stereotypes of Calvinistic thrift and dourness. It should also be remembered that, since the late eighteenth century, the Scottish Highlands, with its mountains and glens, misty isles and loch-side castles, has been one of the most romanticised landscapes in Western literature, art, film and photography, and there is no doubt that this romantic image continues to exert a powerful influence on individuals' choices of which ancestry to identify with. Indeed, the Highland landscape featured in many informants' responses to a question asking *What single experience left the deepest impression with you from your visit?*

> The Highlands and their ineffable beauty. I have seen the Himalayas, the Rockies and many other ranges but there is nothing to compare with the Scottish Highlands. (RG, New South Wales, Australia)

> The landscape. Some of the oldest mountains in the world, rolling and deep green. Damp and hazy, but magnificent and beautiful. (AR, Illinois, USA)

> The timelessness of the landscape. (IG, Auckland, New Zealand)

Performing 'Scottishness' in the diaspora

Although some respondents lived in regions of the diaspora where 'Scottishness is in the air' (AB, Nova Scotia, Canada) and others had recognisably Scottish surnames ('I carry my surname with pride' (LD, British Columbia, Canada)), many more had to resort to more self-conscious means of demonstrating or maintaining a sense of Scottish identity. This was most frequently articulated through the material culture of the domestic home space; through other lifestyle preferences such as music, dress, food and drink; through participation in Scottish heritage organisations, festivals and events; and not least through the practice of family history research itself.

> My home reflects my Scottish ancestry with family photos, maps of the Clans of Scotland, books, fleur-de-lys patterns on everything from pillows to candles, a Matheson coat of arms on display and, along with paintings of castles, there is a suit of armour in the corner. (SF, Georgia, USA)

> We have a Scottish tea cosy, we also have an antique chair which comes from my Great Grandmother Mackintosh. The covering on my loungesuite in our family room is tartan ... plus photographs of grandparents displayed. (BR, Natal, South Africa)

> Cook Scottish foods, read Scottish newspapers, visit Scottish web sites, support Scotland's national football sides and Aberdeen FC, read books by Scottish authors about Scotland, attend the odd Scottish-themed function, i.e. dinners and Highland gatherings. (MM, New South Wales, Australia)

> I wear the Clan pins. I have a picture of Bonnie Prince Charlie leaving Scotland, the Clan MacKenzie tartans are in view, Scottish records, tapes and videos, Scottish friends who sing, member of the Clan – receive newsletters, on several email lists, maps of Scotland on wall and genealogy everywhere. (JM, British Columbia, Canada)

I listen to bagpipe music often, read many books and magazines about Scotland, do family research from Scottish records and display many objects from Scotland in my home. (DS, Oregon, USA)

Several respondents clearly felt that such conspicuous performances of identity were unnecessary or inauthentic; one suggested there were 'far too many "professional" Scots living outside Scotland' (DC, Ontario, Canada):

It's what's in your head, not on the wall or mantelpiece. (BM, Queensland, Australia)

'Scottishness' for me is not related to things or furnishings. It is a spirit, culture and belief system worth preserving. Kilts and thistles are not required. (MM, Virginia, USA)

My sense of Scottishness is an internal thing – I don't want to try and manufacture it by wearing tartans and hanging up contrived coats of arms and stuff like that. (KP, Georgia, USA)

Over half of the questionnaire respondents indicated that they belonged to a Scottish-interest organisation of one kind or another. Thirty per cent belonged to a clan society or association, whilst other popular organisations included St Andrew's societies, Scottish societies, genealogy societies and Scottish music or dance groups. Many reported that they subscribed to email discussion lists concerned with Scottish and genealogical themes. A sizeable minority regularly attended Highland Games, Burns' Night suppers and the like.

Knowledge of family history

There was a huge variation in the level of respondents' knowledge about their family histories. Some had only recently discovered a Scottish connection or were just beginning their research, others had a very comprehensive knowledge about the names and dates of their ancestors, where they had lived, when they had emigrated from Scotland and so forth. Some romantically traced their descent from royal lineages, others were equally proud of their rural labouring heritage.

Have always been told that we were Scots. This is the only information that I have but this has been passed down through the generations. (BA, Texas, USA)

Aside from having the last name Gordon, which we know is Scottish, we have no real information of when our ancestors came to the US from Scotland. We think it may have been during the French and Indian War in the 1750s. (RG, Pennsylvania, USA)

Two of my g-g-grandfathers left extensive family histories behind, from which my sister, a cousin and myself, have managed to trace branches of our families back to Malcolm Canmore [King of Scotland 1058–1093] and beyond. We continue to work on our genealogy to this day, although I have hit a wall on my Fullarton and Reid lines in the 18th century. (MF, Pennsylvania, USA)

Henry McDonald and Una McMaster married in Kilmonivaig nr Fort William in 1839. He was an agricultural labourer. He came from Suddy (Ross and Cromarty) and she from a farm in Kilmonivaig parish (Tomacharrich). Between then and emigration in 1854, they lived in the Inverlochy area. Had 7 kids – two seem to have died in infancy. In Oct 1854 the family emigrated from Liverpool under the auspices of the Highland and Island Emigration Society. Landed at Portland Bay, Victoria, Australia in 1855. The next record I have is the 1864 marriage of their oldest daughter at Wellingrove, New South Wales. The nearest large town was Glen Innes, which was settled by Scots. In this area lived and still live McMasters – prominent graziers – and almost certainly one was the cousin of Una. So they seem to follow out to Australia relatives who had come decades earlier. (DM, ACT, Australia)

How family history knowledge is acquired

Family history knowledge is acquired through a variety of methods. There are a great many published genealogy how-to guides,[1] and each one will advise that the first stage of research should be to gather whatever information is already available within the family: talking to elderly relations, collecting old photographs or family documents, writing down family stories remembered from childhood. Thus, most questionnaire respondents indicated that their family history knowledge was partly handed down from earlier generations, either as stories or items of material culture (a family bible, a photograph album, etc.), and partly acquired through documentary research.

> [*How was knowledge acquired?*] Listening to my grandfather's stories at first when I was young. Then a family member showed me the family history research he'd done on one line of our family, and I decided to find out more and started researching myself. Found another family member who'd kept their old letters and began to feel I knew them. (EL, New South Wales, Australia)

Only 10 per cent of the respondents had engaged a professional genealogist to aid their research, in fact many seemed proud of the fact that they had not needed professional assistance – it was evidently more satisfying to undertake the task themselves.

I have only had to resort to using a professional researcher once. I prefer to do the research myself as it gives a sense of satisfaction, provides insight into their lifestyle since source documents can contain other pieces of information, even if it pertains to other families. There is also the knowledge that if you are wrong there is only yourself to blame. I also like researching, always have done even before I began doing the family history. (SJ, New South Wales, Australia)

Perhaps the most significant development in the practice of genealogical research has come with the popularisation of the internet. Indeed this technology has significantly contributed to the phenomenal growth of interest in genealogy in recent years. There is a profusion of genealogical research resources available on the web, including vast searchable databases of census and birth, marriage and death registration information (the most notable of these are the Church of Jesus Christ of Latter-Day Saints' (LDS) *Family Search* site (www.familysearch.com) and, in a specifically Scottish context, the General Register Office for Scotland's *Scots Origins* site (www.scotsorigins.com)). There are also genealogy 'portals' such as *Cyndi's List* (www.CyndisList.com) and *GENUKI* (www.genuki.org.uk), which provide links to tens of thousands of other genealogy sites, navigable by region, surname and other categories, and thousands of email discussion lists devoted to different aspects of genealogical research. Many questionnaire respondents commented on how they used such resources to gather information on their family histories and forge online relationships with other researchers or newly-found family members ('internet cousins', as they are known among online researchers). The research process does not, however, necessarily begin and end with the internet, as the following statement makes clear:

The search began in the LDS libraries and the Cloverdale Reference Library – which is excellent for Canadian genealogy. When I got online, other wonderful connections were made. Also I inquired to the Clan MacKenzie genealogist and he provided a family link stemming back 5 generations. They were also able to send me information on our family connections. Equipped with the key information, I went to Scotland in the summer of 1999 and explored the Inverness Reference Library using the Findon Tables and other MacKenzie books. Afterwards, the Museum in Ullapool is very good with information regarding the Clearances and family movement all over the world. (JM, British Columbia, Canada)

In the context of genealogical tourism in Scotland, an important observation that can be drawn from the questionnaire respondents' comments is that most serious family history research is pursued at home, not during visits to Scotland. Largely because of the internet and the international network of LDS and other family research centres, much work can be done at a distance and few respondents actually visited Scotland with the express intention of conducting documentary research. Those who did were sometimes disappointed with what they could achieve in the little time they had available. Unsurprisingly, few were prepared to waste an expensive trip to what is perceived as an exceptionally beautiful country sitting in an archives office accessing information that is largely available via the internet anyway. This is not to say that significant discoveries are never made during visits to Scotland, but that the majority of roots tourists are actually looking for something rather different in their journeys – identifying precisely what is, of course, one of the concerns of this book.

Ancestral homelands

Questionnaire respondents were asked whether they had what they considered to be an 'ancestral home', and, if so, where it was located. Around two-thirds indicated that they could identify an ancestral home; many of those who could not nevertheless expressed a desire to find such a place:

> I do not, but feverishly wish I did. (RK, Ontario, Canada)

> If only I knew where to look. This is my dream, to find the land that my ancestors were born on. (MR, California, USA)

For those who did have an ancestral home, the ability to identify its location was dependent on a number of factors including the level of the respondents' family history knowledge, the desire to select one place associated with their family history over another, and variations in the interpretation of what actually constituted an ancestral home. Of the most popular types of location described, 28 per cent identified a particular town or village in Scotland, 17 per cent a particular region or island, 15 per cent a particular house, croft or farm, 10 per cent a castle or clan chief's residence, and 6 per cent a clan territory. 10 per cent of respondents identified Scotland as a whole as their ancestral home.

Generally speaking, the more precise the location identified as 'home', the more powerful the experience of visiting it. Thus, for roots tourists to find and visit an old family crofthouse would result in a more powerful experience than visiting the wider region in which their ancestors appear to have lived according to old parochial records. Similarly, to identify and visit such a parish or region within Scotland would result in a more powerful experience than simply knowing they had some Scottish connection (through their surname, for instance). Having made this perhaps obvious statement, it is interesting to note that Scotland as a whole can also take on a profound significance, as the following statement makes clear:

> As of yet, I don't feel an ancestral family home. I feel the land – Scotland – and felt it many, many years before I actually went there.

Once I arrived, I did honestly feel 'at home'. Perhaps my next visit will allow my heart to pinpoint more precisely where 'home' is. There are likely obvious places, but I try not to be influenced too much on information. My whole goal each time I go to Scotland is to let my heart tell me, not the facts – does that make sense to anyone on this earth besides me?? (BV, Ontario, Canada)

This respondent's fears about making sense are not without justification and, unsurprisingly, the STB is not well equipped to engage with such intuitive and heart-led approaches to planning – or, rather, not planning – an itinerary. Most roots tourists would, however, understand perfectly this desire to relinquish rational control and submit to some kind of 'homing instinct'. Indeed, many roots tourists report having mystical experiences during their journeys, particularly senses of being guided in their quests by their ancestors.

For people such as this Canadian respondent, Scotland is not merely a place: it is an idea and an ideal. Many diasporic Scots identify Scotland as home in a profound sense. In apparent variance with Rapport and Dawson's argument (1998) that, in a postmodern world of perceived movement, home, as 'seat' of identity, is no longer rooted in a particular place but rather located in mobility itself, there is evident in many respondents' comments a nostalgia for a 'lost homeland' – a place of perceived stability, where traditions survive and where time seems to move more slowly. Indeed, the following comments allude to a sense of time travel when visiting Scotland:

The small villages we went through nestled at the bottom of craggy mountains. It was as though, if I'd stepped off the train, I'd be alighting in a different era. (VH, Nevada, USA)

Visiting Scotland was far from a holiday, it was a step back in time. (BC, Texas, USA)

It was a most enjoyable holiday, but it was also a trip back in time to the 1880s visiting the street where my grandfather was born and his parents and siblings walked and worked and went about their daily lives. (PK, Illinois, USA)

This is not just about the accessibility of the past in certain places. Rather, the people of the Scottish homeland are perceived to live more traditional lives, adhering to values felt to have long since eroded in the New World.

I have always been very attracted to Scottish culture. Since I have found out I am of Scottish heritage I understand why I feel so drawn to the older way of life. (A, Florida, USA)

It is interesting to note that the majority of these kinds of comments came from the USA, and it was from a number of American respondents that some explanation of the situation was proffered.

> I believe that with the American society crumbling it is more important than ever before to know who you are. Part of that knowledge will necessarily include a knowledge of where one comes from. This knowledge can give a person a sense of purpose, and a well from which to draw in my efforts to be an honorable man. (BM, Texas, USA)

> I know that too many people in my country are lost, because they have no set of norms or rules to follow, and they are losing their traditions. I think this is hurting us as a whole, and that people need to take pride in the knowledge of where they come from. You have to know where you come from to know where you are going. (SS, Pennsylvania, USA)

> I have found after being in the States for a few months that there is an opinion that the reason a number of people here feel lost and hopeless is the loss of their roots. I have found a great deal of people are realizing this. I have always felt that it is important to know these things and have passed many of the family stories on to my children and plan to write a family history for the benefit of the whole family. I consider myself to be very lucky in knowing where my roots are. (CW, Alberta, Canada – working in California, USA)

In these statements, American society is portrayed as a society in crisis, in which the individual is threatened with senses of dislocation, rootlessness and personal meaninglessness. The respondents seem to find ontological security in their knowledge of their family histories, and the pursuit of genealogical research thus becomes a means of 're-rooting' themselves and their families.

The importance of roots

The following section comprises responses to the question 'Is it important to know where your roots are? Why?' Of course, not every respondent was equally earnest in their interest in their roots. Some felt confident of their identity and heritage:

> It isn't important, but, because I more or less know, perhaps I take it for granted. I often forget I'm Scottish until I maybe hear an accent and think, 'oh yes, my Mum talks like that'. I am aware that I have a Scottish story, but I live in the present. (LE, Wellington, New Zealand)

For others, their roots were a matter of curiosity:

It is 'interesting' to know, but I wouldn't say it was 'important' to know. (GC, Michigan, USA)

It is important to me, personally, to satisfy curiosity, to understand where I came from, how my ancestors interacted with history, and to be able to have information to pass on to younger generations. (RS, Texas, USA)

For others still it was the 'thrill of the chase' that explained their genealogical interest:

I find the search for my roots exciting and challenging. The more I learn of my ancestors, the closer I feel to them. (KC, Ontario, Canada)

However, the vast majority of answers articulated more powerful emotions. Some resorted to poetry, such as Scott's 'The Patriot':

Breathes there the man with soul so dead,
Who never to himself hath said,
This is my own, my native land!
Whose heart hath ne'er within him burn'd,
As home his footsteps he hath turn'd
From wandering on a foreign strand! (quoted by BM, Queensland, Australia)

Other typical responses are provided under the following subheadings.

Giving purpose to travel:

Love history. Roots help explain things. Searching provides a reason for travel which would otherwise be aimless and empty. Gives sense of creating and accomplishing something. (EL, Pennsylvania, USA)

Giving meaning to life:

Without knowledge of my roots, life would be, to some degree, somewhat meaningless. In order to go forward, I need to have a knowledge of my past, and the past of my ancestors. (MM, New South Wales, Australia)

Feelings of connection:

I feel a strong connection to my ancestors and want to know as much about them as possible. When I was in Scotland and especially in the area where they came from I was very aware that they would have seen the same sights and perhaps even walked the same paths. The feeling of connection was very strong. (MC, Victoria, Australia)

I believe that it is important to have a connection to some place in one's 'Mother Country'. Even though I have never been there, I was raised to hold Scotland dearly and to aspire to go there. (MF, Pennsylvania, USA)

Family traits and values:

I feel that it is very, very important for individuals to know where they come from. I think it's wonderful to see how our ancestors were influenced, the world they lived in, the hardships and joys of people so close to us, yet people we've never met. I think we can see the influence with respect to personalities and physical traits common among many generations. (RL, Ontario, Canada)

I've been told many times throughout my life that it isn't hard to tell that I'm Scottish. My families of origin on both sides are Scottish. My father raised us in the morality of Scottish tradition, and he let us know that it was important to remember that we were McLeods. My brothers and father are gone now, and I am the only one left to pass things on to future generations. (JV, Ontario, Canada)

Pride:

Even though I am 4th generation New Zealander I have Scottish blood in my veins and am intensely proud of the fact. Yes, I think knowing your roots is important, it gives you a sense of where you have come from and what your ancestors have experienced. (BG, Wellington, New Zealand)

Cultural diversity in the New World:

Canada was built by people from many different nationalities and cultures and I feel it is important to at least attempt to leave some sense of history for my children, grandchildren and the generations to come. My personal heritage is Scotch/English, my wife's is English/Polish and now one of our daughters has married a fellow of Dutch origin. As these nationalities meld together as Canadians we must remember our forefathers and their customs and heritage. (DA, British Columbia, Canada)

It gives me a feeling of belonging to a historical community, even more now that in Australia we have so many people of varying ethnic backgrounds. (BC, New South Wales, Australia)

In the US today we are more than ever a melting pot of citizens. I need to look back and identify with the land from which my ancestors left. And for what reasons they left. It is a sense of belonging! (TH, Illinois, USA)

Problematic belonging in country of birth:

> It is as important as one wants to make it. For most of my life it didn't matter at all, though a vague wonder came to me from time to time. It is now important because, though a 4th generation New Zealander, there is a feeling of belonging elsewhere. The major importance was in learning about that 'elsewhere' and realizing it did have a real connection for me. I dare to say almost a sense of belonging to a place other than the country of my birth. It is a feeling that is hard to describe. (AS, Auckland, New Zealand)

Understanding oneself and one's place in the world:

> It gives me a better understanding of who I am and what my place in the world is. I am a product of my ancestry and my environment. One I can see, the other I have to look for. (VH, Nevada, USA)

> It is important to know who you are and who your antecedents were. It helps you to understand yourself better and allows you to fix yourself securely in the wider history of all people. (CB, British Columbia, Canada)

A psychological rebirth. Conferring depth to existence:

> When I first visited Scotland in 1986, it was a sort of psychological beginning for me, explaining so much about myself, my family. Never mind the love and addiction I felt towards the land itself. (KW, California, USA)

> It gives one a sense of belonging and I did not seem to have this before I began the family history research. It is hard to describe but there was no depth to my existence – now I feel there is. (SJ, New South Wales, Australia)

The comments continue to range over many other themes: identity; continuity between past, present and future; grievances over being 'exiled'; spiritual callings; completing the 'circle of life'. The examples provided above, however, are adequate to make the point that the search for roots is not a trivial activity.

Homecomings

I should now like to turn to the experience of visiting (or anticipating a visit to) Scotland. As stated earlier, approximately two-thirds of the questionnaire respondents had already visited Scotland. Thirty-nine per cent of this group had visited once only, 23 per cent twice, 8 per cent thrice and 30 per cent four or more times. The percentage visiting four or more times was swelled by those respondents living within the UK, who quite often make annual visits, and also by people who had themselves emigrated and who therefore had close relatives still living in Scotland.

Itineraries

Those respondents who had visited Scotland were asked to name ten places they had included in their itinerary. When the lists were collated and the results analysed, an interesting pattern emerged in which a limited number of places appeared frequently, whereas the majority of places appeared very infrequently – indeed, 63 per cent of places appeared in only one list. Only 14 places appeared in 10 per cent or more of the lists, of these the majority are to be found on the main A9/A82 tourist routes.

What this demonstrates is that the genealogical aspect of these respondents' journeys is one facet of a more general touristic experience, which takes in the main towns and cities (particularly those perceived as cultural or historical), popular beauty spots such as Loch Ness and Loch Lomond (famed through monster and song respectively), iconic sites such as Glencoe and Culloden and a trip out to the islands – either Skye or Mull and Iona. The more personal journeys to places associated with respondents' ancestors are evidently additions to this popular itinerary, involving detours to very specific places, which are often not established tourist destinations: hence the large number of places which appear only once in the collated lists. As would be expected, this trend does not hold true for return visits: having made a more touristic journey, subsequent visits will often be directed to specific areas, either pursuing new, more precise leads uncovered in the process of genealogical research or else getting a better 'feel' for an ancestral place by spending more time in a particular locality.

These observations are significant when considering that this group often defines its activities *contra* tourism, which is characterised as superficial and consumerist. There is no doubt, however, that the boundary between these more profound homecomings and the routine practices of tourism is a blurred one.

Experiences

To explore what roots tourists typically experience in their visits to Scotland, I asked six questions:

1   What did you expect from your visit to Scotland?
2   Were your expectations met? If not, what surprised you?
3   Was it a holiday or something more profound?

4   What single experience left the deepest impression with you?
5   Can you summarise what the experience of visiting Scotland meant for you?
6   What souvenirs do you have from your visit?

Expectations

Many diasporic Scots have never visited Scotland but have nevertheless been raised on stories and descriptions of the old country and are avid readers and viewers of Scottish books, films and web sites. Such people have long imagined Scotland, its historical places, its landscapes, the character of its people:

> To see a beautiful country I've read and heard about all my life. (CO, Alberta, Canada)

> A peaceful, beautiful, friendly land. (BJ, Utah, USA)

> Beautiful scenery as depicted in calendars, post cards, etc. Friendly people who were warm to New Zealanders. (PC, Hawkes Bay, New Zealand)

A large number of respondents anticipated a feeling of returning home or connecting with their roots through visiting places associated with their ancestors:

> To feel as if I was 'going home'. (AM, Victoria, Australia)

> A sense of coming home. (DG, Norfolk, England)

> To visit places the family originated from and stand on the same piece of earth [as them]. (MF, Auckland, New Zealand)

The notion of time travel was also again articulated.

> To see the present, to see the past. (LD, British Columbia, Canada)

> A glimpse of the past. (GM, West Glamorgan, Wales)

A number of people referred to a sense of loneliness, as if the Scotland offered an opportunity to be alone in a way that was perhaps not possible in their ordinary place of residence.

> Just want to be there, to know what it was like centuries ago, to feel the loneliness. (KW, California, USA)

The following comment combines many of these motives:

I expected powerful beauty in nature, misty rains, good down-to-earth people, remote kirkyards, and miles of walking in solitude. I sought out the historical feelings I imagined through all my readings. I anticipated that I would be able to walk in the remote countryside as well as the old towns and catch a glimpse of what others felt many, many years ago. That life moved on yet moved little in the sense of history and pride. (BV, Ontario, Canada)

Expectations met? Surprises?

Most respondents who had visited Scotland were effusive about their experiences. Their expectations had generally been met and surpassed.

Yes, the experience was magical. We keep going back! (DG, Norfolk, England)

Definitely and more. The weather was so misty and romantic in Inverness. I pictured all the life that surely used to go on there. I pictured my relatives' stories about different people. (TG, Texas, USA)

My expectations were met, and way beyond. I have met distant relatives, found two family farms from the late 1700s, early 1800s, found two sets of graves of g-g-g-grandparents, plus graves of other aunts and uncles. I have established friendship with a distant relative, and we correspond regularly. (CL, Illinois, USA)

What surprised roots tourists during their visits? Similarities between the Scottish landscape and the landscapes in which the respondents' families settled in the New World, a recognition of their own traditions or values as being Scottish, realising that they 'looked' Scottish:

Surprised that the scenery was quite identical to British Columbia and see why my ancestors chose to settle here. Also surprised to see many people who looked like me, i.e. freckles, dark hair, light eyes. (JW, British Columbia, Canada)

My biggest surprise was to find, neglecting the difference in speech accents, how easy it was to fit in with those Scots we stayed with. Our opinions on many subjects were similar as was our mode of thinking. There was no doubt on both sides we were among kin. (AS, Auckland, New Zealand)

I didn't have any surprises other than I didn't know how much of a Scottish culture I had grown up in. I grew up in a small town in Eastern Oregon and most of the people there were of Scottish origin. The food, the dances and expressions as well as stories were all much as what I found when I visited Scotland. (JL, Washington, USA)

Others were surprised by the depth of their feelings, the sense of being guided or visiting places that they had somehow always known:

> The areas I went I could not have imagined in my wildest dreams. I spent much of the time by myself just absorbing the places where family would have been. I managed to find three living lines to my family – it seemed like I was guided in my activities. (SJ, New South Wales, Australia)

> It was like going somewhere I always knew. (JS, Ontario, Canada)

A holiday, or something more profound?

It would be misleading to suggest that the experience of visiting Scotland was equally profound for all respondents. For some it was no more – and no less – than a holiday, others felt it to be something special, but not necessarily profound. For the majority of respondents, however, the experience was extremely profound and even 'life-changing'.

Respondents explained this profundity in different ways. Many appealed to a notion of homecoming or a deep sense of belonging.

> Much more profound than a regular holiday. It was a homecoming in every way. (JH, California, USA)

> Much more than another holiday – in fact I never once referred to the trip as such. It seemed more a journey to find my roots and to find me and where I belong. It was nice to finally say, this is mine and this is where I belong. (SJ, New South Wales, Australia)

> We Americans are such a youthful, transient lot in the great scheme of things. I experienced a mystical sense of coming home – of belonging on the land. It was almost as if the chemistry of my body resonated with the geology. (BL, Washington, USA)

> Very profound. I want to go home. I belong there – this I feel in the bottom of my bones. From the food I like to my physical appearance or my temperament. So much makes sense now. (HM, Oregon, USA)

> Both trips were primarily for family research. However, walking around a farm or croft, within a house or around a sorrowful pile of stones was in all cases undoubtedly a profoundly moving set of experiences. No, neither trip was just another holiday. Indeed, I could not visit Scotland just for a holiday. (AS, Auckland, New Zealand)

The journey home can also be a journey of self-discovery and a remarkably emotional experience:

Where do I start? First it was not really a holiday but a journey of discovery. I remember when we first got a glimpse of the Scotland I had been reading about for years. There is a certain corner you turn on the road from Glasgow alongside Loch Lomond, I had Battlefield Band playing on the stereo, my wife turned to me and said isn't it lovely, and myself, my mum, and my wife all started to cry. I couldn't answer anyone. The sun lit up the whole of the glen. The colours and the music and the expectation was all too much! (DG, Norfolk, England)

Even the word 'profound' only minimizes what I felt while in Scotland. It was never designed as a holiday and my mode of travel is witness to that. I simply bought a plane ticket over and just went. I gave my heart and soul permission to guide me only. The only way I can explain it is to say that I never felt such contentment in my life, never felt such warmth within and 'being who I am'. (BV, Ontario, Canada)

Some described their journey as being a spiritual experience, a kind of pilgrimage or a completion of the 'circle of life':

Definitely more profound. For both my husband and for me, it was a very special pilgrimage. We were returning to the land of my husband's birth, where he had close relatives still living, and were also attempting to find the place from which my grandfather emigrated. (PC, Hawke's Bay, New Zealand)

Oh no, not just another holiday. To me it was a pilgrimage. A searching for roots. (IP, Auckland, New Zealand)

It felt good. I really sensed a greatness that attached me to the area. Even though I am not really from there. I felt the circle was more complete. I knew where I fit in the world better. (TG, Texas, USA)

Especially powerful were the strange 'presences' felt at ancestral places and graveyards:

Much more profound than I ever imagined. When I stood at my great-great-grandparents' grave on the Killchollie cemetery at Roy Bridge I 'felt' people surround me, real physical presences. I felt no fear, it was midday on a bright and sunny day. I shall never forget that experience, it was so real. (RG, New South Wales, Australia)

Single experience that has left the greatest impression

What are the most memorable episodes in such homecomings? If these journeys can be described as pilgrimages, it is not surprising to learn that arriving at the 'sacred' destination – an ancestral home or grave site, for example – is the most significant part of the experience. Some of the following statements allude to powerful 'other-worldly' encounters at these places:

Finding my grandmother's grave on Eileen Munda island. A ferryboat man has to take you over to the island. The peace and tranquillity. The unbelievable views. (LZ, Ontario, Canada)

From a family history point of view, the first visit to the farmhouse where my emigrant g-g-grandfather, Alexander Scott, was born in 1830 left me very moved. I momentarily experienced the most irrational desire to contact my people of that past time in that place. (AS, Auckland, New Zealand)

I found a deserted cottage in the Forest of Birse where my Glass family had lived. I knew I was trespassing but I had to go in and the feeling inside was eerie to say the least. It looked like the people who were there before had got up and left 10 minutes before and yet I have since found out that the place was last lived in in 1977. The whole time I was in the house there was the feeling that I was in a crowd of people. There was a hum in my ears as if people were talking to me but just not loud enough to hear. I had never experienced anything like this before so I turned to leave and as I did someone(?) put their arms around me. Needless to say I left straight away. I was really frightened. Fact or fantasy? You decide. This was 'home' and this was certainly not the place I expected to find it! (SJ, New South Wales, Australia)

On my last visit to Scotland, I had a most interesting experience in a visit to Catrine, my mother and grandmother's birthplace. First, you have to know that I am entirely sceptical about thought transference, mental telepathy, or the like. Nevertheless, my son and I stopped at a pub in Catrine in order to ask the whereabouts of St Cuthbert Street. To my knowledge, I have never been shown or told in any way what St Cuthbert Street looked like. I was astonished to arrive on site and feel that I had been there, or could have precisely described the scene, if asked beforehand. (JG, Ontario, Canada)

For others, the most memorable experience was visiting iconic sites such as Culloden.

The battlefield at Culloden was deeply moving. As a child I had been aware of the '45 and knew that Charlie had stayed in Elgin the night before the battle, but actually standing on that windswept moor made the hairs on the back of my hand stand on end. It still does now and it made me so aware of all the Scots had had to put up with. (JO, Auckland, New Zealand)

I was very moved during our visit to Culloden. I had a sense that my ancestors were there. (JH, California, USA)

Contact with local people was also very significant:

I shall never forget meeting the owners of the farm where my Scott ancestor was born and being taken throughout the house, room by room, then the steading, and finally over the fields. (AS, Auckland, New Zealand)

I indeed felt as if I had been home, the warmth and kindness shown by the locals leaves a lasting impression. (AM, Victoria, Australia)

When one of the people we had met in Wick roused me out of bed at 10.15pm on a Sunday evening to visit his house to talk to a long time resident who knew many people that were imagined to be potential relatives. Then at 11.30pm Sunday night we took off to find some of these people! (DM, Kansas, USA)

Unexpectedly meeting an old lady one night having a cuppa by the fire in her loch-side cottage who, as soon as I said I was from America, replied, 'Oh, we haven't had any American visitors since Mary and Georgia!' (This happened to me in 1983. My mother Georgia May visited in 1926. My aunt Mary Evelyn visited in 1930). (EL, Pennsylvania, USA)

As were meetings with distant relatives:

I met 90 year old Malcolm Matheson and his sister, Peggy Ann, with whom I share a common ancestor. They welcomed me into their home and told me stories of what life had been like. (BL, Washington, USA)

Summarising the meaning

Not surprisingly, many respondents had difficulty putting into a few words what the experience of visiting Scotland meant for them.

There are no words to describe the feeling. (SP, California, USA)

Can't describe it in words. Felt somewhere deep inside. (DS, Ontario, Canada)

I honestly can't put it into words. I just long to return. (LB, South Australia, Australia)

This was not merely a problem with the design of the questionnaire.

We have travelled a lot all over the world, and Scotland was an unexpected revelation. It touched into deep feelings and connections that were NOT intellectual and had nothing to do with tourist activities. It was a homecoming and on levels that remain uneasy to explain or translate for people unless they have experienced something similar or are comfortable with those collective parts of themselves. (PP, Washington, USA)

Part of this seemed to be that the meaning of the visit was often so deeply personal that it was impossible to share – an emotional rather than intellectual experience – but part was also a suspicion that others would simply not understand.

Nevertheless, many respondents did attempt to explicate the meaning of their journeys. Examples include:

A feeling of actually belonging to a place and its people. I truly found my identity. (DG, Norfolk, England)

Completing a pilgrimage. (DM, Ontario, Canada)

Coming home. (MC, Victoria, Australia)

I felt like I found a big piece of myself. A piece long-waiting to be put into the void of questions I never asked of my parents, who are deceased. I felt like I belonged there. I told others that I would move there if I could. (PW, Wisconsin, USA)

It was an expansion of experience – a growing web of connection. It made me comfortable with my place on the continuum of life. (BL, Washington, USA)

I think at least for me it is a place of renewal. (DK, Texas, USA)

It gave me an understanding of where my 'people' came from: the sights they saw, the air they smelled, the mountains they walked. As a result I identified with my 'Scottishness' – and in particular my 'Celtic/Gael-ness' – even more strongly. (TS, New Hampshire, USA)

It was life changing. (SM, New Hampshire, USA)

The fulfilment of a lifetime dream. (PM, ACT, Australia)

Closing the great circle of life. I had reached the beginning and I was good. I was better than they had hoped. Perhaps the struggle had been worth it. I am very proud to be an American, but it all came from them. (TG, Texas, USA)

Souvenirs

It is interesting to note what kinds of objects respondents had bought or collected in Scotland to remind them of their journeys. By far the most frequently mentioned souvenirs were the photographs they had taken. In terms of purchased items, books were most popular, followed by clothing (especially woollens), jewellery, kilts and tartan accessories, ornaments, clan mementos and visitor guides or brochures. Many respondents stated that they were not interested in typical tourist souvenirs. A large number of people rated as their most precious souvenirs more intangible entities such as friendships, memories and longings. Others kept diaries or journals during their visit: rereading them allowed them to relive the experience.

The most significant observation, however, to be drawn from the data concerning souvenirs was the number of people who collected more personally meaningful objects during their visits: rocks, stones and pebbles, sprigs of heather, pieces of driftwood, seeds, tufts of wool, moss, pottery sherds and water collected from lochs, rivers and wells. These types of souvenirs were usually collected from ancestral places and may be likened to 'relics' obtained at shrines or pilgrimage centres: there is something especially precious or sacred about them.

> Rocks. Stones. Shells. Sand. Pottery shards. I carry them in all my coat pockets. (PK, Alaska, USA)

> I have heather from places where my family lived, small rocks and other mementos. More photos than I can count. And I wrote a diary/ journal each day of my experiences. In the beginning it was short as I was just starting out, but by the second week of the trip I was writing 4–6 pages on the day's events, mostly descriptions of where I went and what I saw, how I felt. Now that I am back in Australia I only have to re-read my words to relive the experiences. (SJ, New South Wales, Australia)

> A stone from Iona, heather from Culloden. (DL, California, USA)

> A small piece of stone taken from the home of my great-great-grandfather near Loch Fada now part of the Letterewe Estate on Loch Maree. He was evicted with his family in 1878 by the MacKenzie laird. (DM, Victoria, Australia)

> Addresses, appreciation, beauty, books, data, friendships, grief, information, knowledge, maps, memories, names, papers, photos, rocks, sadness, sand, wisdom. (This is a partial list and is in alphabetical order). (EL, Pennsylvania, USA)

Some of the lists included genealogical data: a photocopy of a census entry, for instance, is not merely valued for the information it contains, but also as a tangible 'trace' of an ancestor.

> Six rolls of film, dried wild flowers, census data from the Public Records Office, woollen blankets as gifts for family, Scottish costume

for my niece, sheepskin rugs for my sons, cashmere cape for myself. (NM, California, USA)

Perhaps the most prized of all souvenirs were objects once owned by the ancestors whose homes were being sought:

> An elderly relative presented me the snuff mull which belonged to my great-great-great-grandfather, Alexander Scott. It is a ram's horn with a suitably hinged lid and silver embellishments. On a silver band surrounding the horn near the lid is inscribed his name and the date, 1850. Other articles I consider memorable souvenirs are the photo-copies of the wills and testaments of some ancestors obtained from the Scottish Records Office. (AS, Auckland, New Zealand)

The Scottish heritage landscape

The questionnaire asked respondents to identify five key *events* in Scottish history and five key *places* in Scottish history. There was a remarkable consistency in the results, attesting to the power of certain iconic episodes, which together form a popular nationalistic discourse. Within the historic events lists, many respondents also referred to historical personalities such as William Wallace and Mary Queen of Scots. The most frequently appearing events/personalities and places (those mentioned in 10 per cent or more of the lists) are presented in Table 3.2.

We can conclude from these statistics that the most prominent episodes of Scottish history in Scottish diasporic consciousness are the Battle of Culloden, the Highland Clearances and the Battle of Bannockburn (note also, however, the prominence of the reopening of the Scottish parliament in 1999 in a large number of lists). Indeed, with the exception of the Reformation, each of the events and personalities tells a story of confrontation, victory and defeat in the context of Scotland's struggle to retain or regain its independence from 'England' (this is equally true of the Highland Clearances, which are portrayed in popular discourse as repre-senting the culmination of centuries of English/Saxon attempts to wipe out the Scots/Gaels, e.g. Prebble 1969). Comparing the lists of events and places, it is interesting to note that whereas the battlefield sites of Culloden and Bannockburn can be visited and may be regarded as sacred sites of the Scottish nation (see McCrone *et al.* 1995 for a comparison of these two sites), no similar site 'represents' the Highland Clearances. As I explain in Chapter 7, this has significant consequences for the perception of Highland landscapes more generally.

The prominence of these iconic events and places of Highland history in the diasporic imagination is an attribute of a broader narrativisation of the past: the teleological structuring of events such that they acquire a coher-ence and meaning that is not necessarily intrinsic to the events themselves

Table 3.2 Most frequently listed historical 'events' and historical 'places'

Historical event/personality (date)	Percentage
Battle of Culloden (1746)	54
Highland Clearances (*c.*1790–1855)	53
Battle of Bannockburn (1314)	37
Reopening of Scottish Parliament (1999)	27
Jacobite Uprisings (1715 and 1745)	23
Act of Union (1707)	19
Union of Crowns (1603)	17
Glencoe Massacre (1692)	17
Mary Queen of Scots (1542–87)	16
Robert the Bruce (1274–1329)	13
John Knox (*c.*1514–72)/Scottish Reformation (*c.*1550–1660)	13
William Wallace (*c.*1270–1305)	11
Declaration of Arbroath (1319)	10

Historical place	Percentage
Culloden	61
Edinburgh	51
Bannockburn	32
Glasgow	26
Stirling	23
Inverness	21
Glencoe	15
Edinburgh Castle	13
Scone	13

(H. White 1981, Samuel and Thompson 1990) – a narrative, in this case, which culminates in (and explains) the formation of the diaspora. Questionnaire respondents were asked to recommend Scottish-interest books they had read: by far the most popular author was John Prebble, whose historical trilogy, *Glencoe* (1968), *Culloden* (1961) and *The Highland Clearances* (1969), is widely available, widely read and widely cited on the internet. After Prebble, the second most popular author was Nigel Tranter whose historical fiction works include *The Wallace* (1975) and *The Bruce Trilogy* (1985). The third most popular author was Diana Gabaldon, an American historical fantasy writer, whose *Outlander* series of books involves time travel between the 1940s and the period of the Jacobite Rebellions. The 1996 return of the Stone of Scone (the coronation stone of the kings of Scotland, removed to London by Edward I in 1296) and the 1999 reopening of the Scottish parliament were often conflated in the questionnaires' responses, their inclusion suggesting that many respondents felt that they were witnessing 'history' in the making.

Further remarks

Respondents were invited to make a general statement about their connections with Scotland or to raise issues that they felt I had neglected to address in the questionnaire. Many statements reiterated the depth of sentiment many felt for their ancestral homeland. Included below are a few of the interesting matters arising:

None more Scots than the Scots abroad?

> The perception that I have is that people who are Scottish by descent and living in overseas countries are more devoted to Scotland than Scottish born people. (HP, Queensland, Australia)

Concerns over the attitude of Scots at home to roots tourists:

> I guess my big question is, how do native Scots feel about the rest of us? Do they resent us claiming 'Scottishness'? Are they glad to see their country is so widely loved and admired that people many generations removed from being native still wish to claim a tie to it? What do most think of the folks that travel there searching for their ancestry? (SN, South Dakota, USA)

Calling for stronger ties between Scotland and its diaspora:

> Will it be the tossed out Scots that bring strength back to Scotland as a whole? Leaving might have been a good choice, but a bridge to those in Scotland could strengthen the country. It was the Nova Scotians that taught the Scots their lost music. The Inuit fiddle players have some of the original music to teach both Scots and Maritimers in Canada. I want the people of Ullapool to know what happened to their children who came to the new country over 200 years ago. (JM, British Columbia, Canada)

The blood is strong, the heart is Highland:

> Scotland is in my heart. I would love to go and see the country that is so much in my blood. (JV, Ontario, Canada)

Dilemmas about belonging:

> Indigenous people talk about them belonging to a place rather than a place belonging to them. I hate being a person without a place. So now I have completed the core of my family history research I can say I come from Kilmonivaig Parish in the Western Highlands of Scotland. But I

look at my family tree and see all the other branches stretching back to England, and all those [other] branches that are blank. Maybe I'm just kidding myself about the deep feeling of relief at being able to say to myself (no-one else cares) that I know where I come from, and disregard all the other places. I've tried to rationalize this by asking myself, what if I had found that my McDonald family line led back to a destitute single mum in a Glasgow slum? Would I feel the same about knowing where I come from, compared with 'knowing' now that I come from the heart of the Highlands, the Lochaber District? (DM, ACT, Australia)

Something BIG is missing:

I need some connections. Please direct me. I have no friends or family in Scotland. I need to find both. Is there any way to find people to chat or e-mail from Scotland? I long to know the people with which I share my heritage. I have a deep inner loneliness, a hollow sadness . . . as if something BIG is missing. (MR, Ontario, Canada)

4   Imagineering home

Salman Rushdie begins his well-known 1982 essay, 'Imaginary Homelands', with an observation that is both remarkable and obvious. Describing an old photograph of the house in which he was born in Bombay, which now hangs on his study wall in London, Rushdie is reminded of the famous opening sentence of L. P. Hartley's novel *The Go-Between*: 'The past is a foreign country, they do things differently there' (Rushdie 1992: 9). The phrase has become a byword of heritage studies (e.g. Lowenthal 1985) and acquires a particular literalness in migrant contexts when applied by or to those who have left their pasts behind them in an old country. What is remarkable, however, is Rushdie's qualification of this truism. He writes, 'the photograph tells me to invert this idea; it reminds me that it's my present that is foreign, and that the past is home, albeit a lost home in a lost city in the mists of lost time' (1992: 9). Rushdie's sense of alienation or foreignness is experienced in the present, part of the 'here and now', not the 'there and then'. Despite the 'urge to reclaim', the past remains irrecoverable, and, thus, writing for himself and other Indian 'exiles, emigrants or expatriates', Rushdie concludes that,

> Our physical alienation from India almost inevitably means that we will not be capable of reclaiming precisely the thing that was lost; that we will, in short, create fictions, not actual cities or villages, but invisible ones, imaginary homelands, Indias of the mind. (ibid.: 10)

As 'partial beings', 'wounded creatures' seeing through 'cracked lenses' and 'capable only of fractured perceptions' (ibid.: 12), such fictions must be improvised from a hotchpotch of impressions and dispositions – 'scraps, dogmas, childhood injuries, newspaper articles, chance remarks, old films, small victories, people hated, people loved' (ibid.). Moreover, Rushdie suspects that this sense of alienation and the constructive compensations of the mind are not restricted to ex-pat Indians, but are the universal predicaments of modernity. 'It may be argued', he writes, 'that the past is a country from which we have all emigrated, that its loss is part of our common humanity' (ibid.: 12). It is tempting to posit some kind of Lévi-

Straussian structural logic to this process: the *langue* of the universal myth of the Fall, the *parole* of the particular past felt to have been lost, the latter constructed in the manner of the *bricoleur* from the scraps and dogmas at hand (Lévi-Strauss 1966, 1968).

Scottish diasporic identity is, as I have already argued, largely defined by its relationship to the Scottish homeland. The homeland is situated at the centre of diasporic consciousness, anchoring it spatially and temporally, allowing senses of Scottishness to float diffusely across continents and generations and yet still persist in some coherent form. It is the very materiality of the homeland that guarantees this stability-in-flux: the homeland is perceived as a fact, a given, something unmovable and unequivocal. It is paradoxical, therefore, that the homeland is, as Rushdie powerfully articulates, also a product of the diasporic imagination, a mythic place, a virtual as much as a material reality, a manifestation of the homeless mind. Consequently, throughout much of this book I am concerned with those scraps and dogmas through which diasporic Scots forge their particular imaginary homelands: their Scotlands 'of the mind'. The 'inadequate materials' from which Rushdie creates his India reflect both the public (dogmas, old films, newspaper articles) and the personal (childhood injuries, chance remarks) spheres of the habitus of the imagination. In this chapter I am particularly concerned with the public imagination of Scotland, with what Appadurai terms the 'mediascape': the 'concatenations of images' (and texts, and sounds, and material objects, but *mostly* images) through which the imagined Scottish homeland is produced, disseminated and consumed in the diaspora (Appadurai 1990: 298–9).

Concerning this public sphere, Morley and Robins observe that with globalisation comes a proliferation of 'information and communications flows' (1995: 87) in which, in Richard Kearney's words, 'the real and the imaginary become almost impossible to distinguish' (ibid.: 38). When coupled with the disjuncture with the past described by Rushdie, whereby the 'continuity of identity' is supposedly broken (ibid.: 87), this 'global image space' may have a profound influence on individual consciousness. Thus Morley and Robins argue that 'questions of identity, memory and nostalgia' have become 'inextricably interlinked with patterns and flows of communication', and they suggest that 'the "memory banks" of our times are in some part built out of the materials supplied by the film and television industries' (ibid.: 90). Indeed, Appadurai goes further, positing that not only film companies, but also art impresarios and travel agencies now thrive on the nostalgia of deterritorialised populations and conspire to fabricate 'invented' homelands to take the place of those felt to be lost (Appadurai 1990: 302). Through examining aspects of the Scottish diasporic mediascape I hope to demonstrate that a more complex relationship exists between representation, reality and the desires of producers and consumers. Tourism agencies in the homeland, for instance, do not simply produce images of Scotland that they know consumers in the diaspora will be susceptible to, just as consumers in the diaspora do not simply project idealised images of the homeland onto the Scottish landscape. Rather, I suggest that homeland and diaspora are both bound up in the production and consumption of this discourse, joint-agents in a complex 'imagineering' of Scotland. This imagineering of home may be understood as embracing both the 'innocent' imagining of home described by Rushdie and the more 'interested' engineering of home invoked by Appadurai.[1] But, contrary to the excesses of much postmodern discourse concerning the disappearance of 'the real' and the emergence of a 'hyperreality' of simulations (e.g. Baudrillard 1983), I argue that, whilst the fetishised image-space may be internalised and form the basis of identification, its 'spectacular' nature is also understood as such, and, for many, the mediascape is merely the 'stepping off point' for a journey of discovery and not a destination in itself.

Scott-land: 'the seat of the Celtic muse'

> To speak in the poetical language of my country, the seat of the Celtic muse is in the mist of the secret and solitary hill, and her voice in the murmur of the mountain stream. He who woos her must love the barren rock more than the fertile valley, and the solitude of the desert better than the festivity of the hall.
>
> Sir Walter Scott, *Waverley*

Considering the proliferation of images and ideas that jostle and compete for attention in this mediascape, there is, at first sight, a surprising consistency in the way in which the Scottish homeland is imagined in the diaspora. As part of the online questionnaire discussed in the last chapter, I asked respondents to each list five characteristics that they felt defined Scotland. Respondents interpreted the question differently, some listing perceived Scottish personality traits and values, others listing aspects of the Scottish environment, and, others still, iconic motifs such as whisky, tartan and bagpipes. Drawing from the characteristics most frequently listed, a rough-and-ready description of the Scottish homeland, as perceived in the diaspora, can be assembled. *This* Scotland is above all a Highland country with a wild and rugged landscape of mountains, lochs and rivers. It is a place of great scenic beauty, but also wet and cool. It is an historic land of castles and clans, of traditions and Gaelic language and lore. Its people are proud and fiercely independent, loyal to clan and family, but also hospitable to strangers. They are industrious, inventive and value education highly. Such a composite impression is, of course, somewhat removed from the experiences of the majority of Scotland's inhabitants who live in the towns and cities of the Central Belt and whose landscape is one of urban renewal and industrial decay, commuter trains and motorways, housing estates and retail parks – a reality, one suspects, rather closer to the majority of the respondents' own lives. It is evident, then, that the 'myth of the Highlands' – Scott's 'Celtic muse' – continues to enchant the diasporic imagination.

Before turning to more recent imaginings, it is worth reiterating that the discursive creation of this Highland homeland is neither a new phenomenon nor one associated exclusively with the diaspora. As has already been discussed in relation to Sir Walter Scott and the discourse of Highlandism, the iconography of the Scottish homeland was already firmly established by the beginning of the nineteenth century. As Womack notes, the development of the Highland myth may be regarded as being complete by 1810–11,

> when a flurry of publications, including most notably Scott's *The Lady of the Lake*, both depended on and confirmed a settled cultural construction of the Highlands as a 'romantic country' inhabited by a people whose ancient manners and customs were 'peculiarly adapted to poetry'. (1989: 2, quoting Scott)

In the remainder of the nineteenth century this romantic aesthetic was promulgated by a succession of writers, painters and photographers (see Hart 1978; Pringle 1988; Womack 1989; Harvie 1989; Pittock 1991; Durie 1992; Withers 1994; Cannizzo 2000), and, throughout the twentieth century, it continued to persist in mass media such as film, television, tourist promotions and in other forms of popular cultural transmission such as postcards, whisky bottles, shortbread tins, tea towels and so forth (see McArthur 1982; Gold and Gold 1995; Petrie 2000). The strength and consistency of this discourse (as well as the apparent divergence between the myth and the reality) was evidently sufficient in 1866 for the poet and essayist Alexander Smith to write of 'Scott-land' rather than 'Scotland' – Scott being 'the light in which [the country] is seen' (quoted in Cannizzo 2000: 179). But, just as Said notes that 'it would be wrong to conclude that the Orient was *essentially* an idea, or a creation with no corresponding reality' (1978: 5, italics in original), so it would be naïve to suggest that Scotland was simply a construction of the romantic imagination; after all, each of the motifs of Highlandism – 'bens and glens, the lone shieling in the misty island, purple heather, kilted clansmen, battles long ago, an ancient and beautiful language, claymores and bagpipes and Bonny Prince Charlie' – actually exist or existed (Womack 1989: 1). In a more complex symbiosis, the representation of place and place itself act as distorting mirrors of each other. Thus, whilst the discursive production of the Highlands was (and is) shaped by the geographical and historical realities of the region, so the material reality of the region has been affected by its discursive representation. This is evident, for instance, in the landscaping or Balmoralisation of Highland estates, in the practices of and provisions for field sports and tourism, and, not least, in the marginalisation of the majority of the region's inhabitants who, from the tourist's consuming perspective, become 'part of the scenery' to be gazed upon (Urry 1990).

Differently-authentic imaginaries

As might be expected, the 'tourist gaze' is perpetuated in the promotional material produced by tourism agencies such as the Scottish Tourist Board, which consistently represent Scotland as existing outside time and as modernity's other: a place where traditions survive and people figure small in vast natural wildernesses. From a marketing perspective, the combined motifs of Highlandism constitute an internationally recognised brand identity and, therefore, a significant economic asset. But there is also a concern among homeland Scots that this representation is increasingly incompatible with the modern realities of the country and its inhabitants' lifestyles. Reporting on the findings of a research initiative set up to explore this concern, a Scottish marketing consultant, Russell Griggs, writes,

> Timeless tradition is at the heart of Scotland's equity, so whilst we need to move forward, it must not be done in such a way that it would destroy the cultural integrity on which the perception is based. Others envy Scotland its historic landscape, and what is perceived as its enduring traditions. Scots at home agree with this view, but feel that, whilst their values have not changed, their lifestyles have, and Scotland is a modern country. However, the world thinks, and Scotland fears, that it is in a time warp which stops this recognition. (2000: 239)

For Griggs, the answer is not to again reinvent the image of Scotland, 'throwing the baby out with the bath-water in an attempt to be up to date and "modern"' (ibid.), but to 'weave together old and new images . . . so that the whole remains as one seamless identity' (ibid.: 240).

Indeed, it is a process of refinement of the Highlandist aesthetic, rather than any radical reinvention, that has characterised the changing representation of Scotland in STB promotions over the last 30 years. This process is evident in the gradual suppression of certain elements of Highlandism and the accentuation of others. Thus, in STB posters of the 1980s, alongside images of 'peopleless places' and 'wild, rugged, barren, beautiful' natural landscapes, the element of 'tartanry' still proliferates in photographs of pipers in full Highland dress, kilted and bonneted men playing traditional Highland games such as curling, and so forth (McCrone *et al.* 1995: 80).[2] By the mid-1990s, however, this element has become muted. Note, for instance, the representation of Scotland in an STB television commercial of 1994 entitled 'When Will You Go?'. The commercial is underscored by a contemporary version of a traditional Scottish folk ballad, *The Wild Mountain Thyme*, and features a montage of atmospheric images, including:

- Storm waves pounding the Atlantic sea-shore (Tiree, Inner Hebrides)
- A mountain with cascading streams (Glencoe)
- Speeded-up clouds (and shadows) scudding across the landscape
- A tree in full leaf with a yellow autumnal glow
- A flock of birds taking flight
- Intercity train crossing Forth Rail Bridge with speeded-up effects of night turning into day
- Edinburgh (Castle Hill, Georgian terrace, etc.)
- A boy pushing his bicycle across a wooden Highland bridge (Lower Glencoe)
- A Highland valley with distant hills, a stand of trees in foreground
- A loch-side Highland castle (Castle Ti'Oram, Loch Moidart)
- Speeded up effects of tide coming in
- A pool teeming with wild salmon (Kilninver)
- Thistle-covered field
- Land Rover crossing Highland bridge
- A loch on Rannoch Moor, with an island containing a single tree
- A Highland valley with an isolated cottage (Gold and Gold 1995: 198–9)

These images are intercut with fragments of a narrative involving the parting and reunion of a man and woman. The commercial was intended for the UK market and it is significant that the more overt elements of tartanry are absent (no pipers, no kilts). Indeed, the 'bogus tartan carica-ture' has here given way to an altogether more sophisticated aesthetic: a sophistication epitomised in the inclusion of Norman MacCaig, quoting, in characterful voice-over, from his poem 'Celtic Cross' ('Only men's minds could ever have unmapped / Into abstraction such a territory' (D. Dunn 1992: 106)). Thus, for a UK audience in the mid-1990s, the more obvi-ously inauthentic elements of Highlandism are exorcised while the moody (super)natural picturesque is updated, with digital image manipulation, to include high-speed Intercity rail transport, fashionable 4x4 vehicles and remote, but cosy, holiday cottages.

Examining the images and texts of STB brochures of the 1990s, McCrone *et al.* find a similar divergence in the way Scotland is represented to UK and overseas markets respectively. Thus, in brochures intended for the UK (primarily English) market, 'tartanry and rampant rhetoric' are subdued, and qualities of romance, mystery, friendliness and remoteness are accentuated; whereas overseas brochures remain 'strong on tartanry' and 'a wild, romantic past is continually hinted at through references to clans, to the Highland bagpipes which led them into battle. Celtic symbols and tartan abound' (McCrone *et al.* 1995: 82). There emerges, then, a clear disparity between the way Scotland is presented to itself (and to its close neighbours) and the concessions made to the 'tartan monster' in its presentation to overseas markets. We may conclude that there are, in fact, at least two dominant contemporary Highlandist discourses: a locally-acceptable/authentic version epitomised in the 'When Will You Go?' commercial, which emphasises the natural landscape and the faint-ness of humankind's incursions into it, and the locally unacceptable/inauthentic version in which the perceived sham of tartanry continues to abound.[3]

This evident need to produce differently imagined and differently authentic Scotlands for different regions not only illustrates the marketing strategies of tourism agencies, but also attests to the agency of different consumers in determining the image of Scotland promulgated in the media-scape. This pluralism and the capacity for contradiction becomes more apparent as the mediascape becomes more global, and less differentiated, in its reach. This may be demonstrated by examining the STB's negotiation of that (potentially) most global of media, the world-wide web.

ToScotland, to *VisitScotland* or to visit *AncestralScotland*?

In common with the British Tourist Authority, which was rebranded 'VisitBritain', and the Welsh Tourist Board, rebranded 'VisitWales', the Scottish Tourist Board was recently rebranded 'VisitScotland'.[4] This rebranding entailed a convergence between these organisations' broader corporate identities and their online identities (their respective web site URLs are: www.visitbritain.com, www.visitwales.com and www.visitscot-land.com), reflecting both the influence of the internet on corporate branding more generally, and the perceived importance of the internet in the tourism industry in particular. According to the Scottish Executive's *New Strategy for Scottish Tourism*, for instance, 'travel and leisure currently accounts for 40 per cent of global e-commerce transactions and this is set to grow from two billion dollars in 1999 to 30 billion dollars in 2003 – representing 12 per cent of world-wide travel industry sales' (2000: 15). Responding to such trends, the Scottish Executive has directed much investment towards developing online tourism resources through which potential visitors can access information not only about tourist services such as transport, accommodation and events, but also about Scotland's environment, history and culture (ibid.).

Just as the STB produces different brochures for different regions, so it produces different web sites for different markets. In this section I shall be concerned with three: 'the official web site of VisitScotland' (www.visitscotland.com), 'the official VisitScotland web site for US Travellers' (www.toscotland.com), and VisitScotland's 'genealogy web portal' (www.ancestralscotland.com). In the interests of clarity I shall refer to these as *VisitScotland*, *ToScotland* and *AncestralScotland* respectively. Whilst these sites are all available to anyone with internet access, the STB has clearly attempted to keep them discrete from each other and give them separate identities (reflected in the use of different URLs).

As can be seen in the screenshots reproduced in Figure 4.1, the divergence between the graphic representation of Scotland on the 'global' *VisitScotland* site and that on *ToScotland*, the site targeted at the Scottish-American market, is marked and conforms with that identified by McCrone *et al.* in the brochures of the 1990s. Thus the element of tartanry is all but expunged from the index page of *VisitScotland* (it is there, in vestigial form, in a subtle tartan bookmark graphic and in the 'Scotland' brand logo with its thistle motif) (Figure 4.1, left), whereas the index page of *ToScotland* is emblazoned with a tartan banner, features the slogan 'Savor the past ... Seize the moment', and includes images of pipers, castles and Highland dancers, all set against a dramatic background image of a Highland glen (Figure 4.1, right). Indeed, the most prominent element of the *ToScotland* index page is an animated Shockwave graphic in which the following sequence of images and texts repeatedly dissolve over each other:

- Text: 'Scotland'
- Image: monumental Highland landscape, vast green wilderness, mountains, lochs, wide skies, mist drifting across foreground
- Text: 'The passion of poets'
- Image: massed pipe bands in Highland dress parading in torch-lit castle courtyard
- Text: 'The tunes of glory'
- Image: street theatre, Edinburgh Fringe Festival
- Text: 'The spark of inspiration'
- Image: young Highland dancers (fair-haired, blue-eyed girls, traditional outfits)
- Text: 'The warmth of a smile'
- Image: Edinburgh Castle majestically illuminated, with tartan border
- Text: 'Savor the past. Seize the moment'
- Graphic: 'Scotland' brand logo (www.toscotland.com)

Utilising cutting-edge web design technology, STB's *ToScotland* web site thus forcefully reiterates the (locally inauthentic) Highlandist aesthetic in every way.

In contrast, the main *VisitScotland* site *seems* to eschew not just tartanry, but Highlandism altogether. The index page (Figure 4.1, left) takes the form of a facsimile passport (the text 'Scottish Passport' repeated to form its purple background shading) and appears to have a more functional purpose, acting as a portal to direct visitors in search of particular information or with niche interests to relevant parts of the site. Thus along

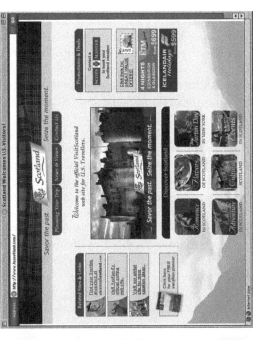

Figure 4.1 Revisioning Scotland at *VisitScotland* (left), reiterating Highlandism at *ToScotland* (right) (VisitScotland)

the top of the page is a series of hyperlink tabs such as 'TRANSPORT', 'GUIDE', 'ACCOMMODATION', and 'WHAT TO SEE AND DO', whilst along the left edge is a number of animated link buttons, one, for example, inviting the visitor to 'Trace your Scottish roots with ancestralscotland.com', another advertising golfing holidays, and so forth. On closer inspection, however, whilst the element of tartanry is undoubtedly suppressed, a more subtle form of Highlandism becomes apparent. At the time of writing, the main window of the index page is devoted to a seasonal promotion which invites website visitors to 'Reawaken [their] senses with a Spring Break' in Scotland. This promotional graphic features a monochromatic image of a still and empty shoreline over which are placed five colour photographs captioned with five statements appealing to each of the senses: 'See it' (general view of landscape of lochs, mountains and blue skies); 'Touch it' (close-up of beach pebbles); 'Hear it' (close-up of golden eagle); 'Taste it' (close-up of lobster); 'Smell it' (close-up of pine cone and needles). Considering the sensorily-limited medium of the internet, it is interesting to note how the web page encourages visitors to shake off the hibernatory slumbers of mediated experience and come to Scotland to use all their senses in experiencing the 'real' (unmediated, natural) world. But here again that reality is narrowly defined by the myth and all the images are associated with the wonders of nature and with the nature of the Highlands and Islands.[5]

This locally authentic version of Highlandism is much more explicit in the 'Guide' section of the *VisitScotland* site, which is accessed by clicking on one of the aforementioned hyperlink tabs of the index page. The main guide page again has the form of a facsimile passport, this time 'rubber stamped' with the title 'Scottish Tourist Board – Guide to Scotland' (Figure 4.2). In the top right, 'sealed' under a repeating thistle motif, is a postcard-like image of a wide, empty beach with a mountain rising in the distance; below this, a relief map of Scotland and to the left a list of eight regions. Placing the cursor over each of the regions in the list or over the corresponding areas on the map causes the image to change to one that represents the region selected (each reproduced in Figure 4.3). Clicking on the region list or map links to one of eight pages, each containing a brief description of the selected region (also reproduced in Figure 4.3) and featuring further links to the local tourist-board web sites concerned with those areas. As can be seen in Figure 4.3, apart from Glasgow (presented as the bustling modern city of culture), each of the images and texts used conforms to the Highlandist aesthetic: Scotland is thus again represented as a country of soaring mountains and heather-covered hills, ancient standing stones and ominous skies, baronial mansions and loch-side castle ruins, empty beaches and turquoise seas, quaint fishing villages and the majestic, historical capital.

Yet another version of the Scottish homeland is evoked in the STB's *AncestralScotland* web site, one that treads a middle path between the

Figure 4.2 The *VisitScotland* 'Guide to Scotland' (VisitScotland)

excessive tartanry of *ToScotland* and the tartanryless Highlandism of *VisitScotland*. *AncestralScotland* was launched on Burns' Day (24 January) 2002 in response to the Scottish Executive's *New Strategy for Scottish Tourism* and is targeted specifically at the overseas genealogy niche market. Whilst it is prominently linked with both the US and global STB sites, it is also promoted strongly on other Scottish heritage and genealogy sites and in print advertisements (see Figure 1.1). Compared to the majority of Scottish heritage web sites, the tartanry presented at *AncestralScotland* is decidedly restrained, but it is there nevertheless. Each page is designed to the same template, which includes a uniform navigation banner (with drop-down menus under the headings: 'Home', 'Who are the Scots', 'Genealogy', 'Visiting Scotland', 'News and Features' and 'Talk to us'), a sepia-toned 'family album' photograph, a series of search forms (which ultimately link to local tourist board web sites associated with the placename, parish or regional surname searched for), a page-specific banner which incorporates images and texts, an 'iconic' colour image, and a few paragraphs of text. Only two of the site's iconic colour images – one featuring two clan chiefs in front of a pipe band, the other a pipe band marching at a Highland gathering – could be described as examples of tartanry (the remainder are exemplars of locally-authentic Highlandism: a thatched croft house; a rugged coast with mountains silhouetted against an evening sky; a mountain stream; a loch and hills at sunset). However, the individual page banners include elements of tartanry in images of kilts, Highland dancers, pipers, a statue of Robert the Bruce, a majestic hilltop castle, hammer-throwing and so forth; and their layered texts include emotive phrases such as 'Clans of Scotland', 'Gaelic', 'Scots

The Highlands of Scotland and the Isle of Skye

'This is one of the last wildernesses in Europe – through the soaring beauty of Glencoe to the idyllic charm of the isles, and from the crashing waves of the northern coastline to the silence of windswept moors'.

Image: sharp peaks of Black Cuillin mountains against blue sky, more accessible heather-covered hills foreground

The Outer Isles – Shetland, Orkney and the Western Isles

'History is layered deep within the northern archipelagos of Orkney and Shetland, in the settlements of the earliest peoples to the Viking invaders ... Lying at the very edge of Europe, the peaceful Western Islands have a rugged natural beauty, with unspoiled beaches, plentiful wildlife and unique culture and traditions'.

Image: standing stones silhouetted against a dawn sky

The Grampian Highlands, Aberdeen and the North East Coast

'Rich in historic castles, royal connections and whisky distilleries, this unique corner of Scotland has hills tumbling down to a dramatic coast with its fishing villages and beaches around Aberdeen, Scotland's city of flowers'.

Image: baronial castle in park land, Lion Rampant flying from turret

Argyll and the Islands, Loch Lomond, Stirling and the Trossachs

'From the romantic isles west of Argyll to the gentle hills east of Stirling, this is the crossroads of Scotland, where the Lowlands meet the West Highlands'.

Image: loch-side castle in rich autumnal sunlight, gold and purple hills reflected in still waters of loch

Perthshire, Angus and Dundee, and the Kingdom of Fife

'This is an area of dramatic contrasts, combining the rich farming patchwork of Fife with the high hills of Perthshire, the city bustle of Dundee with the silence of the Angus glens'.

Image: quaint fishing village and harbour, calm seas in golden dawn light

Edinburgh City, Coast and Countryside

'Edinburgh, Scotland's historic and cosmopolitan capital is embraced by the scenic coastline and rich countryside of the Lothians'.

Image: majestic castle rising above historical buildings, the whole scene bathed in golden sunlight

Greater Glasgow and the Clyde Valley

'Scotland's international gateway, Glasgow is one of Europe's great cultural destinations. Its museums and galleries are complemented by the beautiful countryside along the Clyde from its source, through garden valleys to the sea'.

Image: bustling cultural city by night, three bridges spanning river, buildings illuminated

The South of Scotland

'Rich, rolling farmland, rugged sea coasts and Clyde coast islands characterise the South of Scotland. Robert Burns and Sir Walter Scott both lived in this land of ancient abbeys, castles and historic houses'.

Image: large empty beach, turquoise sea under blue sky, mountain rising in distance

Figure 4.3 The *VisitScotland* 'Guide to Scotland' – images and texts representing each of the regions (VisitScotland)

language', 'Red haired', 'medieval times', 'The Highlands', 'Loch Ness', 'Braveheart', 'Rob Roy' and 'Scotland is a beautiful country, rich in culture and heritage'.

Unlike the *ToScotland* site, however, *AncestralScotland* not only invites its potential visitors to savour Scotland's heritage, it invites them to *identify* with that heritage. Remembering that the site parades as a genealogy portal and not a marketing tool, the potential visitors to whom it is addressed are transformed from potential *tourists* into potential *homecomers*, and the site thus presents itself as performing an important service in reuniting diasporic Scots with their lost homeland. On the index page, for example, genealogists are told that they are undertaking 'a journey of discovery . . . to explore the lives and times of ancestors who lived hundreds of years ago – and perhaps even thousands of miles away' (www.ancestralscotland.com). Similarly, searching for roots is described as 'an intellectual and emotional voyage that can only be completed when you visit the country of your kinsfolk' (ibid.). In this way, the web site itself becomes 'the first step' on this 'journey of a thousand miles' (www.ancestralscotland.com/genealogy/index.asp). Posing such questions as 'Where do you come from?' (www.ancestralscotland.com/visitingscotland) and 'Ask yourself . . . when will you come home?' (www.ancestral scotland.com/scots/index.asp), the site appeals to a contemporary hunger for belonging in which these issues have become both urgent and problematised. Seeming to be sensitive to the existential insecurities of Scotland's 'sons and daughters' scattered throughout the world, *AncestralScotland* presents itself as 'a way home' and promises, through its online search and booking facilities, to make that journey of a thousand miles an easier and more fulfilling one.

A closer examination of two pages of the *AncestralScotland* site may further demonstrate how this appeal to identify Scotland as home is effected. The screen shot on the left of Figure 4.4 is of the web page that poses the question 'Where do you come from?'. The question – which might be more appropriately phrased, 'Where do you *wish* to come from?' – is answered, graphically, in the two photographs on the page: on the right of the screen, in a colour picture of an idyllic thatched croft house, and, more complexly, in the use of the sepia family-album image to the left. Judging from his dress, this sepia image appears to be of an agricultural labourer or crofter of the late nineteenth or early twentieth century and we might imagine such a man living in the pictured croft house. Below the image of the cottage is the statement,

It is estimated that there are more than 28 million people in the world who can claim Scots ancestry, perhaps you are one of them? The pictures on the pages of this site are of real people and events from the 19th and early 20th centuries . . . could they be your ancestors?

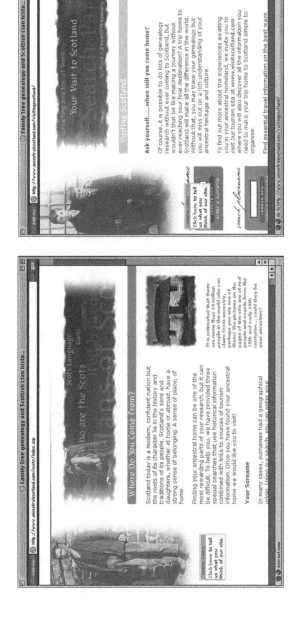

Figure 4.4 Where do you come from? (left) When will you come home? (right) (AncestralScotland)

The sepia image lends a note of documentary realism to the nostalgic dream evoked in the picture of the croft house, but, coupled with the above statement, it also suggests the realistic possibility of personal identification. Implicitly, the page suggests that there is a chance this man is *your* ancestor and, therefore, that this idyllic cottage is *your* home – they are just waiting for you to discover them.

The screen shot on the right of Figure 4.4 is of the page that poses the question, 'Ask yourself . . . when will you come home?'. The sepia image on this page is of two young boys, we might imagine them to be brothers, dressed in their Sunday best to make the voyage by steam ship across the Atlantic. Gazing at the camera, their appeal to the viewer is melancholic: one of homesickness. In the colour image on the right, mountains are seen on the far shore of a calm sea inlet; silhouetted against the setting sun, they conjure thoughts of the magical other-world of the West: *Tir nan Òg* (the place where, in Celtic lore, people live immune to the passage of time). The text is worth quoting at length:

> Of course, it is possible to do lots of genealogy research without ever coming to Scotland, but wouldn't that be like making a journey without ever reaching your final destination? A trip home to Scotland will make all the difference in the world. Without that, you may trace your genealogy but you will miss out on a rich understanding of your ancestral heritage and culture.
>
> To find out more about the experiences awaiting you in your ancestral homeland, we invite you to visit our tourism site at www.visitscotland. com where you will also discover all the information you need to make your trip home to Scotland simple to organise. . . .
>
> With all this information and advice, you can transform your homecoming journey into one of the most exciting and dynamic experiences of your life. (www.ancestralscotland.com/visiting-scotland)

The page suggests to diasporic Scots that genealogical research is pointless without visiting Scotland. Only by visiting in person can they complete their quests and reach their 'final destination' (both of their genealogical 'journey of discovery' and, in the evocation of *Tir nan Òg*, the 'journey of life'). It is only by making this 'homecoming' that roots tourists will be able to gain 'a rich understanding of [their] ancestral heritage and culture' (and, implicitly, of themselves). And, note again how the *AncestralScotland* web site pretends not to be a touristic enterprise: for such profane, touristic matters as room bookings and ferry schedules, the visitor is referred to the STB's 'tourism site', *VisitScotland*.

Through the articulation of a limited number of text and image motifs, it is apparent that in these three web sites – *ToScotland*, *VisitScotland* and *AncestralScotland* – the STB is effectively imagineering different Scotlands for different markets, 'representing back' different visions of Scotland according to its perception of the desires and imaginaries of different interest groups. All three sites demonstrate how the myth of the Highlands still dominates and comes to represent Scotland as a whole, but certain motifs, which the non-Scottish heritage community is perceived to find unappealing, are reserved for the Scottish-American and genealogy niche markets. Thus, members of the Scottish diaspora are subtly invited to visit and identify with a different Scotland to other potential visitors: specifically, an 'Ancestral Scotland'. To 'visit Scotland' is evidently not the same as to 'visit Ancestral Scotland'. Indeed, contrary to the claim implicit in these promotions – that Scotland is, as noted earlier, an unmediated reality, something unequivocal to which is attributed the agency to affect and determine individuals' identities – it is apparent that 'Scotland' is a more malleable destination in which visitors are encouraged to find whichever imagined homeland they seek.

Bringing Scott-land home

I should now like to turn to the representation of Scotland in the glossy Australian print periodical, *SCOTS*. This quarterly magazine was launched in August 1998 by a husband-and-wife team, Bruce MacGregor Sandison (publisher) and Susan Cromarty (editor) – both Australians with Scottish ancestry – with the intent of celebrating 'the unique heritage our ancestors have bequeathed us' (Cromarty 1998: 4). A 2001 promotional circular targeted at potential advertisers summarises the magazine's style, editorial policy and readership as follows:

> *SCOTS* is the only large format 128-page full colour Scottish magazine on the market with a global readership of 150,000 per quarter.
>
> No magazine matches *SCOTS* for the quality of its design, writing and photography. Each issue contains over 20 well-written, beautifully illustrated articles of specific interest to the 40 million people of Scots descent around the world.
>
> *SCOTS* is the only premium quality magazine with a truly global distribution.
>
> 30,000 copies of *SCOTS* are printed and distributed to readers around the world each quarter, everywhere from Iceland to Invercargill. Approximately one third of readers are within Australia and New Zealand, another third are in the US and Canada and a third reside within the UK and Europe . . .
>
> Over three quarters of *SCOTS* readers are professional and business people, members of heritage and cultural organisations, including Historic Scotland and The National Trust for Scotland, St. Andrew's and Caledonian Societies, Burns Clubs and individual Clan organisations around the world. Readers are generally aged between 35 to 65 years. Men and women equally enjoy *SCOTS*. (Scots Heritage Pty Ltd, promotional circular, 2001)

Various slogans are used throughout the magazine: thus, as well as 'Celebrating our Scottish heritage', the publishers claim *SCOTS* is 'More than a magazine: it *is* 'Our Heritage'. Playing on different meanings of home, the slogan 'Bring Scotland Home' regularly features in its subscription advertisements, suggesting that, through *SCOTS*, the sacred/symbolic space of the homeland may be brought into the quotidian domestic spaces of its readers' homes. The subscription advertisement of the August 2000 issue is reproduced in Figure 4.5; this features the 'Bring Scotland Home' slogan against an impressive tobacco-toned photograph of Dunvegan Castle, framed by the branches of Caledonian pines. The advertisement also features images of the front covers of the first eight issues of the magazine – all exemplars of the Highlandist aesthetic.

Reproduced in Table 4.1 is a description of each of the front covers of the first twelve issues of *SCOTS* (1998–2001), those published during the fieldwork phase of my research and upon which my comments here are based.

In terms of the differently authentic imaginaries discussed earlier in this chapter, it is particularly interesting to note that, even in this *diasporic* magazine, the element of tartanry is absent in all but three of the front covers, and in these, significantly, it is only present within historical portraiture. Indeed, a similarly 'refined' Highlandism is evident in the editorial policy. Thus, while many articles are devoted to iconic themes such as tartan, bagpipes, Bonnie Prince Charlie, whisky, shortbread and heather (all key components of tartanry), these are mostly written by recognised Scottish experts in a scholarly manner that generally seeks to replace myths with legitimate histories. It is, for example, Hugh Cheape, curator of modern Scottish history at the National Museums of Scotland, who contributes a series of articles on the history of tartan and another on the history of the bagpipes.

An early precedent is set for this qualified inclusion of tartanry with an article by the heraldist and historian Alastair Campbell of Airds in the first issue of the magazine. Under the title 'Braveheart' and alongside images from the 1995 film, Campbell discusses the 'corruption of Scottish history', particularly, but not exclusively, as promulgated in the Scottish diaspora. As well as criticising *Braveheart* itself, which he describes as 'a classic example of Scottish history being distorted most horribly' (1998: 30), Campbell examines such modern inventions of tradition as the 'Kirking of the Tartan' and the misrepresentation of historical events such as the Glencoe massacre of 1692. He writes,

> One of the first things that hits me whenever I go abroad is the tremendous fervor for things Scottish. That's wonderful, of course, but there are dangers in that, too. The popular view of Scottish history both in Scotland and outwith Scotland tends to be wildly over-romanticised. One finds all sorts of developments in this feeling of being Scottish which actually have no historical background in Scotland at all. (Ibid.: 29)

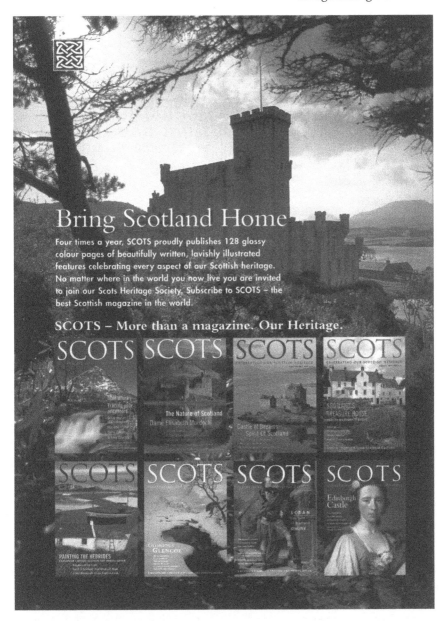

Figure 4.5 Bringing Highlandism home with *SCOTS* (Scots Heritage)

Referring specifically to diasporic Scots, he adds, 'One finds them clinging to the romantic and very often the false aspects of their past. And in so doing they become *more Scots than the Scots*' (Ibid.; emphasis added).

Table 4.1 Representation of Scotland in the front cover imagery of *SCOTS*

#1	Photograph: Snow-dusted mountain and mountain stream Caption: 'Buchaille Etive Mhor, Glencoe, Lochaber'
#2	Photograph: Autumnal sunlight on lochside castle ruin, rich golden hills in background
#3	Photograph: Still inhabited castle on sea loch, misty headlands in background
#4	Photograph: Fishing nets and lobster creels on quayside, quaint seaside cottages
#5	Painting: Hebridean croft house and fishing boat in quiet sea loch with small islands
#6	Photograph: Snowy mountain scene, stream meandering through snowfield Caption: 'Winter in Glencoe'
#7	Painting: Officer in Highland dress, classical ruins in background (18th century)
#8	Painting: Fresh-faced woman with white cockade in hair and tartan cape (18th century)
#9	Painting: Officer in Highland dress, wall-mounted targe and crossed swords in background (18th century) Caption: 'Colonel Alastair Macdonell of Glengarry by Sir Henry Raeburn'
#10	Photograph: Mountains and loch bathed in golden sunlight Caption: Slioch and Loch Maree, Wester Ross
#11	Photograph: Interior of baronial mansion, roaring open fire, stags' head trophies on wall Caption: 'Sitting Room, Mar Lodge'
#12	Photograph: Harbour, quayside buildings and fishing boats, reflections in mirror-like water Caption: 'Kirkwall, Orkney'

This observation that diasporic Scots have become more 'Scottish' than homeland Scots is commonly made (another similar and frequently used phrase is that 'there's none more Scots than the Scots abroad'). Indeed, it is this very enthusiasm for the invented traditions of tartanry, at which Campbell's 'eyes have boggled' (1998: 29), which constitutes the excessive character of Scottish diasporic identity. And whilst Campbell's article does not go beyond challenging the authenticity of this version of Scottishness (he does not, for instance, consider the *local* diasporic context of such performances), it is nevertheless significant that it should be included in the launch issue of a magazine produced in and for the diaspora. It is, perhaps, a more explicit articulation of the editorial policy of the magazine than that stated by its editor in her inaugural editorial.

In contrast to other popular diasporic magazines and newspapers such as *The Highlander* and *The Scottish Banner*, which are often emblazoned with tartans, thistles and Saltires, *SCOTS* is clearly targeted at a more 'discerning' market – identified in the aforementioned circular as 'professional and business people, members of heritage and cultural organisations, including Historic Scotland and The National Trust for Scotland'.[6] This is reflected in the many lifestyle articles in the magazine (Scottish gardens, country-house interiors, cuisine, profiles of clan chiefs, etc.) and in the merchandising products which the magazine offers as its 'Scots Heritage Collection' (coffee-table books, quality knitwear and tweeds, limited-edition prints of paintings and photographs). This refined image has evolved over the years of the magazine's publication, especially since its distribution has become more international. It is evident in the early editions that the magazine was initially addressed to an Australian and New Zealand readership. In the first four issues, for example, many articles are devoted to people and places with Scottish connections in Australia and New Zealand (Highland cattle in New South Wales, Scottish settlers in Otago, profiles of prominent Antipodean-Scots, etc.). In later issues, with distribution now equally divided between Australasia, North America and the UK, the majority of the articles tend to be focused on the Scottish homeland itself (Issue 12, for instance, features articles on the Orkney Islands; Sir Malcolm Innes of Edingight, Lord Lyon King of Arms; Scottish heraldry; the Battle of Bannockburn; the Scottish Crown Jewels; the 'Hebridean Odyssey' of Scottish painter, David Humphreys; a 'photo essay' about the Isle of Skye; and the third part of Hugh Cheape's series on the history of the bagpipes). This change of focus may also be tracked in the classified advertisements: thus, in Issue 3, 81 per cent of the small advertisements are from Australian and New Zealand companies, by Issue 12 this has dropped to 47 per cent. It is also significant to note that the nature of the products offered in the small advertisements has also changed in this period. In the early issues the section is entitled 'Scots Classified' and the products offered are rich in Antipodean tartanry – here one may purchase such items as a 'Scottish Australian flag', 'Highland Heather – grown in the Southern Highlands of NSW from seed imported from Scotland', and portraits of 'your own "young chief"' from 'one of Australia's most gifted artists'. By Issue 7 the section has been refashioned as the 'Scots Business Directory' and much of the tartanry is gone.

It is clear, then, that a very particular image of Scotland is being cultivated in the pages of *SCOTS*, a process which again points to an imagineering of Scotland, a 'program[ming] out of all the negative, unwanted elements' (including, in this instance, the 'unrefined' elements of tartanry) 'and program[ming] in the positive' (Zukin 1991: 222). Indeed, Susan Cromarty admits to such positive programming in her editorial to Issue 11 of the magazine. In the following excerpt, Cromarty is describing being interviewed by a BBC Radio Scotland presenter, Mark Stephens, during a recent visit to her ancestral homeland:

'One aspect of your magazine which particularly appeals to me', Mark said, 'is the very positive tone it contains, something you don't often find in magazines today'. 'SCOTS is a celebration of our Scottish heritage', I replied. 'Yes, we include only stories which are a positive reflection of Scotland and her people. There would be no satisfaction in doing otherwise'.

'And how extraordinary', he said, 'that a magazine which does so beautifully and eloquently celebrate Scotland's heritage, should be published by an Australian rather than a Scot'. 'Well, who better', I replied. 'Who better understands just how important our Scottish heritage remains for those 40 million of us around the world who now live beyond Scotland's shores. Whether we are now Australians, New Zealanders, Canadians, Americans, Argentines, or Zimbabweans, we all understand what it is to value and to celebrate our Scottish heritage'. (Cromarty 2001: 4)

Note also Cromarty's recapitulation of an often-made claim that diasporic Scots are better able to 'value and celebrate' Scotland and its heritage than homeland Scots – a claim that sometimes translates into a diasporic mission to teach Scots how to value their heritage better.

It is perhaps not necessary to perform a more detailed analysis of the images, texts and advertisements of SCOTS to gather that Scott's Celtic muse thrives in this diasporic magazine. The Scotland it purports to 'bring home' to its readers is without doubt a *Scott-land* shot through with Highlandism and a 'gentrified' tartanry. Comparing SCOTS with other Scottish heritage periodicals, however, it is evident that even within diasporic media there is no *single* Scottish imaginary. The tweeds, traditional knitwear and other 'quality' merchandising products promoted in this Australian publication contrast sharply with those offered in competing magazines such as *The Highlander* (in a 1999 edition of this American publication may be found advertisements for teddy bears dressed in kilts; miniature 'hand painted' castles; tartan dog collars; dirks, daggers and *skean dubhs*; clan badges, crests and mugs; sporrans and 'Jacobean' shirts – examples of what is commonly referred to as 'tartan tat' in the Scottish press). Thus, there are not only many Scotlands, there are also many *Scott-lands* – each imagined, objectified and reproduced within the multifarious habitus of a diaspora dispersed not only across geographic space, but also across 'social space' (Bourdieu 1984). Pursuing this invocation of Bourdieu, it will be evident that the 'structuring structures' of taste and distinction and the economies of 'symbolic capital' are manifest in these transnational social imaginings (ibid.).

Ancestral Scott-land: home of the brave(hearts)

If the refined, conservative and authenticated *Scott-land* imagineered in SCOTS is in distinctively good taste, then its inverse, the epitome of bad taste, is represented by the hyperbolic *Scott-land* of *Braveheart*. In the populist tradition of Scott, the 1995 film has grossed some $204 million at the box office worldwide (Internet Movie Database 2002) and, in contrast to the relatively slight impact of a niche interest magazine, must itself be considered partly responsible for the contemporary Scottish heritage revival. In the film, the Scottish-American-Australian producer-director-actor, Mel Gibson, stars as the heroic Scottish 'freedom fighter' William Wallace, who led the Scots to victory over the English at the Battle of Stirling Bridge in 1297, paving the way for Robert the Bruce's more decisive victory at Bannockburn twenty-two years later. With its 'excessive use of patriotic symbolism' and despite its representation of Scottish history which 'at times verges on the ludicrous', this 'medieval action adventure' succeeded in reigniting the cause of Scottish nationalism in the late twentieth century and 'led to the image of Gibson as Wallace being appropriated as an emblem by the Scottish National Party' (Petrie 2000: 209–11; Edensor 1997: 146–9). Of course, this evocation of Scotland as the original 'land of the free, home of the brave' is nothing less that a projection of specifically American nationalistic ideology onto an old country: a melding of Scottish and American nationalist sentiment also evinced, as noted earlier, in the claim that the 1320 Declaration of Arbroath, in which the Scottish Crown asserted its independence from England, was the template for the 1776 American Declaration of Independence (D. A. Bruce 1997: 38–40).

As is apparent in Alastair Campbell's comments in *SCOTS*, the reaction to *Braveheart* among the Scottish *literati* has been unanimously venomous, but this criticism has not stemmed the film's popular appeal. For example, in an article in *Scotland on Sunday* entitled 'Scottish history is being vandalised', Magnus Linklater expresses his exasperation at the *Braveheart*-inspired displays of the Wallace Monument visitor centre near Stirling: 'Since the movie *Braveheart* hit our screens, the place has been refurbished in the Mel Gibson image. Outside, a new statue to William Wallace has been erected, using Gibson's face as the model – all matted locks and painted face' (1999: 17).

The controversial statue was actually defaced soon after being erected, although local opinion is divided as to whether this was a politically-motivated gesture against the Americanisation of Scottish heritage or a 'regular' act of vandalism (Kaiya Marshbank, *Stirling Observer*, pers. comm.). Linklater is, however, even more incensed by the visitor centre's souvenir booklet which, he reports, argues in favour of *Braveheart's* fictionalisation of Scottish history on the grounds that it brings Wallace 'back to life', justifies the adoption of this same approach in the centre's displays and resists the supposedly elitist '"this is fiction" brigade with their synthetic concerns about accuracy'. Linklater concludes,

So there you have it. False history is actually more important than the real thing. Capturing 'the spirit of Wallace' outweighs the facts.

Personally I resent the fact that part of our precious heritage is being subverted to the demands of Hollywood and tourist numbers. Why should our children, in this modern age, be brought up to believe the shortbread tin version of Scotland's story rather than the real thing? Who are the heritage vandals of our day who sell us this pap? And what have we done to deserve a Brigadoon image of our nation?

To paraphrase Tom Nairn, I suggest that Scotland will only be a modern nation again when the last visitor centre is smothered by the last tea-towel version of the Declaration of Arbroath. (1999: 17)

Regardless of the protestations of Linklater and others of the 'this is fiction brigade', it appears that the 'demands of Hollywood and tourist numbers' are being accommodated and that the process of imagineering Scotland continues in the material heritage landscape of the homeland itself, not least through the medium of the visitor centre. In a very literal sense, we may thus see how certain places in the Scottish landscape come to be remade 'as objects for the tourist gaze' and how identity comes to be 'produced partly out of the images constructed for tourists' (Urry 1995: 164–5).

Indeed, just as Scott's *The Lady of the Lake* and *Waverley* inspired the first Scottish tourism boom in the nineteenth century, so *Braveheart* has had a significant impact on Scottish tourism in the present day. In 1997, for instance, Stirling Council and Forth Valley Enterprise commissioned a study to measure the effect of films set in Scotland on visitor generation. Of the 1,540 visitors surveyed in the region, 55 per cent reported that they had seen *Braveheart* and 39 per cent stated that seeing it had indeed influenced their decision to visit Scotland (Seaton and Hay 1998: 230). The STB calculated that, in terms of tourism revenue, the films *Braveheart* and *Rob Roy* together generated the equivalent of nearly £11.5 million of free advertising (Petrie 2000: 220), and Seaton and Hay conclude from such remarkable figures that 'international feature films could be a better promotional medium for Scotland than mainstream commercial advertising' (1998: 230). Capitalising on such free publicity, the area around Stirling was promoted as 'The Land of Braveheart' and 'Braveheart Country' in tourism marketing materials (the irony being that, due to favourable tax incentives, much of *Braveheart* was actually filmed in Ireland).

Despite its not inconsiderable impact in Scotland itself, the influence of *Braveheart* has perhaps been most conspicuous in the USA. Here it has given rise to what has been described as 'claymore culture' and the reinvigoration of the image of Scotland as 'an elemental land of warrior men and wan maidens, of breast beating heroes fighting the overtly rational [and effete] English' (Pat Kane quoted by Edensor 1997: 141). These heroic, masculine identities are performed, most literally, by the now-ubiquitous *Braveheart*-inspired re-enactment groups at countless Highland gatherings throughout the States. Ray observes that, in the aftermath of *Braveheart*, men attending such gatherings in North Carolina would often appear with their faces painted in the (spurious) manner of the warriors in the film's battle scenes, and that 'movie posters and cardboard images of Mel Gibson as William Wallace appeared in many clan tent displays' (2001: 205, 231n29). The influence is evident, too, in the choice of period costume that Scottish-American clansfolk elect to wear at these gatherings. Thus, the warrior-like *feileadh mor* or 'big kilt', complete with leather jerkin, spiked targe and claymore, has become preferable to the more genteel *feileadh beag* and its accoutrements, which have become perceived increasingly as Victorian inventions (Ray 2001: 26–7; Trevor-Roper 1983; Edensor 1997: 149).

Whilst many homeland Scots find it easy to lampoon the enthusiasm of many members of the Scottish-American community with their theatrical outfits and naïve rallying cries of 'Freedom' for their imaginary homeland, the impact of *Braveheart* on its audiences must be taken seriously. As with other media discussed in this chapter, our concern ought not to be with the authenticity of the film's representation of Scotland and its history, so much as to understand how the film comes to inspire and represent the sentiments of a significant number of people. Thomas Elsaesser, in his discussion of the cinematic representation of the Holocaust, argues that the relationship between 'representation and affect, and affect as representation' is articulated in a 'forcefield of the said and the unsaid, the excessive and the repressed' and that, in an era in which 'public history has inevitably superseded personal memory', it is through the deployment of excessive devices such as melodrama and spectacle (epitomised in Hollywood cinema) that audience identification is brought about (1996: 147–9). The consequence of this mirroring of representation and affect is one of recognition: the movie, for example, appears to speak one's own story, one's own history. This somewhat abstruse reasoning may be clarified in the example of *Braveheart*. Consider the following North American testimonials posted to a 'Braveheart Experiences' message board on a web site devoted to the film:

> This film, and the legacy of William Wallace's quest for freedom, has had a profound effect on my own life. For some reason, his story stirred something in me that drove me to delve into Scotland's tumultuous history. I became drawn to things Scottish, and later found to my surprise that I had Scots blood in my own ancestry. I am compelled to come to Scotland now. I don't know why, but *Braveheart* has become the stepping-off point for my own Scottish odyssey. (www.macbraveheart.co.uk/messages/bhexp-02.htm)

> I'm an American of highlander descent, and spent the last couple of years researching my family, which originated in the glens around

Glen Shee. I had discovered where they lived, found the ship's passengers logs for them, etc., all very exciting for a bagpipe-playing, trying-to-learn Gaelic Yank like me. I LOVED *Braveheart* ... Then, two Novembers ago, I had the opportunity of a lifetime: I got to take my entire family to Scotland for two weeks. ... I drove up A93 towards little Glen Shee to find my ancestor's homelands. Just as we came up on a rise, I saw a bunch of stuff at once – a little sign telling me I was 'there', a huge mist crawling over huge, yellow larch and green spruce and red heather covered mountains, the site of my clan's gatherings, and THEN – with the soundtrack to *Braveheart* in my car's tape deck – the music of the main theme crescendos as the panorama opened around me. It was absolutely BREATHTAKING ... I will NEVER forget it, and it truly cemented something in this Gaelic Soul! (www.macbraveheart.co.uk/messages/bhexp-04.htm)

As I watched the movie I was completely immersed in the experience. I suspended all of disbelief and was 'there' in a sense that I cannot remember ever having in a movie theater. At the end of the movie, I was unable to stand and simply sat and wept for about five minutes. Later, in the car on the way home, I continued to weep. This was such a profound experience for me that I began to do some research on the story and on William Wallace. Sure enough, I discovered through my family history that the MacKinnons had surely been a part of the battle to win the Scots' freedom. I knew I was there in some way or shape – but this information helped to explain the depth of my feeling during the movie. (www.macbraveheart.co.uk/messages/bhexp-04.htm)

Note how, in the first message, an identification with Gibson's Wallace and his 'quest for freedom' leads the poster to discover her own Scottish heritage and feel compelled to journey to her new-found ancestral homeland. The second message demonstrates that such journeys, contrary to expectations, involve not simply a departure from the artifice of discursive realms and a discovery of the authentic, material homeland, but often involve a melding of both, such that the emotion-inducing techniques of cinematic '*mis*representation' (a stirring soundtrack, for example) may be employed to enhance the experience of the real. In the final example, the poster's identification with the film is so complete that, through positing the presence of her ancestors in the historical scenes portrayed, *Braveheart* literally becomes her own story. This poster, despite her knowing suspension of disbelief, becomes transported 'there' in a most powerful manner – not only into the film's *mise-en-scène*, but (through her genetic heritage) also into Scotland's history itself. Each of the posters alludes to a mysterious sense of connection with this historical homeland of the brave. Thus the last poster knows she 'was there' (fighting for the freedom of her kinsfolk at the Battle of Stirling Bridge) 'in some way or shape'; and the second poster's orchestrated encounter with his clan's ancient gathering place 'truly cemented something' in his 'Gaelic Soul'; and even the first poster, hitherto unconscious of her Scottish ancestry, felt 'something' stirring within her when she first saw the film, something she only later discovered to be her Scottish blood.

Through such expressions of 'genealogical rhetoric', agency for this profound identification with Scotland is diverted from the rational 'mind' of the self and directed to the more obscure emotions and substances of the 'body'. Intuited as a kind of genetic memory, it is thus the soul or blood of the self that is perceived to recognise home in such moving images as *Braveheart*'s. This sense of embodied identification enabled through such unembodied media as the cinema, or indeed STB web sites and diasporic magazines, calls into question any straightforward distinction between the roles of virtual and real worlds in the processes of identity formation.

Consistencies and inconsistencies

Before going on to explore the relationship between these two realms in more detail, it is perhaps worth pausing to review some of the issues that have emerged in the explorations across the Scottish diasporic mediascape undertaken in this chapter. Despite being a modern nation with a varied landscape, Scotland has become identified in the popular imagination with its Highland region, which, in turn, is imagined precisely according to a set of long-established conventions. Scotland has, in short, been 'colonised by the empire of signs' and transformed into *Scott-land*, that paradigmatic land of romance. With its misty isles and heather-covered mountains, its castle ruins and ancient customs, Scotland has become a territory of desire: modernity's other, a dream of nature – and, specifically, 'nature as left behind, as lost wholeness' (Womack 1989: 174). If the Highlands are 'imagined', argues Womack,

> it follows that the non-Highlands (the Scottish Lowlands, or the metropolis, or anglophone Britain generally) are real. The consumer of the myth partakes of the 'pleasing enthusiasms which the wilds impart' and quits them 'with regret': to move back across the Highland line is to leave Fancy's Land and re-enter . . . the realm of factual truth. (ibid.: 166)

Although Womack's structuralist analysis is largely based on the late eighteenth- and early nineteenth-century literary texts through which the Highlandist myth was first constructed, it is evident that the structure of the myth has not been dislodged in the new 'patterns and flows of communication' which characterise the contemporary mediascape. 'The story', as

Womack puts it, 'is by no means over' (1989: 175), and the same few *Scott-ish* motifs are reproduced with banal consistency in countless web sites, magazines, films, and in many of my questionnaire respondents' comments.

The Highland myth is, of course, widely consumed, and a diverse array of people – Scots and non-Scots, Highlanders and non-Highlanders – seem to 'find in the Highlands an idea which they love' (ibid.: 177). Considering the consistency of the representation of the Highlands, it is tempting to suggest that the idea articulated in the myth does not reflect the diversity of those consuming it. In other words, the nature of the metropolitan core may vary, but the *nature* of the Highland periphery seems to remain constant. This is actually a consequence of the structuralist methodology, whereby the persuasiveness of its binary logic obscures more subtle encodings of meaning. If, as Tim Edensor argues in his reading of *Braveheart*, global culture is consumed differently by differently situated actors (1997: 154), it would be reasonable to expect meaning to be contingent upon the particular habitus of each actor and to be modified over time according to changing experiences, influences and circumstances. Such migrations of meanings are explored in subsequent chapters.

The apparent clarity of a straightforward structuralist analysis of the Highland myth is also muddied if we re-envisage the basic Highland/non-Highland (Scotland/non-Scotland) opposition in specifically diasporic terms: that is, as an opposition between homeland and diaspora. Where, for instance, should we situate the diasporic Scot, who, as we have seen, is often considered more Scots than the Scots? And along what lines is difference to be drawn? Diasporic Scots *contra* homeland Scots? *Contra* the dominant culture of their host societies? *Contra* other putative diasporas or heritage communities in their midst? *Contra* diasporic Scots in other host countries? Given the plurality of even diasporic situatedness and the multiplying others against whom actors may be defined as diasporic Scots, one might wonder why this inconsistency does not result in an inconsistent imagining of Scotland. What emerges, instead, is an interplay of consistency and inconsistency according to scale. The consistency with which Scotland is imagined in the diaspora may be understood as a *necessary* component of diasporic consciousness. As Robin Cohen argues,

> transnational bonds no longer have to be cemented by migration or by exclusive territorial claims. In the age of cyberspace, a diaspora can, to some degree, be held together or re-created through the mind, through cultural artefacts and through a shared imagination. (1997: 26)

Thus, a diaspora is cemented through a *shared imagining* of its homeland, and we may conclude that the Scottish diaspora *is* a diaspora to the extent that its members imagine the same 'Scotland of the mind'. In constructing an 'us' in opposition to a 'not us', where the postulated opposites are not necessarily spatially or, indeed, cultural distinct or self-evident, the Scottish diaspora is forced to imagineer its consensual homeland from a familiar assemblage of cultural artefacts which have become '"emblematical" of themselves' (Womack 1989: 48). Waters observes something similar in her study of white ethnicity in North America, where she notes that, in choosing their ethnic identities, her informants need simply to 'learn the appropriate symbols' (1990: 92), selecting them from 'a cultural grab bag of . . . stereotypical traits' (ibid.: 115). The mediascape therefore becomes a repository of symbols and a resource through which diasporic Scots learn what it is to be diasporic Scots, a key component of which is learning how they should imagine their lost homeland.

The journey home is, however, also a journey of discovery and part of this process is the acquisition of an increasingly more authentic local knowledge (i.e. locally-authenticated knowledge), including the ability to discern truth from myth, a refined Highlandism from unrefined tartanry. Enabled through the rigours of genealogical research and, most especially, by visiting the homeland itself, this may be understood, in Bourdieu's terms, as the acquisition of symbolic capital. Thus, within the necessary homogeneity of collective imagining is evident a heterogeneity of subtle, but codified, distinctions through which sub-diasporic social identities are 'defined and asserted through difference' (Bourdieu 1984: 172). At this scale, the meaning of any one of these emblematic cultural artefacts becomes highly nuanced according to complexes of differentiations in social and geographic space (and, of course, the divisions of social and geographic spaces need not be congruent with each other). In this way, the precise choice of colour and quantity of a tartan design on a web site or the items offered for sale in the classified advertisements of a magazine point to differences in the way Scottishness is practised, not only in different regions of the diaspora, but also among different social groups: differences evinced in matters of taste. That is to say, whilst being Scottish in Australia is not the same as being Scottish in America, some Australian Scots may have more in common with some American Scots than with certain other Australian Scots.

As will be seen in the more detailed explorations of particular homecomings provided in Chapter 8, the journey of discovery may ultimately entail a complete rejection of the stereotypical *Scott-land(s)* represented in the public mediascape and lead to the identification of and identification with an increasingly more localised and personally-meaningful homeland. In the postings to the 'Braveheart Experiences' message board we have already seen how the affective public image spaces of the mediascape may be employed by individuals as a medium for the expression of more personalised Scottish identities. In the next chapter I shall pursue this theme further, investigating how the internet may be considered as a space in which these identities are not only expressed, but also challenged and contested.

5 Home spaces, homepages, homelands

> The project of modernity is, then, 'to make oneself at home in the maelstrom'. .... It is this idea of 'home' that interests us. Home in a world of expanding horizons and dissolving boundaries.
>
> David Morley and Kevin Robins, *Spaces of Identity*

With the unfathomability of its electronic networks, the fluidity and bi-directionality of its information flows, the proliferation of such flows, its resistance to censorial control or definitive expression, its potentially global reach, the internet epitomises the 'maelstrom' of late modernity like no other technology. Here one many find the 'vociferous confusion' and 'cluttering up of cultural space' described by Kenneth White (1999), here one may find an intractable milieu in which identity has become disembedded from the body and the body disembedded from place – identity reduced to the level of a text message. As Judith Donath notes,

> Said Sartre in *Being and Nothingness*, 'I am my body to the extent that I am'. The virtual world is different. It is composed of information rather than matter. Information spreads and diffuses; there is no law of the conservation of information. The inhabitants of this impalpable space are also diffuse, free from the body's unifying anchor. One can have, some claim, as many electronic personae as one has time and energy to create. (1999: 29)

Actually, Donath reiterates this familiar assertion in order to argue the opposite. '"One can have . . . ?"' she continues, 'Who is this "one"? It is, of course, the embodied self, the body that is synonymous with identity, the body at the keyboard' (ibid.). Indeed, much of the 'millennial rhetoric' which characterised earlier studies of the internet has now given way to more sober analysis which recognises that the internet is merely another 'site among many in the flow of economics, ideology, everyday life, and experience' (Sterne 1999: 282) and that 'it is essential to treat telecommunications and computer-mediated communications networks as *local* phenomena, as well as global networks' (Shields 1996: 3). Discussing the internet as both 'culture' and 'cultural artefact', Christine Hine similarly argues that the internet has 'multiple temporal and spatial orderings which criss-cross the online/offline boundary' – she concedes, however, that the interaction between these various social spaces remains to be adequately explored by academics (2000: 27; see, however, D. Miller and Slater 2000). I suggest that the contemporary practices of genealogical research and roots tourism cannot be explored except in these terms and that the journeys of discovery with which I am concerned typically move across this online/offline boundary, involving migrations between homepages, as it were, and homelands.

Despite – or, perhaps, because of – its expanding horizons and dissolving boundaries, spatial and orientational tropes proliferate on the internet. The very profusion of data that this communication technology makes available transforms its users from passive receivers of information into active explorers and navigators of discursive space. The most fundamental of such 'cyberspatial' tropes is that of 'home'. Thus the index page of a web site is its homepage, the starting point from which further excursions into uncharted discursive realms may be undertaken. The homepage is that to which most other pages in a site will be linked, often via the word 'Home' or a picturebook icon of a house. In a paper discussing the metaphor of home in personal homepages, Hugh Miller notes, 'if we are lost and confused in navigating around a site, we can always safely return home and start out again' (1999). He observes that the metaphor may be invoked in personal and family web sites in a variety of ways, often going beyond hospitable 'welcome to our home' messages on homepages, and sometimes providing structuring schemata for whole sites. He describes examples of such sites thus:

> Images of houses, gardens, and picket fences marked the 'outside' (earlier) pages, with links to different rooms for different family members (which could sometimes be reached by clicking on the windows of the image of the house presented). Inside, wallpaper-like backgrounds, flower arrangements, coffee cups, and pictures in frames on the 'walls' defined the 'homely' space. (Ibid.)

An even closer melding of online/metaphorical and offline/literal homes in personal homepages is evident in the use of live 'web cams' by some site owners, such that 'by visiting their [web] pages, you can (really) look inside their (real) homes (in real time)' (ibid.).

But there are also other ways of thinking about home, identity and the internet. There is, as Donath suggests, the body at home at the keyboard; then there is the idea of home as a close-knit community (a community of subscribers to an email discussion list, for example); and there is the material homeland that may lend its substance to the otherwise insubstantial identities that form around it. Note how these various ways of thinking about home are articulated in the following few messages, selected from hundreds like them, posted to an online guestbook at *Gael-net*, a tourism web site focused on Skye and the Western Highlands (www.gael-net.co.uk/tourist.html):

> Hi. What did we do before the Internet and Web pages? I love being able to find information about Scotland. While I am now an American, my soul belongs to my native country. I am looking forward to visiting Scotland this summer and plan to spend as many days as is possible on Skye. (AG, Delaware, USA) – *internet as place to learn about home, home as native country.*

> Glad to find your web site. I was on Skye in June '98. It was love at first sight. Am going to get back there to spend more time. It exceeded anything I ever read about it or saw. Truly a little bit of heaven here on this earth. Loved Scotland so much! Must be my Scottish heritage. (FL, Virginia, USA) – *experience of material homeland surpassing that of mediated homeland; attachment to homeland attributed to heritage (i.e., genetic inheritance of body/blood).*

> I always enjoy learning about the land of my ancestors and hope to travel there some day. I would love to see a chat room for gael-o-philes like myself to chat with folks in the old country (CC, Tennessee, USA) – *desire for communication with kinsfolk 'back home'.*

> My husband and I had always hoped to visit Scotland one day but events here at home prevented that. He has since passed away and the possibility that I will be able to do so is very small. I was so pleased to be able to visit this way. I will revisit often to see what changes will be made. I love the photographs and hope to see more bagpipes and kilts and tartans. My mother was a Robertson and I'm digging away to find all I can about our roots. I always feel like I'm searching for home when I read and explore about Scotland. Thank you so much, Scotland, for coming to visit me (MK, Texas, USA) – *home as both place of ordinary residence and as (inaccessible) symbolic homeland; imagined homeland constructed from emblematic motifs; genealogical research as 'search for home'; internet as medium through which homeland can 'travel' to diasporic home.*

> I am scouring the net for information that will help me in planning my long desired trip to Scotland. Funny thing is, my family has Irish roots, and yet I have always thought there was a Scot inside me! I have since found out thru research that the Irish relatives actually came to Ireland from SCOTLAND! ... I KNEW IT!! So my trip to Scotland will be my homecoming in a sense! (CP, Florida, USA) – *'genetic memory' substantiated through research; visiting Scotland as homecoming.*

These various articulations of being at home, searching for home and coming home, as well as the more and less implicit assertions of distance between one kind of home and another, should be kept in mind throughout the discussions of this chapter.

Genealogy and the internet

It is somewhat paradoxical that the internet, this globalising technology *par excellence*, should prove such an effective facilitator of individuals' localising strategies, enabling many people to re-embed their identities and find a way 'home' in the 'new and disorientating global space' in which they exist (Morley and Robins 1995: 87). Nowhere is this paradox more apparent than in the contemporary practices of genealogy and roots tourism, and it is no exaggeration to say that the internet has revolutionised the process of family history research worldwide. As Judy, an informant from Victoria, Australia, explains:

> Using only the Internet, I unearthed the raw data of the family trees of my three Scottish grandparents, and traced their families back to around the 1750s. I found out who my ancestors were, where they were born, where they lived, who they married, the names of their children, what their occupations were, when they died, and what they died of.

Indeed, genealogy is often cited as one of the great success stories of the internet and is reputedly the second most common leisure use of the technology after pornography (Warren 1999). Shortly after its launch in May 1999 the LDS *Family Search* site (www.familysearch.com) was, for instance, reported to be receiving an astounding 100 million hits a day (C. Bennett 1999); whilst, in an article discussing the remarkable popularity of the genealogy internet service provider *RootsWeb* (www.rootsweb.com), a journalist in *The Scotsman* remarked that, 'amid this hive of relative tracing activity, few countries outside the United States are attracting as much attention as Scotland, with thousands of emigrant Caledonians from across the globe using the digital highway to stake their claim in the nation's past' (I. S. Bruce 2000).

What is equally clear, however, is that many journeys begun on the 'digital highway' are continued by air, rail, ferry, hire car and on foot. We have, for example, already seen the claim made at the STB's *AncestralScotland* web site that, whilst 'it is possible to do lots of genealogy research without ever coming to Scotland', this would be like 'making a journey without ever reaching your final destination' (www.ancestralscotland.com/visitingscotland). Indeed, the assertion that only by visiting Scotland will family historians with Scottish ancestry gain 'a rich understanding of [their] ancestral heritage and culture' (ibid.) is supported by many informants. Thus, Judy continues:

All those dates and all that information on certificates just gives you the bare bones. They don't tell you what these people were like, how they lived, or the nature of the landscape they lived in. By going to Scotland I can start to put the flesh on their old bones. By taking this journey I can see where they lived and worked, and try to discover what it must have been like to be them. I want to know *what* they were, not just *who* they were. I want to know what formed them.

Reiterating a commonly used metaphor, another informant describes the internet as 'a fascinating beginning step' on an 'exciting journey' to discover her roots (MD, Arkansas, USA).

But neither do these migrations simply begin online and end offline in a visit to the old country: they frequently include multiple movements back and forth between these different domains. As already noted, every genealogy how-to guide will advise its readers to begin their research 'at home' and in the present, collecting information that is readily at hand, interrogating their own memories and those of older relatives about more recent generations, assembling certificates and photographs in the family's possession, and so on. Information collected offline thus becomes the basis for researchers' initial investigations using online genealogy resources.

There are a vast number of such online resources, from searchable databases of parochial and statutory records to place- or name-specific discussion lists through which 'virtual communities' of genealogists exchange information and experiences. These resources are often indexed, categorised and cross-referenced at genealogy portals such as *Cyndi's List* (www.cyndislist.com) or, relating to the UK and Ireland in particular, *GENUKI* (www.genuki.org.uk). When I last viewed it, the page-view counter at *Cyndi's List* reported that some 41,610,400 'fellow genealogists' had visited the site since it was established in 1996; elsewhere it is claimed that the site includes links to over 240,200 other genealogy-related internet resources.

Although the STB's *AncestralScotland* web site (www.ancestralscotland.com) is primarily a tourism promotion tool and only parades as a genealogy portal, it provides a simple demonstration of the link between homepage and homeland. As mentioned in Chapter 4, the site includes a facility at which visitors may search its online genealogy database for their ancestors' surnames. Inputting the surname 'Macpherson', for instance, returns a list of occurrences of the name in the 1881 census (Table 5.1).

The list provides the top ten counties or towns in which the name is most frequently recorded, ordered according to the percentage of the total population of each region in 1881 and including links to the web sites of the regional tourist boards concerned with promoting these areas. Whilst this may be of only limited value to genealogists concerned with the particularities of their family histories, the broad association of surname and

Table 5.1 AncestralScotland surname search results for 'Macpherson'

Surname	County/Town	Occurrences	Regional tourist board
Macpherson	Inverness-shire	615	Highlands of Scotland
Macpherson	Sutherland	78	Highlands of Scotland
Macpherson	Argyll	155	Argyll and the Trossachs
Macpherson	Nairn	13	Highlands of Scotland
Macpherson	Ross	107	Highlands of Scotland
Macpherson	Caithness	42	Highlands of Scotland
Macpherson	Elgin	44	Aberdeen and Grampian
Macpherson	Edinburgh	238	Edinburgh and Lothians
Macpherson	Perthshire	49	Perthshire
Macpherson	Bute	6	Argyll and the Trossachs

place is clear – and, as we shall see in Chapter 6, Badenoch in the county of Inverness-shire is indeed recognised as 'Macpherson country'.

Much more significant online research tools are available at the afore-mentioned LDS *Family Search* web site, at which researchers can freely search the 'International Genealogical Index', and, for those with Scottish ancestry, the General Register Office for Scotland's *Scots Origins* site (www.scotsorigins.com), launched in 1998, which, at the time of writing, includes indexes to births, baptisms, marriages, burials and deaths in pre-1855 parochial registers and post-1855 statutory registers, as well as indexes to the 1881, 1891 and 1901 censuses.[1] *Scots Origins* also hosts its own genealogy email discussion list and offers a service whereby researchers can purchase and have sent to them copies of certificates and extracts from records relating to their ancestors. Judy, again, stresses the importance of obtaining such certificates, partly because the online indexes contain only abbreviated data and are therefore not reliable sources in themselves, but also because these documents contain leads to earlier generations. She describes how the arrival of certificates ordered from *Scots Origins* at her home in Australia occasions 'a little ritual' and how she has been introduced to some of her ancestors through these documents:

> The day the certificate arrives in the post is a joyous occasion. I've now made a little ritual of it. I get myself a cup of coffee, get my family history files out, and while drinking my coffee read the certificate through a few times, making sure every detail fits into what I already know. This is the important cross-referencing that is essential if you are to avoid accidentally claiming the 'wrong' people as your ancestors. Every new certificate you acquire provides you with new information. My grandparents' marriage certificate gave me my first 'meeting' with four of my great grandparents.

Needless to say, prior to the internet and computerised databases, this kind of research would have been extremely laborious and would have necessitated either personal visits to records offices in Scotland or else employing a professional researcher to carry out the work by proxy.

Whilst some researchers proceed with celerity, for the majority, even with these online resources, the process may take many months depending on the amount of time devoted to the search and the number of 'dead-ends' encountered. Hypothetically, however, having pieced together the raw data of a family history through these resources, researchers are perhaps in a position to again cross the online/offline boundary and visit some of the places they have been able to associate with their newly-discovered ancestors: the parishes or villages in which they lived, the graveyards in which they are buried, and so forth. As well as putting 'flesh' on the 'bare bones' of the pedigree chart by exploring the environment which 'formed' their ancestors, such journeys also enable researchers to access more local sources of information unavailable online: maps, estate records and catalogues of monumental inscriptions held at local libraries, for instance, or insights gained from contact with local inhabitants and historians. The acquisition of this new information inevitably raises as many questions as it answers, and sends roots tourists back home to their online research with a new set of queries to pursue.

The research process itself thus entails a migration between online and offline realms which, in theory, might repeat indefinitely depending on the individual researcher's funds and inclinations. Many roots tourists return to Scotland frequently (typically every two or three years) either progressing to an increasingly more precise and localised identification of their ancestral home or moving sideways, pursuing other associated branches of the family tree. Indeed, the process of family history research is, by definition, unending and many researchers describe themselves as 'detectives' merely moving from one mystery to another, with no prospect of reaching any 'final destination'. Judy describes this in terms of an ever-expanding puzzle: 'It's like doing a huge, giant jigsaw puzzle except this one has no edges, no boundaries. You want to fill in every piece but the more pieces you slot into the right place, the bigger the jigsaw becomes'.

At home at the keyboard

Considering the seemingly boundless task of genealogical research, many roots tourists inevitably spend a great deal of time online. But these computer-mediated explorations, as much as their non-mediated (or, at least, less mediated) equivalents in the Scottish homeland, cannot be reduced to mere fact-finding missions. What is sought is not only a substantiation of individuals' genealogical research, but also a substantiation of their genealogical *identities* – identities excavated intuitively from the self rather than from certificates and census records (note, for example, the Floridian *Gael-net* guestbook poster, quoted above, who *knew* she had Scottish roots and whose genealogical research simply confirmed her belief). In their online and offline journeys of discovery, roots tourists desire both to legitimate their identification with their ancestral homeland through documentary evidence and to effect an increasingly more substantial identification with that homeland through an increased familiarity with its landscape, history and culture.

As the focus of many of these processes, the computer becomes quite literally a portal through which roots tourists can be transported to Scotland and through which Scotland can be transported into their diasporic homes. One consequence of this is that the computer often becomes highly charged and imbued with qualities of the homeland. For example, Anna, also from Victoria, describes how her computing experience is infused with the personality of her ancestral homeland:

> I go out of my way to add that 'place, color, texture, history and emotion' to my virtual experience. For example, my computer is a kind of virtual Scotland, even before I get online. When I turn it on it plays a verse from Capercaillie's '*Fear a'Bhata*',[2] and my mouse cursor has a little rotating Celtic knot instead of an hourglass. And the desktop background is a picture that my mother took of our ancestors' home in Pabbay in the Outer Hebrides. So even though I can't imagine virtual space as such, I'm doing a great job of imagining parts of it as Scotland!

This corner of the diasporic home which is 'forever Scotland' frequently extends to the space around the computer and to whole rooms, typically including shelves loaded with Scottish-interest books, framed photographs of the ancestral home, family tree charts, clan crests and family heirlooms displayed on walls, mantelpieces, and so forth (cf. D. Miller 2001). Of particular value among such collections are souvenirs obtained during visits to Scotland, notably 'found objects' such as stones, shells and pottery sherds, which function as relics, introducing into the mundane space of the domestic home something of the 'sacred' substance of the homeland.

Two further examples of this transference of qualities of the homeland into the diasporic home space are worth elaborating. Reproduced in Figure 5.1 are photographs of the room in which Sharon, another Australian informant, works on her family history research. 'I seem to spend my whole life on the computer', she explains,

> I write to family who are on the Internet, it makes them so much closer and you can correspond much more quickly. I also use it to keep in touch with researchers in Scotland [and] transfer files to the Aberdeen and North East Scotland Family History Society – I am an active member and transcribe censuses which are published and placed on their shelves.

Figure 5.1 Sharon's office in her New South Wales home. Images of Birse and
    sprigs of heather collected on homecoming journeys crowd around the desk
    at which Sharon works on her family history research

Sharon's office in her New South Wales home is painted 'the colour of the
Scottish thistle', and on its walls are hung many framed photographs and
pressed sprigs of heather taken at and collected from places associated
with Sharon's ancestors in Birse, Aberdeenshire. Describing her office,
Sharon adds:

> Now there is a wooden sign hanging from the middle group of photos
> above the desk which says 'Auchabrack' [the name of one of her ancestral
> homes]. I think there will be a sign post in the corner behind 'Alex' [a
> teddy bear mascot named after Sharon's great-great grandfather] which
> will have some of the family croft names on it – just for something orig-
> inal. Still to come is an old map of Scotland and also one of
> Aberdeenshire which is being framed at the moment. Plus, if I can find
> space, I want to put up some sort of cork board with a map of the area on
> it and then somehow attach the different family trees I have constructed.

It is interesting to note that included in her displays are a number of
photographs that I took while accompanying Sharon on her second homecoming journey in 2000 (Sharon specifically asked me to send a
photograph of her laying flowers at the grave of Alexander, an ancestor
with whom she feels a particular affinity). In these images in particular,
Sharon is thus placed 'within the frame' of her imagined homeland, rein-
habiting the landscape of her ancestors – and, indeed, it is very common

for roots tourists to hand their cameras to passers-by and ask to be photographed in front of ancestral places. I asked Sharon whether she found herself gazing at her photographs when working at her desk. She replied, 'Yeah, well Auchabrack is just above the computer where I sit . . . just having a little drift along there Sharon! A little visit back'.

Similarly, for Brenda, from Ontario, Canada, the internet is not only an important research tool, it is also the key medium through which she maintains her sense of connection with her ancestral homeland:

> The net is my lifeline to the world I really feel I am part of. I can be there via photos of scenery, web cams, radio, TV, writings, even voices of people in Scotland that I share daily life with. I can continue to explore daily until the day I walk back onto the peat. I can let almost any emotion hit me with regards to my wanting to be in Scotland and then go to my computer to quench that thirst somewhat until the next trip over.

Brenda describes in some detail how she is surrounded by Scotland in her Canadian home, but the distance between her 'daily world' and the world she 'really' feels 'part of' is also clear. In the following comments, she refers to a red stone which she found in a river bed in Glencoe, the scene of a particularly powerful homecoming experience (see Chapter 8), which is now placed on the mantelpiece of her living room 'to look at as I pass by in my daily world here'. Even more than the internet or her photographs and books, this stone, embodying the substance of the old country, enables Brenda to be transported back to Scotland.

> First and foremost, I hold my red stone and close my eyes. I can go back in my heart and the feelings come to the forefront once again. My photo album is always on the coffee table for me to look through or share with anyone who will listen. My books continue to grow and surround me and are scattered around my home. I listen to Scottish music daily. I have many sayings and quotes on paper off the Internet floating around regarding Scotland's history. My mantelpiece in the living room is like a shrine: my stone, a sheep's tooth [another found object], pence coins, pebbles, shells, maps, print outs on MacKinnon Clan history off the net, books . . . On my computer desktop a picture of the MacKinnon castle, in my computer room more maps printed off the net, photos of Scotland I took, and endless [web site] bookmarks on Scotland.

Such local practices, focused around the global networks of the internet, remind us of the presence of 'the body at the keyboard'. However, we should also be cautious about accepting uncritically Donath's suggestion that this 'embodied self' is necessarily 'synonymous with identity' (1999: 29). We might, instead, question the efficacy of the body as the 'unifying anchor' of identity. Rather than rooted in the body, the identities described by Brenda and other informants seem to be routed elsewhere – in an ancestral homeland which, as we have seen, is largely imaginary. Thus, perhaps we should understand the use of these Scottish screensavers and web site print-outs, these photographs, maps, genealogy charts and, especially, stones and sprigs of heather as attempts to re-embody identities which are felt to have become disembodied and to give substance to the virtual worlds on which they are based.

At home with the virtual community

Online genealogical research is not only a matter of viewing web sites and extracting information from databases, it is also about exchanging information with other researchers, particularly via email. Some of the most important resources for online genealogists are therefore email discussion lists, a popular form of computer-mediated communication in which individual list subscribers send messages to a collectivity of co-subscribers via a group email address.

Even within the field of genealogical research there are many thousands of such lists: at the time of writing, *RootsWeb*, for instance, claims to host some 29,356 genealogy-related discussion lists (www.rootsweb.com). The majority of these are focused around specific surnames or regions, but others are devoted to more general genealogical themes. Discussion lists are usually indexed and categorised by their host organisations together with paragraphs describing their foci and character. Examples of Scottish genealogy lists hosted by *RootsWeb* include:

SCOTS-IN-CANADA. A mailing list for anyone with a genealogical, historical, or cultural interest in people of Scottish descent in Canada.

SCOTLAND-GENWEB. A mailing list for anyone with an historical or genealogical interest in Scotland and its people. Includes surname research queries.

GEN-TRIVIA-SCOTLAND. A mailing list for anyone with an interest in Scotland and the Scots through genealogy. This list does not focus on surnames and family trees, but addresses the culture and lifestyle of subscribers' Scottish ancestors and their descendants.

SCT-INVERNESS. A mailing list for anyone with a genealogical interest in the county of Inverness-shire, Scotland.

CLAN-MACKAY. A mailing list for anyone with a genealogical or historical interest in the Scottish Clan MacKay. Topics include searches for MacKay ancestors; discussions of Clan history; notices of Clan gatherings and meetings; rebuilding the Clan Castle, etc.

MACPHERSON. A mailing list for the discussion and sharing of information regarding the Macpherson surname and variations in any place and at any time.

Roots tourists typically subscribe to a number of such discussion lists, and, of course, these need not all be exclusively focused on their genealogical research – many will be concerned with Scottish history and culture more generally.

Bound by the mutual interests of subscribers, senses of community often emerge among the otherwise dispersed members of discussion lists, and this has led to the discussion list and other similar forms of computer-mediated group interaction becoming the focus of much academic research concerning the nature of online sociality. Considering the 'placeless' context of such interaction, much of this work has drawn heavily from Benedict Anderson's conceptualisation of the imagined community (1991). Indeed, if Anderson was concerned with the technologies of print capitalism in forming national consciousness in the nineteenth and twentieth centuries, it is tempting to suggest that the internet and, particularly, the email discussion list or newsgroup are the key technologies informing transnational and diasporic consciousness at the beginning of the twenty-first. Researching the use of Indian discussion lists by members of the Indian diaspora in North America and Western Europe, Ananda Mitra observes,

> The construct of the 'imagined' community becomes powerful in thinking of the communities being formed in the electronic forum. The electronic communities produced by the diasporic people are indeed imagined connections that are articulated over the medium of the Internet, where the only tangible connection with the community is through the computer, a tool to image and imagine the group affiliation. (1997: 58)

He adds, 'The "imagination" that binds the members of the electronic group is the common memory of the same putative place of origin from which most of the posters came' and suggests that, since the Indian homeland is now inaccessible to the dispersed migrants, 'the Internet space is coopted to find the same companionship that was available in that original place of residence' (ibid.: 70). The virtual space thus comes to act as a surrogate for the physical place, or, as Mitra puts it, 'the loss of geographic proximity is the *raison d'être* for the mobilization of the Internet space' (ibid.: 71).

Although Mitra does not consider those born within the diaspora, for whom the notion of an 'original home' is surely more complicated, a similar sense of 'commonality' is certainly evident in some Scottish discussion lists. This is sometimes articulated in terms of being 'at home' among the community of list members: at home, that is, among those who share the same lost home. Bill, a Californian subscriber to the Homecomings list, articulates these different notions of home in the following messages:

All of us on this list are interested in our Scottish heritage, whether we were born there or are several generations removed. Some are interested in music, some in literature, others in history, etc. Ultimately though, I believe it is the land itself that draws us. There seems to be 'something' inbred that recognizes that particular spot on the globe as home (Bill, homecomings@onelist.com, 08-Nov-99).

This list seems to serve a similar purpose as many clan societies. For those of who are just starting to discover their heritage it offers not just a starting point to 'Scottishness' (a highly individual thing anyway), but a community in which to find support and feel 'at home'. (Bill, homecomings@onelist.com, 27-May-99)

Home here is both a physical entity, a native or ancestral place, and a community of kinsfolk: a family. But there is, on some lists, sometimes a self-consciousness attached to this latter assertion that betrays its insubstantial foundation. This is demonstrated in the following typical discussion list exchange at scotland@onelist.com:

Hi Folks. I've been meaning to join for a while, and here I am at last. We live in Inverness, Scotland. I'm married with 4 kids and at the last count we have 6 grandkids. Been retired for 8 years and seem to spend my life at the computer!! I'm looking forward to seeing what goes on here on the Scotland List and putting in my 'Pennies Worth'. Aw ra Best, Eddie. (Eddie, Inverness, Scotland)

Eddie, Welcome. This list is like a family. Little squabbles at times but when the time comes to stand up for each other all voices are heard. I hope to learn much from you and other native Scots joining as I have from the current members. Yours aye, Gary. (Gary, Massachusetts, USA)

Welcome Eddie. I lurk most of the time. Do learn a lot. Enjoy yourself here. Libbi. PS Kids are back in school! It's hot here (100+). From San Antonio, Texas. (Libbi, Texas, USA)

Hi Gary. Thanks for your welcome message. It'll be like coming home, all families have their squabbles but there is nothing like being the member of a strong family, who back up and look after each other. Eddie. (Eddie, Inverness, Scotland) (scotland@onelist.com digest #319, 15-Aug-1999)

One could unpack much in this, like any, seemingly banal 'conversation': the native Scot's elevation as someone to learn from, the apparent need to identify 'where' the poster is speaking from (geographically, climatically, as a grandparent or mother of schoolchildren, etc.), the use of an innocuous strand to assert one's membership of a group that one does not normally contribute to, the use of Scots words such as 'aye' (always) to signal identity and demonstrate the possession of 'local knowledge', and so forth. However, the idea of a mutually supportive community is, in this case, a fantasy and, though there was plenty of squabbling on the list, there was little evidence for such 'standing together'. Indeed, after this welcoming exchange of bonhomie, Eddie never posted a message again. But the posters are not unaware of the fantastic nature of their interaction: the list is, after all, only *like* a family and, for Eddie, it will only be *like* coming home. Similarly, for Bill, the Homecomings list member quoted above, the discussion list serves only a *similar* purpose to clan societies, and for the bereaved Texan woman whose guestbook message is quoted earlier in the chapter, the internet is merely a *substitute* for the anticipated visit to Scotland, which she now believes to be impossible. My point is that each comment refers elsewhere, to a context outside the internet, to something somehow more real, substantial and unequivocal: 'homepage' invokes 'homeland'.

Negotiating Scottish identity online

The equivocality of email discussion list communities and identities is not surprising considering that list members' interactions occur primarily within text-based environments. Such environments lack the social context cues provided by bodies, vocal intonation, gestures and so forth routinely used in understanding 'face-to-face' interaction (Hine 2000: 15). This 'poverty of signals' is both a limitation and a resource, making certain kinds of interaction more difficult, but also enabling individuals to represent themselves online 'in ways quite different from their offline personae' (Kollock and Smith 1999: 9; Hine 2000: 15). Identity in an email discussion list is thus transformed into a 'discursive performance', and the persuasiveness of posters' performances largely determines the value placed upon their contributions in a given discussion.

Despite the poverty of textual identity cues relative to face-to-face interaction, on closer examination the average email discussion list message may be shown to contain a wealth of identifying information. In Goffman's terms, this includes both information 'given' (i.e. intentionally presented) and information 'given off' (that which 'leaks through' unintentionally) (Goffman 1959; H. Miller 1995). In addition to the main 'body' of a message, which may convey many identity cues in the poster's written 'voice' and vocabulary, much information is also provided in the 'header' automatically attached to the top of a message and in the 'signature' with which the poster 'signs off'. This may be illustrated with reference to a typical posting to the SCT-INVERNESS genealogy list:[3]

Header:	Subject:	Glenelg, Scotland
	Date:	20 Mar 2000 14:08:38 –0600
	From:	John McRae <jmcrae@sympatico.ca>
	To:	SCT-INVERNESS-L@rootsweb.com

Body: I am looking for information on Glenelg, Inverness, Scotland. My ggggrandparents were married January 25, 1827 in Glenelg. They were Farquhar McRae and Elizabeth McLennan. Farquhar was also born there by my information. Can anyone help me with some research, as I have hit a dead-end, because I cannot find any information on these two people.

Thank you

Signature: John
Saskatchewan, Canada
Visit my genealogy pages at
http://www.freepages.sympatico.ca/~jmcrae/

The most straightforward form of identification in any discussion list message is the poster's name and email address that appears in the 'From:' field of the header. In the above example, the poster is thus identified as 'John McRae <jmcrae@sympatico.ca>', which suggests (but *only* suggests) that the poster is male (forename), has Scottish ancestry on his paternal side (surname), and is posting from Canada (the '.ca' suffix of the poster's internet service provider). In this case these observations are confirmed in the body and signature of the message, but this is not always the case. Indeed, it is common for posters to use 'aliases' in their email addresses, a practice that often obscures certain aspects of their identities (e.g. name and gender) whilst accentuating others (e.g. desired ancestral affiliations). The following few examples are taken from postings to the Homecomings list:

Beth Kerman <cruachan@xxxxxx.ca>
Belinda <celticlady@xxxxxx.com>
Joyce <skyemcleod@xxxxxx.com.au>
Frank MacEowen <mac@xxxxxx.com>
Doreen Krava <nippythistle@xxxxxx.com>

These email aliases all connote 'Scottish' or 'Celtic' affiliations that are not necessarily apparent in the names of those who use them (to the degree that their names are given at all). 'Cruachan', for example, is the 'war-cry' of the Clan Campbell and the name of a prominent mountain in Lorne, the area associated with Beth Kerman's Campbell ancestry; while Joyce's paternal grandmother's family were McLeods from the Isle of Skye.

In the signature of the example SCT-INVERNESS message, the poster signs off using his forename and identifies where he is writing from. The name and place concur with the information automatically added in the header, demonstrating a 'transparency' in the poster's identity and inspiring confidence in the reader that the poster is who he claims to be. In this example, the poster additionally includes the URL of his personal homepage which, judging from his invitation to the recipient to visit, is devoted to his family history research. Readers who share ancestral connections with the Glenelg area might be especially interested in visiting the web site to find out whether they have any common ancestors. It is through such chance 'meetings' in the social spaces of discussion list communities that many 'dead-ends' are indeed overcome, and it is not unusual for distant relations ('internet cousins', as they are known) to become acquainted in this way – many go on to meet 'in the flesh' on mutual ancestor hunting trips to the old country. By including links to personal web sites in their signatures, posters invite other discussion list members to explore their more intimate 'identity spaces', which may include photographs of themselves, their families, ancestral places, and so forth.

Posters may also use their signatures to convey other identifying information. Some list ancestral family names or places that they are researching, whilst others demonstrate their possession of local knowledge through the use of Gaelic or Scots phrases. Example signatures from the Homecomings list include:

Becky
Beathag Nic Donnachaidh (Rebecca, Daughter of the Children of Duncan)
Garg'n Uair Dhuisgear (Fierce when Roused)

[Gaelic version of name; Clan Donnachaidh affiliation; use of clan motto]

Sarida
xxxxx@celtexas.com
Celtic roots run deep
Our branches spread afar
Our acorns are scattered
Among the stars

[personal aphorism expressive of diasporic melding of Celtic and Texan identity]

Patti Heimsness
Whose mind and body reside in Montana, but whose heart and soul are in Scotland – Searching for Matheson-Irvine-MacGillivray-MacLean-Ross connections.

[articulation of diasporic identity; list of ancestral names being researched]

From the header to the signature, identity cues are thus scattered throughout the email discussion list message. But the discussion list not only provides an opportunity for the discursive performance of identity, it also enables the contestation of such performances. In Scottish-interest discussion lists, an 'authentic' Scottish identity is often performed through the articulation of local or expert knowledges: for instance, in the display of a nuanced understanding of Scottish history rather than one which merely reflects the hackneyed myths, or in the 'correct' use of Scots or Gaelic language. Since Scottish-interest discussion lists are open to both homeland and diaspora Scots, these tend to be the lines across which most contests over authenticity are fought.

This can be illustrated in a message sent to the SCOTLAND-GENWEB list by a native Scottish subscriber in response to what he termed the 'inaccurate rubbish' that other subscribers had posted on the subject of the Highland Clearances. 'This posting is going to offend some of you', he states, before providing a long disquisition on the topic, authenticating his argument with details of his local knowledge of the lands in question and evidence of his critical reading of historical sources. Challenging the diasporic romanticisation of the pre-Clearance Highlands and the demonisation of the English, he writes 'You are free to subscribe to the "Braveheart" school of Scottish history', but rhetorically asks 'Have any of you seen a real black house? . . . Have any of you actually been to Strathnaver or Strath Halladale? I suggest that before you condemn people you actually see the ground in question'(scotland-genweb@rootsweb.com, 19-Oct-00).

Another topic over which such contests are commonly fought is the nature of clanship in Scotland. Exasperated at what she characterises as the 'tartan tomfoolery' that masquerades as Scottish culture on the internet, a Scottish subscriber to scotland@onelist.com writes:

> I can honestly say I have never read so much crap about clans since I came online, and all of it comes from across the pond. I recently disillusioned a poor soul that there was no such clan as the Clan Hamilton. He insisted there was, but I live 5 miles from Hamilton and I can bloody well assure you there is no such clan as Hamilton. It exists only in the minds of Americans. (scotland@onelist.com, digest #262, 22-Jul-99)

In such 'discussions' most diasporic subscribers simply defer to those living in Scotland or to those raised in Scotland who subsequently emigrated; the assumption being that native Scots will necessarily be expert in their own history and culture. Occasionally, however, this implicit rule regarding the right to arbitrate over authenticity is challenged and questions arise regarding the ownership of cultural property. Responding to the above message and other similar postings to scotland@onelist.com, a North American subscriber writes,

> It seems, lately, that some participants have begun expressing a view that Scotland is for native Scots only, and all the rest should keep their noses out. There have been some statements derogatory of Americans who are interested in things Scottish – not because they're Americans, but because they're interested in things Scottish. Americans have been accused of having essentially 'invented' the current view of clans and tartans and kilts and all that. . . .
>
> We [Scottish-Americans] want more than just a Scottish name – we want something we can point to and say, 'This is where my ancestors came from'. It's not cooking (I doubt that most Americans of Scottish descent could prepare peculiarly Scottish food if their lives depended on it). It's not appearance (we look just like any other 'average white folks'). It's not ethnic enclaves (as far as I know there's never been a Scottish neighborhood along the lines of LA's Koreatown or Boston's Irish districts). What we Scottish Americans look to is something less tangible. We look to our ancestry, and to the language(s) of those ancestors, and to the clothes they wore. . . .
>
> And from there I turn to Scotland, and my Scottish heritage, and this mailing list, hoping that here I'll be accepted as someone who isn't from Scotland, and doesn't know everything there is to know about Scotland, but who is genuinely interested in that part of my ancestry – and hoping that I'll be encouraged in that. And it seems that there are those who reject me, not because I'm an American of Scottish descent, but because I want to 'get into' that Scottish heritage. . . .
>
> Well, I'm here, and I plan to stay. And I continue to be proud of where I came from. I plan to continue my efforts to learn Scots, and perhaps someday when I have the time and undivided attention it deserves to learn Gaelic as well. I plan to someday, if I can ever afford it, own a kilt and wear it when appropriate. I do not plan to toss all my Scottishness in the drink, abandon my clan and forget my tartan and reject my ancestors' tongue(s), just because some think we Americans are paying too much attention to Scotland. (scotland@onelist.com, digest #275, 25-Jul-99)

Back came the response from the homeland, this time apologetic and accepting of the diaspora's right to be 'interested' in Scottish culture. But, even here, the matter of ownership of cultural property is spelt out with some condescension.

> I may point out that a lot of the culture you are being fed is too romantic and express that it does not reflect the Scotland I live in, but

that is an opinion of circumstance and does not reflect any sort of opinion I may have about you or your desire to learn about *our* culture. Frankly I am tickled by your interest. (scotland@onelist.com, digest #278, 25-Jul-99; emphasis added)

Within the discursive spaces of the email discussion list, identities are thus being contested in novel and unique ways. The discussion list is evidently not merely an arena for the playing out of desires and fantasies, where individuals may perform whatever identities they choose, or lay claim to national histories and cultures without meeting checks and resistances. As with other kinds of communities, such resistances are grounded in group politics and dynamics. What is particularly significant in this context, however, is the way in which this politics straddles the online/offline boundary, and the online authority of the respective posters is itself grounded in their physical proximity to the homeland (whether through birth, dwelling, 'non-touristic' travel or thorough research). Identity in the discussion list is therefore not so much performed as negotiated in the ongoing conversation of the virtual community. Indeed, it is this dialogic and democratic quality of online discourse that sets the internet apart from the more regulated spaces of established national media (print, television, etc.) and justifies our considering it as a key facilitator in the imagining of new, specifically *trans*national, communities.

The discussion list does not, of course, replace other more or less mediated identity spaces, but the experience of this particularly equivocal environment – one in which the constructedness of identity is manifestly apparent – may have an influence on individuals' confidence in these other supposedly more concrete contexts. The 'place ballets' of individuals' negotiations of identity are thus rarely elegantly choreographed movements and more often involve faltering steps between online pillars and offline posts in the search for home. Marion, another Californian member of the Homecomings list, describes the quandary as follows:

The homeland where everyone 'belongs' is now the Internet space where people have common goals and interests, and frequently help each other in their search for information. It coexists with our current space of residence, to which we also belong. It also coexists with our 'imagined' or (in the case of native Scots) 'remembered' spaces of residence, the 'national homeland'.

Those of us who join discussion lists and research groups should, and probably do realize that the 'underpinnings' of this 'virtual community' are fragile and potentially fleeting. The middle-aged spinster one corresponds with could actually be a 20 year old male truck driver. With this understanding safely tucked away for future reference, we enjoy the benefits of the community, taking everyone at 'face value' until something indicates otherwise.

So what is it that creates this strong sense of 'Homeland' in a place I have only visited twice? The sense of belonging to Scotland is stronger than the sense of belonging to the 'virtual community', though not as vivid as the ties to my physical community here in San Diego. I migrated to California in 1975 after living 30 years on the opposite coast of the US in New Jersey. Do I have any sense of 'homeland' in thinking about New Jersey? Not one shred. (Marion, homecomings@onelist.com, 24-Jun-99)

Whilst Janet, from Victoria, Australia, recognises that even the 'underpinnings' of this *Scott-ish* homeland are unsound:

I wonder if the 'idea' of Scotland, especially the Highlands, is itself a sort of Virtual Reality, and has been for much longer than the Internet has been around. It seems to have been so for the Victorian English, from whom the current stereotype of Scotland seems to have been derived. (Janet, homecomings@onelist.com, 26-Jun-99)

It appears, though, that the 'actual' reality of the homeland is able to transcend the ideas from which it seems to be constructed, and, in a later post, after having visited her McLeod homeland in the Western Isles, Janet explains to the list,

I am still reflecting on what it meant. I know one thing has happened very definitely, and that is now I have had a 'hit' of the real thing, I have much less need of the Virtual Reality. (Janet, homecomings@onelist.com, 06-Sept-99)

Virtual homelands

Michael Benedikt refers to cyberspace as both the 'etherealization' of the world we live in, 'the real world of people and things and places', and the 'concretization' of the world we dream and think in, 'the world of abstractions, memory and knowledge' (cited in Fernback 1999: 218). Nowhere is this play of homeland and homepage, substance and insubstance, 'real thing' and 'virtual reality', more evident than in the personal web sites created by genealogists and roots tourists.

As the titles of genealogy guidebooks such as *Web Publishing for Genealogy* (Christian 1999) and *Publishing Your Family History on the Internet* (Wilson 1999) attest, the internet has become a popular medium for individuals to disseminate their family histories. Evinced in this autobiographical practice is the desire to weave together disparate strands of research and present the 'prehistory' of the self as a coherent narrative. The intangibilities of genetic inheritance are thus made concrete in texts detailing the names and dates of ancestors and in old family photographs (often presented in the virtual space as if pasted into scrapbooks or hanging upon walls); whilst the more tangible places with which ancestors were associated are photographed, digitised and uploaded, so becoming part of the ethereal world of the electronic mediascape (Figure 5.2).

Personal genealogy web sites vary a great deal in style and content: some include merely skeletal lists of names, dates and places, others feature detailed narrative histories with old family album photographs, images of ancestral places and transcriptions of wills and other certificates. Often, at these more detailed sites, along with the family history narrative is the narrative of the researcher's own genealogical quest. Such quest narratives include accounts of journeys to the ancestral homeland. These are mostly written up after the event from notes and journals kept during the homecoming, although I did meet one Californian roots tourist who was exploiting the medium more fully by uploading daily journal entries and digital photographs to a Scottish-heritage web site he managed so that clansfolk in the USA could follow his journey as it unfolded.

Considering the open-ended nature of the genealogical research process, in which the narrative of the family is perpetually evolving (both backwards in time with every new discovery and forwards with new births, marriages, deaths and reunions), it is particularly well suited to being told via the medium of the internet. Many researchers thus proclaim that their sites are 'works in progress', with labels and links announcing the addition of new features and details of the latest 'updates'. An interesting example of such a site 'under construction' is that of Sharon, the informant from New South Wales whose office I discussed in an earlier section of this chapter. The homepage of Sharon's site is entitled 'Birse, Aberdeenshire' after the name of the parish to which she has traced her eighteenth-century Glass, Gordon, Coutts and McKondach ancestors (www.geocities.com/sharemslie/index.html). The page includes several components: an introductory statement of objectives; a photograph showing a general view

Figure 5.2 The faces of ancestors gaze out from genealogists' homepages

looking towards Auchabrack and the Forest of Birse (the area with which Sharon feels most strongly connected and in which most of her Birse ancestors lived); a short descriptive excerpt from Sharon's journal of her 1999 visit to the Forest of Birse; a site contents list (with links to other pages in the site); a page-view counter and a note of the date the site was created.

By including complete transcriptions of old parochial registers and statutory records (births, baptisms, marriages, deaths, censuses, etc.) that are not directly related to her own ancestors on her site, Sharon provides much information that will be of interest to other researchers with Birse connections. Indeed, in the introductory statement on her homepage, Sharon explains that the web site is not only concerned with her own family history, but also with the wider historical community of which her ancestors were a part:

> Branches from the various families of Birse have spread themselves far and wide to other places, other lives and other times. I would hope that the information on this site can help those researching the area to develop a greater knowledge (and understanding) of the place our folk left behind.

Sharon intends to elaborate her own particular genealogy within an as yet unfinished 'My Ain Folk' section of the site, but, as she explained to me in an email, one of the reasons she has not completed this section is that she is not sure *how* to write it: 'I know I don't want to put up just a family tree – names and dates – I want to make it more personal, but how? Do I speculate online like I do in my head?' It appears that the story Sharon feels more inclined to tell is not about her ancestors *per se*, so much as her own sense of connection to those ancestors and, particularly, her sense of connection to the Forest of Birse where they had lived. Thus, while the 'My Ain Folk' section remains unfinished, an 'Impressions of Birse' link features prominently at the top of the contents list. By clicking on this link, the visitor is taken to a page in which Sharon describes her homecoming to Birse in 1999. She introduces her account as follows:

> In 1999, I made my first trip to Birse to see the land of my ancestors. I had scoured the Parish Registers for information pertaining to my various families of Glass, Coutts, McCondach and Emslie. I had searched each of the census[es] to see who was living where and with whom. I knew the names of the crofts and in most cases I knew who lived in them – but nothing prepared me for what I saw on that first trip . . .

Sharon continues with a moving account of some of her experiences, notably her discovery of 'Auchabrack', the croft house in which her Glass ancestors once resided:

Auchabrack was deserted, the windows were boarded up and parts were in ruins. The ruins looked as though they may have originally been two more houses attached to the main building, after all three families are recorded as living here in the 1891 census. A step through that door was a step into another world, a world filled with ghosts of past generations, each whispering not quite loud enough to hear, whispering stories of their lives in a time gone past. The kitchen was small; a table stood in the middle of the room still surrounded by chairs. There was a sink to one side and a fireplace at the back where the sway still stood firm awaiting the return of the black kettle and the crackle of the open fire. Another room at the opposite side of the hall, and between a staircase ascending to the upstairs bedrooms, a staircase now weak with time and certainly not safe to walk on.

As I walked around, I touched the walls and the doors . . . I walked through doorways, the same doorways they walked through and I looked out on the same hills that they would have seen – I was living their past in my present.

The account concludes with an excerpt from a self-penned poem:

And home embraced this restless soul
And now held close there, whispered in softest voice
Of lives in crofts and hills and glens

Sharon explained to me that, in fact, the genealogical content of the site was really just 'the bait', and her main objective was to 'catch fish' – that is, to find others who might share her deeply felt sense of connection with Birse. Sharon further explained,

The present folk of Birse, well the ones I have made contact with, don't understand this need to be a part of the area. I seem to have a gap in my life, I was born in Australia yet I do not feel Australian. I can find no connection to this country/this land [i.e. Australia] – yet Australians accept me as one of them. I feel a very strong connection to Scotland, and Birse in particular, yet I am not seen as a 'Birseite'. They see me as an Australian: I live here [in Australia], I talk like one – yet inside I feel like I belong there.

So the genealogical data is the worm. People always want information for free. . . . The majority of people will only want names and places and when you provide this sometimes you don't even get a thank you in return – part of the deal I suspect. But hopefully along the way there will be someone to share this feeling with – hence the 'Impressions' part of it.

Rather than simply providing a medium for the 'publication' of family histories or a venue for the exchange of genealogical information, it appears therefore that the personal genealogy web site has, in some cases, a more profound function. The photograph with which Sharon chooses to represent Birse on her homepage is of an empty landscape with a lonely road, louring clouds and heather-covered hills rising in the distance (Figure 5.3). We are left in no doubt that this, Sharon's homeland, is the land 'our folks left behind', abandoned by all but the 'ghosts of past generations', where even the wind 'whispers of days gone by'. And yet here in the ethereal realm of the internet, in transcriptions of valuation rolls, censuses and parish registers, surely those ghosts are enumerated and given back their names and dates and residences. Thus Sharon repopulates the Forest of Birse with its past generations, reconstructing the intricate relationships of its communities (the Cattanachs and the Gillespies, the Couttses and the Glasses), and, in a way, inscribes herself into their company. The Forest of Birse – etherealised, concretised – becomes Sharon's own place, the place she calls home. Throughout its 'homepages', hyperlinked to her email address, are repeated the words 'contact me': poignant invitations to the countless lost children of those families who 'have spread themselves far and wide to other places, other lives and other times' to join her there.

The ghosts of Birse's past generations are also gathered in a section of Sharon's web site entitled 'Birse Kirkyard' (Figure 5.4, left). Under a photograph of the parish church, Sharon provides images and transcriptions of the graves of Forest of Birse families. Such 'virtual cemeteries' are quite common

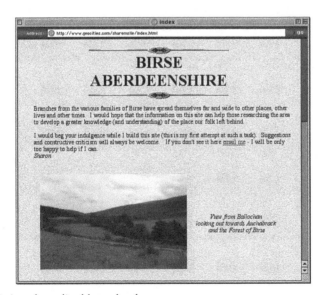

Figure 5.3 An etherealised homeland

Figure 5.4 Virtual cemeteries. From left to right: 'Birse Kirkyard' on Sharon's web
site, Genealogy.com's 'Virtual Cemetery Project'

features of personal genealogy sites. The genealogy internet service provider,
Genealogy.com, has, for instance, devised a 'Virtual Cemetery Project',
described both as 'an invaluable source of genealogical information' and 'an
electronic memorial to our ancestors' (www.genealogy.com/vcem_welcome.
html). Visitors to the 'Virtual Cemetery' are encouraged to participate in the
project by uploading images and transcriptions of their own ancestors'
graves to its expanding and searchable database. If the monument or memorial may be understood as the concretisation of the memory of the dead,
then, at such virtual cemeteries, these material manifestations are again etherealised. Passing back and forth between substantial and insubstantial
realms, memory becomes revivified and, indeed, in remembrance, the ancestors are in some sense brought back to life.

An t-Eilean Sgitheanach – The Isle of Wings

One final example of this fascinating interplay of substance and insubstance on- and offline may be found in a personal web site entitled
'Soraidh air Deireachd – A Last Farewell' (www.geocities.com/Paris/2350/
index.html). This site is constructed as a virtual memorial to its author's
late wife, also named Sharon/Sìaron:

> She has no grave, but she lives on in the memory of myself, our chil-
> dren and our friends. I swore on a knife to honour her memory *fad' ré
> mo là* – all my days; our custom. With this small memorial I am
> honouring my promise.

In commemorating the life of his wife, the author – evidently a Gaelic-
speaking Canadian, with ancestral roots in the Hebrides – also
commemorates their common Scottish heritage. Thus, as well as photographs

of his wife, a few biographical details and a poem which recalls their love, the site also contains images of Jacobite clan chiefs, accounts of 'Bonnie Prince Charlie' and the 'Year of the War against England, 1745–1746', and a link to the web site of Sabhal Mòr Ostaig, the Gaelic-medium college on Skye.

Prominent on the site's homepage is a page-view counter positioned adjacent to the sentence fragment: '. . . people have travelled this road so far'. When I viewed the site in March 2000, the counter had recorded 24,357 'hits' and thus the complete sentence read: '24,357 people have travelled this road so far'. An explanation is provided thus:

> It is our custom in the Highlands to build a small rock pile called a cairn to memorialize someone special, always beside a path, so that passing strangers can add a rock, and indeed all Highlanders add a rock to any cairn they pass, so the memorial becomes permanent. Because I am far from home and the custom of building a cairn and passers-by adding to it is unknown here, I saw no point in building one. Instead, my wife's webpage is her cairn and the numbers added to the counter are the rocks placed by the people who pass by. When I go home to Scotland I will build a cairn for her. If I cannot, my children will.

It appears that husband and wife shared a distant ancestor, a Jacobite survivor of the Battle of Culloden. Perhaps not unexpectedly, the account provided of the '45 Rebellion and Culloden perpetuates the familiar myth that this was a war between England and Scotland, and that to be a Gael is to have survived a genocide and to live in exile.

> One of the men who fought for Bonnie Prince Charlie at Culloden and escaped was our great x8 grandfather. Had he not managed to survive, neither of us would ever have been born. Our very lives were due to a musket ball that missed, a sword cut that didn't go too deep, a ditch that hid our fleeing ancestor while the death squads of King George cantered by, looking for fugitives to kill. A blessing on our ancestor; a curse on the English murderers.

Such pronouncements are interspersed with recollections of days passed at the couple's lakeside hideaway in British Columbia and with moving accounts of their life together. Hyperlinks in these texts lead to verses of favourite Gaelic songs and photographs of favourite places. The final section, however, is perhaps the most intriguing in the present context. This is devoted to *An t-Eilean Sgitheanach*, the Island of Skye (though it is not referred to by its Anglicised name within the section itself). For the author, the island is equated with the 'Gaelic Paradise', *Tìr nan Òg*:

> *An t-Eilean Sgitheanach* means The Isle of Wings, because the clouds stream from the peaks of the Cuillins. Set amid the jewelled Hebridean

isles, homeland of our ancestors, Sìaron and I planned to live here when we retired.

In our culture, we do not go to Heaven or Hell; we go to *Tìr nan Òg*, Land of Youth, the blessed Isles of the West. The Hebrides lie to the west, so for us they were *Tìr nan Òg*.

Clicking on '*An t-Eilean Sgitheanach*' in the text leads one to a postcard-like image of Skye, complete with sea loch, mist and towering Cuillin hills (Figure 5.5).

The couple had evidently imagined what life would be like in such an idyll: they would find a cottage, 'in a sheltered bay, with a good view, a sweet well close by', where they would sit outside enjoying a dram, until, 'as the half-dark took over the bay', they 'would retreat to the peat flames to dream and muse before smooring the fire and climbing into bed'.

Sìaron was strangely comforted by the idea and we spent many of our last days together planning our cottage and its furnishings for our stay in Eternity. She swore we would never speak English again; only the lovely *cànain a'Phàrrais; teanga ar sinnsear* – language of Paradise; tongue of our forefathers – *Gàidhlig*.

After quoting a verse from Psalm 23 in both Gaelic and English, the page closes with a Gaelic proverb:

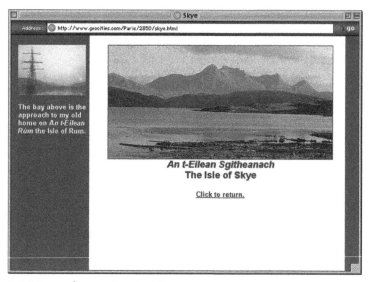

Figure 5.5 Tìr nan Òg – a virtual reality?

The three most beautiful phrases in the world:
  Mo bhean fhein – my own wife
  mo chuidse fhein – my own goods, and . . .
  rachamaid dachaidh – let's go home.

My objective in citing this final example is not to labour a point that is self-evident, that its representation of the Scottish Highlands and Islands, severed of all modernity, is a fantasy, but rather to highlight the way in which the fantasy is projected onto a 'real' landscape. The web author's dreams are given substance in Skye (there is the photograph to prove it), but Skye itself becomes the ethereal, timeless dream of *Tir nan Òg*. The play of substance/insubstance, homeland/homepage, is also manifest eloquently in the metaphor of the cairn/counter, such that, in visiting the site whilst researching this chapter, I have added a stone or two to that already considerable monument, and, somehow, in the most ephemeral of media, have contributed to its permanence.

6 Clanlands

Stepping through the door of the old parish church of Latheron, Caithness, gifted to the Clan Gunn Society in 1974, its museum since 1985, one is confronted by a somewhat moth-eaten, but still impressive stag's head hunting trophy. Below it, placed in front of a length of Gunn tartan, a board on which is printed two quotes. The first is taken from William Morris's introduction to his 1888 translation of the Norse *Volsunga Saga*:

> It would seem fitting for a Northern folk, deriving the greater and better part of their speech, laws and customs from a Northern root, that the North should be to them, if not a holy land, yet at least a place more to be regarded than any part of the world beside, that howsoever their knowledge widened of other men, the faith and deeds of their forefathers would never lack interest for them, but would always be kept in remembrance.

The second is a Gaelic proverb credited to one Alexander Makay, although I have seen it elsewhere cited as being of unknown provenance: '*Leanaibh gu dlu ri cliu na'r Sinnsir*' (Closely follow your ancestors' fame).[1] Not only does the juxtaposition of these texts reflect the 'Nordo-Celtic' heritage of the Gunns and many other Highland clans, it also articulates powerfully the twin ideologies of Highland clanship as it is popularly understood today: that the fame of the forefathers and the fame of the land are as one.

The Gaelic word *clann* literally translates as 'children', 'offspring' or 'descendants' (MacLennan 1979: 86), but clanship does not only evoke a sense of belonging to an extended family with a common ancestor (a people 'of one blood'), it also implies a marriage between that common blood and the territory it has historically occupied. The 'golden age' of Highland clanship is generally bracketed between *c.*1500 and 1746 (ending abruptly, so the myth goes, on the battlefield of Culloden). In fact the system was already well in decline by the end of the seventeenth century, and we should therefore treat with caution Samuel Johnson's account of the 1770s, in which he portrays the clan as an archaic, tribal survival:

> The inhabitants of mountains form distinct races, and are careful to preserve their genealogies. Men in a small district necessarily mingle blood by intermarriages, and combine at last into one family, with a common interest in the honour and disgrace of every individual. Then begins that union of affections, and co-operation of endeavours, that constitute a clan. They who consider themselves as ennobled by their family, will think highly of their progenitors, and they who through successive generations live always together in the same place, will preserve local stories and hereditary prejudices. Thus every Highlander can talk of his ancestors, and recount the outrages which they suffered from the wicked inhabitants of the next valley. (Chapman 1970: 42)

Such a view of territorial stability and close blood-ties has been challenged by more recent commentators and characterised as part of the romanticisation of the Highlands discussed in Chapter 4. Michael Lynch, for example, argues that,

> The nineteenth- and twentieth-century cult of the Highlands – of clan tartans, clan maps and clan societies – have all tended to obscure what a clan was. Few clans had a compact block of territory, either in the medieval period or later; 'clan maps' at best indicate where surnames occurred, but not a clan territory. ... In most cases, kinship and a common surname obtained only to the inner circle of the chief's family or to cadet branches of it. The notion that all members of a clan were descended from a common and distant ancestor is a nonsense. ... Clan society was fluid and eclectic. (1992: 69)

Drawing on more ethnographically informed analyses of kinship systems, Robert Dodgshon stresses that the Highland clans should be understood not as literal descent groups, sustained 'by inertia or conservatism', but rather as 'changing, responsive institutions' able to adapt to unfolding socio-political and economic conditions (1989: 170–1). He notes that such hybrid systems of alliance must, however, lean more heavily on an *ideology* of kinship and 'on self-conscious displays of unity and self-justification' (1989: 170) – an observation as relevant for the understanding of modern, international clan societies as for the 'traditional' social structures Dodgshon is concerned with.[2]

In popular Highlandist discourse, academic quibbles over the historical constitution of clan society and the inventedness of its traditions are, however, largely irrelevant, since it is the 'romantic ideology' of clanship that continues to be promulgated and consumed with enthusiasm. This is

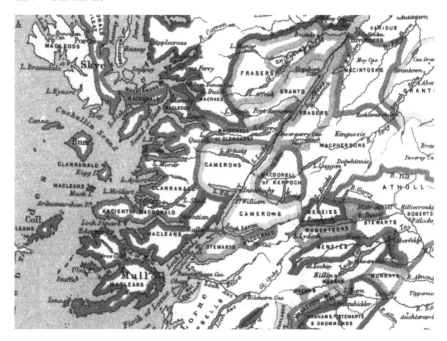

Figure 6.1 Detail of a 'clan map', identities inscribed onto the landscape
  (Edinburgh Geographical Institute)

particularly true in the Scottish diaspora, and especially among members of the North American Scottish heritage community, for whom affiliation to a clan society is frequently central to the practice of 'being Scottish', and clan duties are performed with a seriousness that baffles homeland Scots. In North America, this devotion to clan is often founded on a number of erroneous assumptions: the assumption, for instance, that a shared surname is a reliable indicator of shared kinship (that every MacDonald, for example, is biologically related and descended from Donald of Islay, grandson of Somerled, progenitor of the clan). Indeed, the ostensible purpose of genealogical research for many such clansfolk is to find the 'missing link' that connects their own family histories to these chiefly lineages that emerge dimly from Scottish mytho-history. As Ray observes, 'most Scottish Americans join clan societies that share their surname or are part of their family history; and, as clan has come to mean "family", clan history becomes their family heritage' (Ray 2001: 77; see my discussion of Don's homecoming in Chapter 8).

Although Dodgshon has demonstrated that powerful descent groups effectively 'grew down' into a territory through 'infiltrating the land-holding hierarchy' (1989: 174), the ideology of clanship portrays the clan emerging autochthonically from the land. This is reflected in the celebrated notion of *dùthchas*, a Gaelic term that has no exact English equivalent and which can be used to refer to a person's native land, hereditary rights of tenure to land, and to more general senses of cultural heritage. Noting the marriage of clan and land evinced in 'territorial sobriquets' such as *Dùthaich Mhic Aoidh* (Mackay country) and *Srath Mhic Fhionghuin* (Strath of MacKinnon), Michael Newton argues that *dùthchas* 'ties together a sense of inheritance and territory':

> One's *dùthchas* is one's set of hereditary qualities, one's culture, one's homeland. The adjective *dùthchasach* describes that which is indigenous, native and inherited, and the same word can refer to a native of some particular place. This demonstrates that place is integrated into a sense of identity and ancestry in Gaelic tradition. (2000: 209)

The resonance of this concept has been exploited in various heritage initiatives in the Highlands and Islands. Sharon Macdonald has, for instance, examined its use at the *Aros* visitor centre on Skye, which is also known as *Dualchas an Eilein*, meaning 'the heritage of the Island' – where heritage may be understood as an uncommodifiable, 'inalienable possession' of the islanders, something that may be 'kept' while yet being given away (Weiner 1992; Macdonald 1997a: 173).

The traditional integration of place, ancestry and inalienability represented by *dùthchas* is also evident in the war-cries or slogans of many clans. Such slogans, part of each clan's 'sacra', are thought to predate heraldic conventions and originate quite literally as rallying calls used in battle. Many refer to clan strongholds, gathering places, or prominent hills, mountains or lochs in the clan territory: places that symbolise the wider clan homeland and for which the clansmen were presumably prepared to die (examples are provided in Table 6.1). These slogans are now often called during clan ceremonials and parades, and are sometimes employed as the titles of clan newsletters or annuals: thus the Clan Macpherson annual is entitled *Creag Dhubh* and that of the Clan MacRae, *Sguir Uaran*.

As the Scottish heritage revival has gained momentum over the past thirty years, so too has the cult of the clan, and there are now many hundreds of clan associations throughout the world, each recognising a particular Highland lineage, and each identifying a specific region within the Highlands and Islands as its ancestral homeland. In addition to more localised gatherings within diasporic countries, many clan societies organise regular tours to Scotland to visit their postulated clan territories and participate in international gatherings. Such gatherings generally follow a standard programme including marches through the clan territory; parades at local Highland Games; excursions to places of interest associated with the clan; formal dinners and *céilidhs*; lectures on clan history and genealogy; church services; and quite often visits to Culloden battlefield. As Ray notes, the Scotland they come to visit is mapped 'not by current economic or popula-

Table 6.1 Examples of the use of placenames in clan war-cries or slogans

Clan	Slogan	Notes
Buchanan	Clar Innis	Clarinch, an island in Loch Lomond
Campbell	Cruachan	A prominent mountain by Loch Awe
Fraser	A 'Mhor-fhaiche	'The great field'
Grant	Stand Fast, Craigellachie	Craigellachie is a rocky eminence in Strathspey
MacBain	Kinchyle	Clan territory on the south side of Loch Ness
MacDonald	Fraoch Eilean	'The heathery isle'
MacDonell	Creag an Fhithich	'The raven's rock', badge depicts a raven on a rock
MacFarlane	Loch Sloidh	Loch Sloy, Dunbarton
MacGillivray	Dunmaghlas	Dunmaglass, the clan territory in Strathnairn
MacGregor	Ard-choille	'The high wood'
MacIntyre	Cruachan	As Campbell, indicating allegiance to feudal superiors
Mackintosh	Loch Moigh	Loch Moy, Strathdearn
MacLaren	Creag an Tuirc	'The boar's rock'
MacLennan	Druim nan deur	'The ridge of tears'
Macpherson	Creag Dhubh	'The black rock', a prominent hill in Badenoch
MacRae	Sguir Uaran	A prominent mountain in Kintail
Morrison	Dùn Eistean	'Hugh's Castle', a stronghold near the Butt of Lewis
Munro	Caisteal Folais'n a Theine	'Castle Foulis in flames', the seat of the clan chief
Stewart	Creag an Sgairbh	'The cormorant's rock'

tion centers, but by places of historical relevance to the[ir] heritage' (2001: 128). This 'clanscaping' of the Highlands may be understood as 'a further evolution of the way Scottish landscapes . . . have been invested with varying meanings by and for various "others": elite others, tourist others, even returned others' (ibid.: 138). Thus, as places come to be remade as objects for the tourist gaze (in this instance, the gaze of the 'returning' clansfolk), the boundaries between mediascape and landscape are further blurred and, in tours, museums and monuments, the process of imagineering the ancestral homeland may be said to continue in the homeland itself.

In this chapter, I should like to examine this clanscaping of the Highland heritage landscape in more detail. My interest here is to highlight the relationship between landscape, narrative and identity, and to explore how, in the process of 'learning' the clan's 'place-stories' (through the body as much as the mind), a sense of personal identification with both clan and territory is effected in the individual.

'Be of this land'

Historically, the 'focus' of the clan was the residence of the clan chief, a castle or mansion at the 'heart' of the clan territory. More recently, however, there has been a tendency to establish more widely accessible museums or heritage centres at nearby locations to fulfil this role. The first of these dedicated clan museums was established in 1952 in Newtonmore by the Clan Macpherson Association. Other examples include the afore-mentioned Clan Gunn Museum in Latheron, Caithness; the Clan Cameron Museum at Achnacarry, Inverness-shire; the Clan Donnachaidh Centre in Bruar, Perthshire; and the Clan MacKay rooms at the Strathnaver Museum in Bettyhill, Sutherland. Though open for general tourist trade in the summer months, because of their narrow field of interest, such centres have limited attraction for many more casual visitors. There are, however, two notable exceptions, which, with either significant private sponsorship or public funding, have attempted to attract a wider audience whilst still retaining a clan identity or theme: these are the Clan Donald Centre at Armadale, Skye and 'Clanland' at Foulis Ferry, Easter Ross.[3] In this section I am concerned with the Clanland visitor centre, and particularly with the way in which its clan-themed exhibitions define the relationship between a clan and its territory and how its displays encourage diasporic visitors to identify with such territories.

It should be noted that these displays form only one part of the 'Clanland' experience: there is, for instance, also an impressive *son et lumière* tableau telling the story of the rent house in which the centre is based, and a seal interpretation and viewing gallery. These other exhibitions sit somewhat uneasily with the clan-themed sections and were evidently included to attract visitors with more general interests. Indeed, even within the clan displays there is a tension between telling the specific story of the Clan Munro, in whose 'clanlands' the centre is located, and telling a story that articulates the connotations of clanship generally. Thus, the name 'Clanland' was chosen rather than the 'Clan Munro Centre', for example, because this was felt to be more widely appealing to visitors. It is ironic, therefore, that the enterprise began in the early 1990s with an appeal to members of the Clan Munro Association for £80,000 to convert an old farmstead behind Foulis Castle, the residence of the clan chief, into a modest clan museum; and that, as the project escalated in ambition and cost over subsequent years, this was the very element that was sacrificed. Driven by a more commercial agenda, the resulting £1.5 million Heritage Lottery Fund-supported centre must now compete with other major tourist attractions in the area with its more broadly appealing displays, its restaurant and gift shop; the casual visitor is, one assumes, provided with a more satisfying experience, but arguably the clan still does not have its museum.

At the time I interviewed Clanland's then-manager, Julian Dow, there *was* an ambition to establish a Clan Munro archive and library for clan members and family historians, but this was now contingent on the financial sustainability of the visitor centre itself or else the discovery of a clan benefactor willing to sponsor it.

> That's a long-term thing, and a long-term undertaking, because the centre has only been open a year, and obviously we have to be economically viable and stable and on a good footing before we can afford to put money into that side of things. But I am hopeful that that will happen. And there's also the possibility of getting sponsorship for something like that, particularly in the States. You know, we might get lucky as the Clan Donald Centre did – find an Elice McDonald called Munro or something! (Julian Dow, pers. comm.)

That diasporic Scots are prepared to invest financially as well as emotionally in their ancestral homeland is made clear in Dow's allusion to the North American benefactor of the 'Clan Donald Lands Trust', which owns Armadale Castle and the Clan Donald Centre.

Upon entering the clan-themed areas of Clanland, the visitor triggers the playback of a sound recording that seems to emanate from a dimly lit mural of a traditional storyteller or *seanachaidh*. As the *seanachaidh* begins to speak, so the visitor joins a painted audience of eighteenth-century clansfolk gathered to hear his tales:

> I am the *seanachaidh*. I bear the Clan through the ages. With me lie the stories. I recount our chief's family line; I am the holder of our history. Others who came before me told and retold the stories of our Clan to keep them alive through time. I pass them on to you and to those who follow.
>
> From the River Roe in County Derry came a man called Donald O'Ceann, son of the Prince of Armagh. He came with his sister who married Angus Og mac Donald of Islay, and with her came a dowry of seven-score men, of whom several became chiefs of Highland clans, including ours: the Munros. Our chief, Donald Munro, called his place Foulis, after Lough Foyle in Derry, and the lands of Donald became Ferindonald, home to the Clan Munro.
>
> But these stories were not written, we pass them from generation to generation. Oh yes, there are charters, pieces of parchment, which say that the King gives us these lands for a pair of white gloves, three pennies or a bowl of snow in mid-summer, which Ben Wyvis could always provide. These stories were spoken, passed on in our Gaelic tongue, and I give you them as I heard them. (Recorded from display.)

Accompanied by a soundtrack that dramatises the scenes he relates, the *seanachaidh* then goes on to tell some of the stories of the Munros: tales of cattle rustling, of skirmishes, the heroics of chiefs, murderous schemes, and a famous battle with the Mackenzies at Bealligh-na-Broig, the Pass of the Shoes, which became the inspiration for a *pìobaireachd*. 'Ah, but there were good times too', the *seanachaidh* concludes, 'when we sing and play and tell stories at our *cèilidhs*. But do not forget, these stories, these histories: they *are* our Clan. They are the Munros' (ibid.).

The story of the origin of the clan and the naming of Foulis are, not unexpectedly, apocryphal. One recent writer on clan lore comments that the account of Donald O'Ceann's sister, Aine Ní Cathan, arriving with 140 retainers, the progenitor of the Munro line among them, is 'sustained by no evidence whatsoever' (Roberts 1999: 6), and other sources suggest that 'Foulis' is not derived from 'Foyle', but from the topographical *Foghlais*, meaning 'sub-stream rivulet' (W. J. Watson 1916: 458). Such nit-picking is, however, to miss the point. What the *seanachaidh*'s tales convey is a sense of the clan's association with their place from time immemorial, a sense of being the original settlers of that place – the ones to name it – and a sense of how the identity of the clan is bound with their territory through their narratives. This genre of historical narration, a telling of 'history' through place, will be familiar to anthropologists working in diverse fields – Elizabeth Tonkin's (1992) description of 'geochronology' in Jlao story-telling is just one example. That an awareness of this mnemonic consciousness is communicated through the trickery of infrared sensors, digital sound files and graphic display panels, attests to both the art of effective exhibition design and to the power of narrative to transcend genre and context. In the Scottish Highlands, the heritage centre has become the public storytelling place *par excellence*.

The motifs of territory and kinship are repeated throughout the clan displays. Indeed, the centrepiece of this exhibition is a revolving 'sculpture' entitled 'The Clan', in which the symbolic figures of a clan chief, a harpist, and a crofter are portrayed as emerging from the land itself (Figure 6.2). An accompanying text provides the following interpretation for the visitor:

> The central sculpture represents the essence of a clan. The clan chief watching over his kinsfolk, the *clarsach* player to illustrate the culture of the clan, and the woman working the ground with a *caschcrom* denotes the strong practical and emotional ties to the land from which the figures symbolically emerge. The chief's extended plaid with incised world map represents continuing membership of the clan for those who dispersed from the clan homeland.

The display could be more accurately described as representing the romantic ideology of autochthonic clanship. It is not surprising, therefore, that the interpretation offered provides no commentary on the economic basis of feudal relations within the clan or the gendered division of labour so apparent in the sculpture. What is apparent in this benevolent and

Figure 6.2 'The Clan' sculpture (Paul Basu)

paternalistic depiction of clanship is a desire to reconnect with clan members in the diaspora: the warmth of the chief's/clan's protective plaid encircling the world, offering the security of home from the heart of the homeland. Of course, we might question this cosy sense of belonging and instead wonder why the clan should be dispersed in the first place.

A series of text panels around the walls appear to answer such questions but actually reveals more complex contradictions. One introductory panel announces, 'You are in the heart of Ferindonald, the area of land with which the Clan Munro is absolutely bound'. Other panels juxtapose the general story of clanship and the specifics of the Clan Munro. Thus, a panel entitled 'What is a Clan?' is placed adjacent to another which gives a brief history of the Munros; 'Fighting Clansmen' is placed next to 'Fighting Munros'; 'The Clans Dispersed' next to 'The Munros Abroad';

and 'What's in a Name' next to 'A Clan in Name', which explores the origins of the name Munro itself.

This device of juxtaposing the general and the specific serves other purposes too. An interesting example is apparent in the sections dealing with the issue of dispersal. As I have already touched upon, and shall explore more fully in Chapter 9, what one might neutrally describe as 'structural change' in the Highlands – the transformation from a subsistence to a capitalist economy, the commodification of land, the decline of kinship-based allegiances and dependencies, 'landlords and tenants' replacing 'chiefs and clansmen' – is more commonly evoked in Scotland as the *destruction* of a traditional way of life and is bound up with the Hanoverian (rationalistic, colonising and evil) crushing of the Jacobite (traditional, colonised and benign) cause at and after the Battle of Culloden. 'The Clans Dispersed' panel reads as follows:

> The clan system was crushed following the Jacobite rebellions of 1715 and 1745 with the passing of Acts to: break the ties between Chiefs and their men; disarm the clans; outlaw the wearing of tartan and the kilt; and to take Jacobite clanlands into crown hands (for nearly 40 years). The system ended with the 'clearing' of tenants from some Highland estates to make way for sheep during the first half of the 19th century. At that time over 100,000 people left for Canada and the USA.
>
> Today a clan system still exists in dispersed form. All around the world people with the same or associated surnames lay claim to clan membership and often 'come back' to Scotland in search of their Highland roots.

The Jacobite rebellions, the defeat at Culloden, the Disarming Acts, the Clearances: these are some of the key narratives of modern Highland identity. Nowhere are they more avidly consumed than in the diaspora where they delineate an émigré identity based on exile rather than expansionism. What is fascinating about this particular articulation of these themes, however, is the fact that the Munros, along with many other Highland clans, were actually loyal to the British/Hanoverian/Protestant Crown during the rebellions.

> The Munros weren't Jacobites, and, although a couple of senior members of the family fought at Culloden, as a clan they didn't fight at Culloden. So that sets us apart slightly from many others, because most people assume that everybody who was a Highlander fought on the Jacobite side at Culloden and was for Bonnie Prince Charlie. But the truth is, of course, quite the opposite and it was as much a civil war as anything else. (Julian Dow, pers. comm.)

The panel adjacent to 'The Clans Dispersed', entitled 'The Munros Abroad', is therefore conspicuously silent on the issue of the rebellions and carefully exonerates the Munro chiefs/landlords from 'clearing' their tenants from the lands with which they were, as we have seen, 'absolutely bound'. Instead, the panel asserts that the Munro clansfolk *chose* to emigrate of their own accord.

The contradiction evident in these two panels – the general story explaining the 'crushing' of the clan system through the Jacobite defeat and the Clearances, the particular revealing that neither of these was particularly relevant to the Clan Munro – is typical of the confusion that abounds regarding these still-contentious episodes in Highland history. It also demonstrates that a dilemma exists in the representation of these important 'identity narratives': should the heritage centre displays challenge the problematic, but deeply ingrained beliefs of its diasporic visitors regarding their own cultural heritage? If, as Dow suggests, most such visitors come believing that to be a Highlander is to be a Jacobite (i.e. the underdog, the victimised, the exiled, the virtuous – and such beliefs are often profound to a sense of self), then is it right to present a more complex and contradictory story? In other words, it is appropriate for a heritage centre to shatter the 'myths' its visitors live by? (Samuel and Thompson 1990).

The problem of either fulfilling visitors' expectations or providing a more educative experience remains unresolved at Clanland. A tension thus exists between those panels that bolster the romantic Highlandist stereotypes that are often central to diasporic visitors' senses of what it means to be a Scot/Highlander/Munro and others that present a more complex story which might threaten to destabilise identity and cause visitors to question the moral certainties on which it is constructed. The dilemma is avoided, however, by deflecting attention onto the romantic ideology of clanship, and particularly onto the association between clan and territory. Ignoring the complications of the narratives that explain the displacement of the clansfolk from 'their' land, the exhibitions instead extend an invitation at every opportunity to those 'dispossessed' to reconnect with their heritage and even, perhaps, to finance its perpetuation.

This invitation is powerfully evoked in a video presentation in an adjacent auditorium, the doors of which introduce these sentiments and bear the words 'Be of this land'. The video follows the journey of a young Glaswegian woman to her ancestral homeland in Ferindonald. With her grandmother's stories leading her on, the woman's heritage becomes alive to her as she begins to identify with the Munro lands over which she walks. This is conveyed in the elegiac declamations of a battle-weary eighteenth-century clansman, as he makes a parallel journey to the heart of the clanlands. Gordon Lyall, the exhibition designer responsible for the interpretative strategy at Clanland, explained to me that the idea for the video came to him when he was invited to attend an international Clan Munro gathering at Foulis Castle. Only after participating in the gathering did Lyall realise that this close association between kinship and territory was not only a matter of tradition, but also a burgeoning contemporary phenomenon: something very real to its professors.

The sense of a recovered continuity with the past, of the connection between personal history/identity and the broader narratives of social history/identity, the mediating role of the landscape, and the significance of the journey itself is articulated in the closing scenes of the video which take place at a ruinous chapel beside a river at the heart of the Munro clanlands. Anna is the contemporary Glaswegian character, Sean the eighteenth-century clansman:

SEAN: ... As for me, my words must make a bridge between what has been and what will be, so that others can cross from times to come and sense what happened here and taste the past. The land will hold the past secure, so that always when we see the land we see ourselves.

ANNA: A thousand years, then me. A million journeys by hundreds of thousands of travellers all across Ferindonald. Then my wee journey. So, wee journeys as well as great ones, wee folk and camp followers as well as chiefs and heroes, masses of them doing ... I don't know, whatever they did. Whoever they were.

SEAN: *(fades in)* ... died seventeen hundred and two. William Munro, tacksman of Katewell, died seventeen-hundred and eighty-six. John Mackenzie, ferryman, eighteen hundred ... Alexander Munro, ferryman, eighteen hundred and fifty. Hugh Urquhart, sawmiller, eighteen hundred and sixty. Reverend Harry Robertson, minister, nineteen hundred and fifteen ... *(fades out)*

ANNA: John Munro, shipwright, died Glasgow, 1965, buried at Kiltearn. Anna Munro, nurse, grand-daughter of John, born Glasgow 1974 ... A thousand years. Then me. What's that? I kept asking myself, all the way into the hills, into the past. Not knowing what I was looking for until at last I came to that wee chapel lost in its wood. As soon as I saw it ... I don't know, that was it. It was like following that dark river had led me to some kind of source. I just wandered around, touching the old stones. Feeling them, almost hearing them tell me their story. Stones that tell stories! ... Then it dawned on me. This is my place too. I own this land too! Nooooo ... no ... NO! Not that. The opposite. The land owns me. The very land was laying a claim on me.

Story telling stones, wash your stories down to the sea!

SEAN: Be of this land as the eagle is of the mountain air.

We look at the land and we see ourselves.

The land is the bone. We are the blood. (Crumley 1997)

Macpherson country

The territory historically associated with the Clan Macpherson is the old Lordship of Badenoch in the Central Highlands, which has as its capital the town of Kingussie. The name Macpherson is derived from the Gaelic *Mac a' Phearsain*, meaning 'Son of the Parson', and, according to one account, the progenitor of the clan was a twelfth-century prior named Muireach Catanach. The Macphersons were part of confederacy of clans known as the Old Clanchattan which originated in the Lochaber area and migrated east across the Highlands between about 1350 and 1450, gradually disinte-grating as the various branches (including Macphersons, Mackintoshes, MacMillans and MacNivens) competed for dominance. The Macphersons came to prominence in Badenoch after first ousting the hitherto powerful Comyn overlords and then displacing their own erstwhile allies, the MacNivens, who had previously settled in the area. Acquiring the clan seat, Cluny, by marriage bond, the Macphersons emerged as a new elite in the area, finally gaining the *dùthchas* – in this context, the legal 'right of ancient possession' – to the territory in 1600 (A. G. Macpherson 1993: 11–19). Through the granting of lands to cadet branches of the family and through strategic marriage practices (generally speaking, males marrying exoga-mously, females marrying endogamously), the history of the Macphersons in Badenoch provides an excellent example of a kingroup 'growing down' into a territory (Dodgshon 1989: 174; A. G. Macpherson 1966).

The Clan Macpherson has thus been 'mapped' onto the Badenoch land-scape, not only in the names of townships and estates associated with the various branches or *sliochdan* of the clan (so that one gets the Macpherson *of* Cluny, the chiefly line, the Macphersons *of* Pitmain, *of* Glentruim and so forth – and the heads of these families become known simply by the placenames: i.e. Cluny, the chief, Pitmain, Glentruim), but also in those sites which may be said to 'bear witness' to the clan's history and around which stories continue to be told. For instance, in the shadow of Creag Dhubh, the clan's totemic hill that stands sentinel at the heart of Macpherson country, there is the site of the fourteenth-century Battle of Invernahavon, a conflict fought against the raiding Clan Cameron, the Macphersons' neighbours to the west. And then there is the Iron Age souterrain at Raitts near Kingussie, known locally as the MacNivens' Cave: a name which recalls a grim story that dates to the feud between the Macphersons and MacNivens, in which a group of MacNivens used the souterrain as a hideout until, through the cunning of Cluny's men, they were discovered and promptly dispatched.

Another often-told Badenoch story is that of the infamous Captain John Macpherson, the 'Black Officer of Ballachroan', who was killed dramatically in an avalanche in 1800. The ruins of his once-impressive farmhouse, said to have been built from stones taken from Kingussie's old parish church, remain shrouded in superstition. As Meta Scarlett, a local writer, explains,

> From my earliest childhood I heard tales, the oral tradition handed down by my great-great-grandmother who was his contemporary, in which he was represented as the incarnation of evil, the hated recruiting officer called black not for his dark colouring but for his black heart, who tricked the local lads into enlisting in King George's

army, who trafficked with the Devil and who came in the fullness of time to his inevitable doom.

He sounded like a character from a ballad or a ghost story, but he was real enough. I had only to open our sideboard to see his cream jug and sugar bowl, simple homely things bought at the Ballachroan sale in 1821. (1988: 124)

In addition to being reviled for his deviousness in enlisting recruits and his other misdemeanours, the Black Officer was also responsible for introducing improved methods of agriculture to the area. By adding lime to the peaty soil around Ballachroan and introducing a turnip crop, the Captain prospered as a farmer, but his success was attributed to his being in league with the Devil. Indeed, even today, visiting the ruinous farmhouse occasions the telling of a tale in which the Captain successfully outwitted the Devil himself.

The Evil One agreed to give the Captain whatever he might desire and his first wish was that the lands of Ballachroan might for their fruitfulness be a wonder to all who saw them. To this Satan agreed provided he would get half the crop. That year Captain Macpherson sowed a grain crop as usual, reaped in a wonderful harvest and when the Devil came to claim his due offered him the roots. Satan protested and was told that the following year he would get the crop and the Captain would keep the roots. Next spring Macpherson planted only potatoes and turnips which gave a marvellous yield and when the time came to fulfil his bargain he gladly surrendered the 'shaws'. (Scarlett 1988: 129)

Needless to say, Macpherson of Ballachroan's death at the Gaick avalanche catastrophe on 'Yule Eve 1800' was seen by many as the Devil's revenge, and it features prominently in local folklore, gruesomely elaborated in every telling. The site where Macpherson's body was found is marked by a cairn on which the last poignant stanza of an elegy by a contemporary bard is inscribed:

O duisgibh-se mu'm fas sibh liath,	Oh waken before you grow grey,
'S dlùithibh bhur cas risant-sliabh	Quicken your foot towards the moor,
Feuch gu'm bi bhur fasgadh deant	See that your shelter is made
Mu'n teid a' ghrian a laidhe oirbhe.	Ere the sun sets on you.

(Clarke 1994: 31–5)

As Keith Basso has compellingly argued with reference to the Western Apache: through the telling of narratives, places in the landscape become transformed from geographical sites into 'something resembling a theater, a natural stage upon the land . . . where significant moral dramas unfolded in the past' (1996: 66). Such Macpherson place-stories demonstrate vividly how 'wisdom' comes to 'sit' in the Scottish Highland landscape too.

Perhaps the most significant of the 'moral dramas' to have unfolded across the Highland landscape is that of the Jacobite Rebellions – particularly the Rebellion of 1745–46. A drama shot through with motifs of love, loyalty, exile and loss, the story of 'the Forty-five' is recalled not only at those iconic sites such as Glenfinnan, where Charles Edward Stuart ('Bonnie Prince Charlie') first raised his standard, or Culloden, where the Jacobite army was finally routed by government forces, but also in countless other less prominent sites connected to 'that arduous and unfortunate enterprise'.[4] Most prolific of these are those sites associated with the flight of the defeated Bonnie Prince Charlie and his supporters after the Battle of Culloden, and, indeed, there is no shortage of these in Macpherson country (unlike the Munros, the Macphersons *were* Jacobite supporters). It was at Ruthven Barracks, for example, across the River Spey from Kingussie, that the Jacobite armies regrouped after Culloden, fully expecting to renew hostilities until the message came from the Bonnie Prince advising them that the cause was lost and that every man should 'seek his own safety in the best way he can' (Chevalier Johnstone's account, quoted by S. Gordon 1995: 207). As the government forces launched a massive manhunt across the Highlands, the Jacobite rebels fled to the hills and hid until passage could be secured to carry them to safety in France. The tales of their adventures and exploits in hiding constitute one of the great bodies of Highland folklore and song, later to be appropriated in the Hanoverian romanticisation of the Highlands and published in collections such as James Hogg's *Jacobite Relics* (1819–21).

Every Jacobite clan has its Jacobite hero, and the Macphersons' hero is its chief of the time, Ewan or Cluny 'of the '45'. In the aftermath of the Rebellion, those chiefs who would not swear allegiance to the Hanoverian crown remained outlaws and had their estates confiscated: Cluny's was among them. Thus Badenoch effectively became an occupied territory with upwards of 1,000 government troops stationed on the banks of the Spey at Sherramore, Cluny Castle fired, and a bounty of 1,000 guineas placed on Cluny's head. Cluny spent a remarkable nine years in hiding in Badenoch before fleeing to exile, and many of the places in which he reputedly hid may still be visited and form key sites in the Macpherson clanscape (Figure 6.3). The two most famous of these hideouts are *Uamh Chluanaidh* (Cluny's Cave) on Creag Dhubh and 'Cluny's Cage' on Ben Alder. Cluny's Cage is especially famous since it was here that the chief sheltered Bonnie Prince Charlie for six days while he awaited news of a vessel to take him to France. The Cage is also the setting of a much-celebrated scene in Robert Louis Stevenson's 1886 novel *Kidnapped*, demonstrating how tales of Jacobite derring-do remained popular throughout the nineteenth century. It was not until 1755 that Ewan himself finally escaped to France; he died there in 1764 and was buried in the grounds of a Carmelite

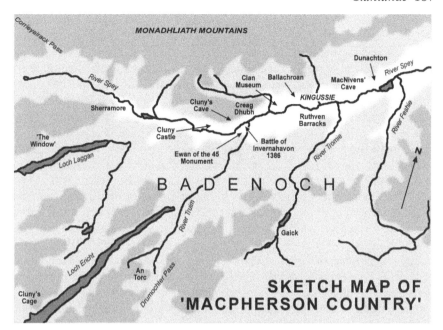

Figure 6.3 Sketch map of Macpherson country (Paul Basu)

Monastery near Dunkerque, the exact location of which is now unknown. The Macphersons were eventually restored to Cluny in 1784 and Ewan's son had the family castle rebuilt. After the long, charismatic 'reign' of Ewan's grandson, however, the fortunes of the family began to decline and, in 1933, the estate finally went into receivership. Writing soon after, Seton Gordon comments, 'Truly the glory of the house of Cluny Macpherson has gone on the hill wind' (1995: 221).

Such, then, is the *topographie légendaire* of the Clan Macpherson (Halbwachs 1941). I should now like to examine how these place-stories are effectively, and affectingly, 'performed' in the Badenoch landscape. Surprisingly, this role is not fulfilled by the clan's museum in Newtonmore. Unlike the Munros' 'Clanland' visitor centre, the Clan Macpherson Museum was not established explicitly to tell a story so much as to house those 'relics and memorials' of the clan that were salvaged by the nascent Clan Macpherson Association when the Cluny estate was sold off in 1942. The association was formally inaugurated at its first annual rally in 1947, and it officially opened its museum at 'Clan Macpherson House' five years later. Since then, the constitution of the clan association has altered significantly. Thus, in the 1950s, no more than 10 per cent of the association's members were based outside the UK; whereas today, of the 3,000 strong membership, over 60 per cent reside overseas (there are currently eight branches of the association: one each in Scotland, England, Canada, the

USA, New Zealand and South Africa, and two in Australia). This reflects the more general growth in Scottish diasporic consciousness and, to a large degree, has determined the function currently demanded of the museum as a 'focus' for a clan no longer acquainted with its own lands. A jumble of curios, it could be argued that, whilst providing this focus for the dispersed clansfolk, the museum actually diverts their attention away from the infinitely richer mnemonic landscape outside its doors, and we must therefore look elsewhere for the practice of Macpherson place-storytelling.

We may look, for instance, to the main event of the clan association's calendar: its annual gathering in Badenoch. This rally may be understood as a 'commemorative ceremony' or 'ritual form' (cf. Kapferer 1988: 149–82; Connerton 1989) in which the individual 'bodies' of the clan gather together as 'one body' in the clan's homeland. In this corporeal act of gathering, the otherwise dispersed clans folk 'perform' their membership of the clan, assuming its heritage as their own (see Fortier 1999). This performance of heritage (a laying claim to a past and a place) is perhaps most explicit in the central event of the rally, in which the clan marches from a place called Old Ralia, across Spey bridge, to 'the Eilean', Newtonmore's sports ground, where they parade at the town's annual Highland Games (the gathering and the games are organised in tandem around the same weekend in August). The clan members are led by a pipe band and march in full Highland dress behind the clan insignia, their chief and other senior clansfolk. The march usually draws a large crowd of spectators (locals and tourists alike), which forms a witness to the ceremony – as, indeed, does Creag Dhubh, within sight of which the event takes place (Figure 6.4).

After attending the games, the clan members then make their way to the clan museum, where there is an opportunity for them to socialise more informally and enjoy a dram together. That this 'open house' takes place at 'Clan Macpherson House' is significant in itself and demonstrates that the museum acts as a substitute for the lost clan seat, Cluny Castle, where such gatherings would have traditionally taken place. But, given that the clan members here mingle not only among themselves but among the clan's relics and memorabilia, it is also fascinating to observe how this part of the event may occasion the telling of clan stories, usually in casual conversations between more and less knowledgeable clan members as they linger over the displays. In this respect the poor labelling of objects in the museum becomes advantageous, since this provokes additional commentary and explanation. If particular interest is shown, more experienced clan members may recommend books about clan history to novices, or introduce them to other clansfolk who are recognised for their expertise on certain aspects of clan lore. Through such informal social interaction newcomers thus become increasingly acquainted with the clan's stories: to learn these stories is, in a sense, to become initiated.

Among other events, a clan walk is organised as part of each year's rally. Again, these walks are ostensibly occasions for informal social interaction,

Figure 6.4 The Clan Macpherson marching to 'the Eilean', near Newtonmore, in 1999. Creag Dhubh can be seen in the background (Paul Basu)

where members may enjoy each other's company as well as seeing more of the magnificent Badenoch scenery than their travels by road and rail allow. Beyond its sociable surface, however, these walks also constitute a form of corporeal commemorative practice through which Macpherson place-stories are 'experienced' bodily as much as cognitively. The destinations of these walks are usually places connected with Macpherson history: places that, in the words of the clan member who organises them, have 'become *totems* to go and visit'. Recent destinations have thus included Cluny's Cave (1986), the Corrieyarrick Pass (1990), Glen Banchor (1992), Ballachroan and Gaick (1993), Cluny's Cage (1996), and Creag Dhubh (2000). Although many male participants walk dressed in their kilts of Macpherson tartan, this event is a far less 'spectacular' performance of identity than the clan march. Indeed, its performance is directed inwardly rather than outwardly, both at an individual level, through the development of a more intimate physical relationship with Macpherson country, and at a collective level, through the shared endeavour and the conversational telling of clan stories in the very places where they happened. A 'write-up' of each walk usually appears in the following year's *Creag Dhubh*, the clan's annual journal. In these articles, the story of the site visited and the story of the walk itself are combined, such that the 'historical' event and the 'commemorative' event become interwoven and new meanings accrue in old places. As a commemorative practice, the *walk* 'remembers' the past event; in remembering the walk, the *walker* recalls both the past event and the event of the walk – individual heritage thus becomes closely associated with collective heritage, and the polysemic 'site of memory' becomes a site of personal identification (E. Bruner and Gorfain 1988; Nora 1989).

In 1996, to celebrate the fiftieth anniversary of the founding of the Clan Macpherson Association, it was decided that a special golden jubilee gathering would be organised. As well as staging an extra-large rally, with lots of guests and special events, it was felt that the clan should also have something more tangible to mark the occasion. The jubilee would coincide with the much anticipated 250th anniversary of the Battle of Culloden (McArthur 1994), as well as with the period in which Ewan of the '45 harboured Bonnie Prince Charlie in his celebrated hide-out on Ben Alder. Since there was no other memorial to their esteemed Jacobite chief, it was decided that this 'tangible something' should take the form of a cairn erected in his honour, and that its ceremonial unveiling would be the centrepiece of the gala (Figure 6.5, bottom). Whilst the dedication to 'Ewan Macpherson of Cluny, Colonel of the Badenoch Men in the Forty-five' inscribed on a plaque set into the cairn makes clear its primary commemorative purpose, a closer reading of this monument reveals it to be a far more complex and fascinating 'memorial text'.

The land on which the cairn and its enclosure is located was gifted to the clan association by Euan Macpherson of Glentruim at another ceremony at the clan's forty-ninth gathering in 1995 (i.e. the year prior to the planned jubilee). This slightly elevated site, with its views across the Badenoch landscape, is key to the success of the monument, and it is worth reproducing part of Glentruim's address to the clan delivered during this ceremony to explain why:

Cluny, Lady Cluny, Clansfolk –

Welcome here today. The very last time I stood here on this piece of ground was on the 12th of January this year when Ewen, Bruce and I met here to decide whether this was the right place to build a Commemorative Cairn to Ewan of the '45.

The three of us stood here and we looked out there over the Upper Spey, the broad fertile valley where our ancestors lived and worked, cultivated the fields and tended their cattle. Right at the head of the valley is the ancestral home of the Head of the Clan, the House of Cluny. And over there beyond Torr na Truime where the rivers Spey and Truim join is the place where our forebears bravely fought and won the Battle of Invernahavon 600 years ago. On the cliff over there is Cluny's Cave, the place where Ewan of the '45 hid from the English. I like to think that on a day like today he would come out of the cave and lie down in the heather and watch the English Redcoats marching up and down in search for him in vain.

And standing over us now, as then, is Creag Dhubh, the sentinel and guardian of our Clan through all the ages.

Figure 6.5 The cairn commemorating Ewan Macpherson of the '45. Images include detail of inscribed stones, diagram illustrating the 'place-story' dial, and, at the bottom, a photograph of the gathered Macpherson clansfolk taken after the unveiling ceremony in 1996 (Paul Basu, Jerome Le Roy Lewis)

On that day in January this year when Ewen, Bruce and I met here it was a bitterly cold day with snow lying all around. There was not a breath of wind – utter silence. It was Ewen who suddenly turned to me and said, 'You know, if you listen very carefully you can almost hear the silence'. The three of us stood together for some moments without speaking and, listening carefully, I think that what we heard were distant echoes from all the centuries past in the long, proud history of our Clan. (E. Macpherson 1996: 7–8)

The sight of the Macpherson clanlands is thus central to the site of the cairn – indeed, like Creag Dhubh itself, the cairn site seems to be at the very centre of the territory, the point at which the echoes of the clan's place-stories are collected and focused as if through a parabolic reflector. For the uninitiated visitor to the site, these place-stories are 'gathered in' and hinted at in a compass-like dial attached to a large boulder within the cairn's enclosure (Figure 6.5, centre). The particular significance of the places included on this dial is established through their very inclusion, but explication is withheld, and the visitor whose curiosity is aroused is thus encouraged to visit the clan museum to enquire.

Perhaps the most remarkable aspect of the monument, however, is the fact that it is constructed from stones sent by clan members from twenty-six different countries throughout the world. Some of the stones are inscribed with the names or initials of those who contributed them, but the majority are anonymous within the fabric of the cairn. Records were kept, however, of every stone donated, noting the donor and details of where each stone was sourced, and these have been compiled into a commemorative 'Book of Gold', which is on display at the clan museum as a memento of the jubilee gathering.

The cairn incorporates stones sourced both in the homeland and in the diaspora, literally uniting disparate fragments into one body. As Robert J. Macpherson, the architect of the memorial, explained at the unveiling ceremony, in contributing these stones, 'clansmen and women have donated a part of their country, culture and personal history'; and, within the form of the cairn, the 'layers of meaning' embodied in the individual stones intricately overlap with one another. A few examples of the notes compiled in the 'Book of Gold' may give some insight into the specific meanings represented in each of the stones:

- Medium size grey stone found in direct proximity of Fort Ticonderoga (French Fort Carillon), N.Y. Still has traces of masonry on it. [The present] Cluny's direct ancestor, Allan Macpherson, was with the Black Watch at this location with Abercrombie in 1758. Given by C. Peter McPherson Fish, Keene, NY, USA.
- Piece of brown rock from near the bachelor officers' quarters, bldg 40, near the north east boundary of historic Fort McPherson, Atlanta, GA,

USA. Obtained by Donald and Dodie McPherson and family, Roswell, Georgia, USA.

- A large yellow coloured rectangular limestone inscribed 'McPherson Kansas 1995'. The state rock for Kansas and is found in the Flint Hills that extend in the eastern edge of McPherson County. This rock was used in the construction of a very early home in McPherson. Robert W. and Debra J. Macpherson. Robert is the Vice Chairman, McPherson Scottish Society, McPherson, Kansas, USA.
- A tiny piece of black coal and a tiny piece of red stone from McKeesport, PA, USA. Gt Grandfather MacPherson settled in the township of Elizabeth just outside of McKeesport to mine coal and the family are still in the area. The sender, Sue Anne MacPherson, of McKeesport has four sons and a daughter who are proud of their Scottish background.
- An Aboriginal axehead from Western Australia. From Douglas & Margaret McPherson, Western Australia.
- A very large, black and white stone with flakes of real gold glistening. The face is polished and has eighteen first names inscribed on it plus the first initial of seventeen other members. From the Western Deep Levels Gold Mine in South Africa, being the deepest mine in the world. Sent by Allan D. MacPherson of Rivonia, South Africa on behalf of the South African Branch of the Clan Macpherson Association.
- A small piece of brown petrified wood and polished at one end. From Mount Abundance Station, Roma, Queensland, Australia. Settled in 1847 by Allan Macpherson of Blairgowrie, Scotland. He abandoned the Station in 1856 because of droughts and attacks by Aborigines on stock and settlers. Allan was an ancestor of the present Chief. Given by Peter Keegan, Roma, Queensland, Australia. (Clan Macpherson 'Book of Gold')

Each stone thus represents, metonymically, its own place-story: each tells an individual family narrative, but each narrative is also a fragment of a wider story, that of the Macpherson diaspora. Just as the fragments of rocks are conglomerated into one in the cairn, so the personal histories they each embody are fused in the cement of a shared heritage into the collective history of the clan.[5]

It seems, therefore, that this cairn is not merely a memorial to a Jacobite hero; it is, rather, the clan's memorial to the clan itself: on the one hand, an acknowledgement of its essentially dispersed nature (a clan 'gone on the hill wind'), on the other, an emphatic assertion of the resilience of its attachment to the place it still identifies as home. In a medium as substantial as stone, the monument makes tangible the intangible relationship between a people and its place, and 're-presences', despite its continued absence, the clan in its clan lands. Furthermore, as the place-stories of homeland and diaspora are interfused and articulated within the panorama of the monument, Macpherson country seems to extend far beyond the bounds of

Badenoch to embrace, as we have seen, coal mines in Pennsylvania, gold mines in South Africa, and abandoned sheep stations in Queensland: territories (and identities) delineated not so much by the *dùthchas* of dwelling as by the itineraries of ancestral migrations.

Living in a new (Macpherson) country

Another fascinating way in which Macpherson country may be seen to extend far beyond Badenoch's bounds is in the remarkable number of places named 'Macpherson' (or 'McPherson') throughout the world. As we have already seen in the excerpts from the 'Book of Gold', there is a McPherson County in Kansas and a Fort McPherson in Georgia – these are named after the American Civil War hero James 'Birdseye' McPherson, as is McPherson County in South Dakota. There is another Fort McPherson at the head of the Mackenzie River in Canada's North West Territories, this time named after Murdoch McPherson, a factor of the Hudson's Bay Company. To these we may add a further eight McPherson/Macpherson Lakes, two McPherson Points and a Glen McPherson in Canada; a Macpherson's Strait in the Bay of Bengal; another McPherson Point on the coast of Christmas Island; and, in Australia, a Macpherson's Pillar, a McPherson mountain range and no fewer than three Mount Macphersons (A. G. Macpherson 2000: 25–6).

Natural features of the New World landscape were often named in honour of those who funded expeditions during the process of European colonisation. Thus, Bill Macpherson, an informant from Western Australia, writes in his family history how his great-grandfather, Donald Macpherson, who emigrated from Badenoch to Western Australia in 1839, had a mountain named after him in acknowledgement of his sponsorship of an expedition led by his land surveyor, F. T. Gregory:

> In 1861, Gregory led an expedition through the North West of the State, largely financed by five settlers of whom one was Donald Macpherson. Gregory reached a point about 160 kilometres east of present-day Nullagine before being forced back by lack of food and water. Near that turning point he named Mt Macpherson. Expedition sponsors could expect to get their names on the map, although the records of the Geographic Names Section of the Dept of Land Administration state only that Gregory chose the name of an early settler. One of the family legends had been that a more famous explorer, Sir Lord John Forrest, named Mt Macpherson after Donald. (R. W. Macpherson n.d.: 37)

The expansion of this more literal Macpherson country in Australia exemplifies the 'rhetorical colonization' of the New World described by Paul Carter, a colonisation in which 'the historical space of the white settlers emerged through the medium of language' – and, more precisely, through 'the language of naming' (1987: 67). Through naming, Carter argues, undifferentiated space, itself rhetorically constructed as *terra nullius*, becomes transformed into an 'object of knowledge': 'something that could be explored and read' and thereby appropriated (ibid.). Carter is keen to emphasise that such colonisations should not, however, be understood exclusively as the acts of famous – and not so famous – explorers such as Sir Thomas Mitchell (another Scot who, incidentally, named the Mount Macpherson on the Darling River in New South Wales), Sir Lord John Forrest, or, indeed, the likes of F. T. Gregory.

> To understand the settling process we need to bear in mind that contrary to the imperial paradigm of colonization, in which settlement follows on smoothly from discovery and exploration, the settlers inhabited the new country strategically. They were themselves discoverers and explorers. (Carter, 1987: 138)

Thus Carter cites the example of a Mr and Mrs Austin, who, in planning the development of a township on their land selection near Geelong, *first* name it 'Chilwell' after their old home in Derbyshire, England. In the anticipatory act of naming, Carter argues, the Austins create a new place where meanings and associations can accrue (ibid.: 137–8). We may see the same processes at work in the *new* Macpherson country: thus we find an Alexander Macpherson naming his property in New South Wales 'Kingussie' after the Badenoch town from which his father emigrated in 1838; or that same Donald Macpherson, namesake of Mount Macpherson in Western Australia, naming his sheep station 'Glentromie' after Glen Tromie in Badenoch (and indeed, my informant, Bill Macpherson, named his own house 'Glentromie', not after Glen Tromie, Badenoch, but after his great-grandfather's *Australian* property, thus continuing the toponymic migration).

Carter maintains that the 'spatial histories' these settler-explorer-discoverers were making were orientated towards the future, not invocations of the past. The fact that the Chilwell in Derbyshire which gives its name to the Austins' anticipated township in Victoria has its own etymological roots is not, he suggests, particularly significant. Carter is more concerned with the manner in which the intentional act of naming brings into being a new 'communicable space' and how this constitutes the true 'settling' of a new country. Whilst not disputing the substance of Carter's argument, I believe the significance of these old country names – names such as 'Kingussie' and 'Glentromie', or, for that matter, the township of 'Badenoch' in Ontario – are much more than mere etymological curiosities (Carter 1987: 137).

Topographically, whilst the Grampian Mountains in Victoria (again named by Mitchell; see Birch 1996) may bear some passing resemblance to the Grampian mountains in Scotland, the same could not be said of Donald Macpherson's parched 'Glentromie' in Western Australia and its namesake in the Central Highlands (Figure 6.6). 'When I think of Tromie', recalls Meta Scarlett, 'I think of fishing picnics far up the glen on luminous summer evenings; of bathing in brown-dappled pools on lazy afternoons' (1988: 73). It is in the heights of Glen Tromie that Gaick is to be found, the place where the infamous Black Officer of Ballachroan was killed, and it was in this same glen that my informant Bill Macpherson's great-great-grandfather, 'Old Aeneas', father of Donald, was born in the 1780s. According to Bill's family history, Aeneas married into a family of McIntoshes at a place called Dunachton, across the Spey from Glen Tromie, and it was at Dunachton that Donald himself was born in 1815. As a 24 year-old emigrant, Donald was no doubt well acquainted with his father's native glen – its 'dappled pools' as well as its darker associations – and he evidently carried the memory of that place with him to Western Australia. A further 20 years after his emigration, the significance of that memory was still sufficient for Donald, now a successful farmer with a flock of 4,000 sheep, 'a fine herd of cattle' and a homestead consisting of 'several substantial buildings', to change the name of his estate from the 'aboriginal' *Murra Murra* to Glentromie (R. W. Macpherson n.d.: 36).

Actually, it was the name of his great-grandfather's sheep station in Western Australia, sold after his death, that provoked Bill Macpherson's interest in his family history in the first place and inspired him to set off in search of its old-country namesake. Thus, in 1989, Bill made a journey to Badenoch, not so much to see the generic Macpherson country of the clan as to find his own Macphersons' country. He explained to me, 'We didn't know why great-grandpa Donald Macpherson named his Western Australian sheep station Glentromie, and when I eventually did find out, I knew I would have to see the glen'. Of Old Aeneas's four sons, three emigrated to Western Australia, and it was interesting for Bill to discover that his was not the first homecoming in the family. Indeed the continuing

Figure 6.6 'Glentromie' sheep station, Victoria Plains, Western Australia (Bill
 Macpherson)

connections between this particular Macpherson diaspora and its home-land were evident in two nineteenth-century gravestones that Bill came across during his visit: the first, now lying broken in Kingussie's Middle Cemetery, was erected in 1853 by Donald's older brother, 'John Macpherson of Western Australia', in memory of their father, Old Aeneas, who had died in 1840; the second, in nearby Alvie churchyard, was dedi-cated to Duncan and Mary Macpherson, Donald's younger brother and his wife, who died at Carnamah in Western Australia in the 1890s. As Bill observes, 'there must have been someone in Badenoch who remembered them kindly and who had enough money to erect the stone'. 'Or', he adds, 'did Duncan provide for it out of his own estate?' (suggesting that the old country remained home for him in some profound sense).

Perhaps the most poignant part of Bill's journey to Badenoch, however, was his visit to Dunachton, the farm, originally subdivided into smaller townlands, on which Donald and his brothers had been born and raised in the early nineteenth century (Figure 6.7). Bill explained,

> It is all laid out as shown on the Ordnance Survey maps. I was surprised to find that the little groups of squares and lines on the map are actually the remains of the cottages and enclosure walls of the villages that were there in the time that Old Aeneas raised his children there.

Figure 6.7 Donald Macpherson (1815–87), pictured alongside the 'squares and lines' of Dunachton as represented on the 1st edition Ordnance Survey map (Bill Macpherson)

The story of Donald Macpherson and his brothers is, of course, just one among thousands of similar migrant tales. In its specificity, it lends credence to Carter's argument that colonial history must be understood, not as the unfolding of some epic narrative, but in the minutiae of thousands of individual actions and intentions. In naming their new homesteads after old homelands, however, surely these individual colonists were not only making spatial history, as Carter argues, in the sense of mapping out their futures onto what was, for them, an uncharted and abstract territory (1987: 137); I suggest that they were also historicising that supposedly 'unhistoried' landscape by importing place names that were already highly charged with memories and associations with the past. May we not conclude that whilst they contemplated new horizons, these colonists were also attempting to make their new country old? And, like the Aboriginal 'dreaming trails' that the settlers knowingly and unknowingly overwrote, may we not perceive in these spatial histories a kind of conduit connecting new lands and place-stories with their ancestral counterparts? Thus, travelling from Macpherson country to Macpherson country, Bill is able to reconstruct his genealogy from its linguistic as well as material traces in the landscape and, among the grassed-over ruins of Dunachton, to make sense of the puzzling 'squares and lines' of his maps – to discern in their hieroglyphs a particular meaning of home.

7 Sites of memory, sources of identity

David Lowenthal's observation that 'the locus of memory lies more readily in place than in time' (1997: 180) is certainly borne out when considering the relationship between landscape and memory in the Scottish Highlands. Neil Gunn, for example, provides a wonderful account of storytelling *through* the Caithness landscape in his 1942 novel, *Young Art and Old Hector*. Towards the end of this fable, the avuncular Old Hector takes his young friend, Art, to 'the River', the magical 'far country' up the strath that Art has heard so much about, but to which he has not yet dared venture. Art's elder brother has recently emigrated and Art wonders why Hector did not want to leave the village and 'go away off into the world' like so many others.

> 'Well, if I had gone away, I wouldn't have been here walking with you, for one thing. And for another, I like to be here. You see, I know every corner of this land, every little burn and stream, and even the boulders in the stream. And I know the moors and every lochan on them. And I know the hills, and the passes, and the ruins, and I know of things that happened here on our land long long ago, and men who are long dead I knew, and women. I knew them all. They are part of me. And more than that I can never know now'.
>
> 'That's a lot to know, isn't it?' said Art wonderingly.
>
> 'It's not the size of the knowing that matters, I think', said Old Hector, 'it's the kind of knowing'. (1976: 250)

Hector explains that 'every little place, every hillock, every hill and slope' in the strath has its name, and he agrees to teach the names to Art: to know the names is, in some senses, to keep the 'little places' alive (ibid.: 250–1). He follows Art's gaze to a small ravine,

> 'That's where I saw the gaugers go up first', Art explained in a low voice, his eyes round.
>
> But there was no-one there now, and as they journeyed on, Old Hector gave Art the name of the burn that issued from the ravine, and

explained how once, long ago, there had been a bothy near a spot high up the burn where stone cists, that were prehistoric graves, could still be seen. About that spot he told so fabulous a story that Art forgot to ask questions until it was finished. (Gunn 1976: 253)[1]

An *Allt Bothain* – a 'stream of the bothy' – does indeed issue into the upper reaches of the Dunbeath Water, although I suspect, on this occasion, inspiration for the scene came not only from 'Neil Gunn's country' and the Strath of Dunbeath, but also from 'Macpherson country' and Strathspey, and, particularly, from two nineteenth-century texts. Thus, of the Spey and its hinterland, John Longmuir writes that there is,

> Not a turn of the river, not a pass in the mountains, or the name of an estate, that does not recall some wild legend of the olden, or some thrilling event of more recent times; not a plain that is not associated with some battle; not a castle that has not stood its siege or been enveloped in flames; not a dark pool or gloomy loch that has not its tale either of guilt or superstition; not a manse that has not been inhabited by some minister that eminently served his Master. . . . Or, turning from the castle to the cairn, from the kirk to the cromlech, what a field is opened up to the investigator of the manners of the past! (1860: 2).

And Alexander Macbain, in an article in the 1890 *Transactions of the Gaelic Society of Inverness*, notes that,

> The Ordnance Survey maps, made to the scale of six inches to the mile, contain for Badenoch some fourteen hundred names; but these do not form more than a tithe of the names actually in use or once used when the glens were filled by people, and the summer shealings received their annual visitants. Every knoll and rill had its name; the bit of moor, the bog or blàr, the clump of wood (badan), the rock or crag, the tiny loch or river pool, not to speak of cultivated land parcelled into fields, each and all, however insignificant, had a name among those that dwelt near them. Nor were the minute features of the mountain ranges and far away valleys much less known and named. The shealing system contributed much to this last fact. But now many of these names are lost, we may say most of them are lost, with the loss of the population, and with the abandonment of the old system of crofting and of summer migration to the hills. (1890: 170)

These three texts – Gunn's, Longmuir's and Macbain's – attest to the density of 'place-stories' that have accumulated in the Highland landscape, and demonstrate that it is not only in those 'exotic' landscapes, still prioritised by anthropologists, where such remarkable mnemonic and toponymic practices occur or have occurred. But these texts are also indicative of a transformation that has taken place in the way such landscapes are experienced and perceived. In this respect, we may agree with the French historian, Pierre Nora, and say that these landscapes no longer constitute *milieux de mémoire*, 'real environments of memory', but have become complexes of *lieux de mémoire*, 'sites of memory': places where memory 'crystallizes and secretes itself', venerated traces 'of that which has already happened' (1989: 7–8). This 'historicisation' of a mnemonic consciousness is related to the decline in oral traditions and the corresponding expansion of literacy. 'As traditional memory disappears', Nora argues, 'we feel obliged assiduously to collect remains, testimonies, documents, images, speeches, any visible signs of what has been' (ibid.: 13), and it is the textual, architectural and performative spaces where such vestiges are inscribed, stored and re-enacted that constitute the *lieux de mémoire*. These sites of memory are 'many and diverse', writes James Young, 'they range from archives to museums, parades to moments of silence, memorial gardens to resistance monuments, ruins to commemorative fast days' (1993: viii). The 'lived-landscape' (in which memory, too, is 'alive', permanently evolving, and 'unconscious of its successive deformations' (Nora 1989: 8)) thus becomes a 'heritage landscape': a landscape of monuments of the past, which venerate the past because it is past.

Whereas, in French historiography, the definitive moment of transition between 'memory' (tradition) and 'history' (modernity) may be dated to 1789 and the Revolution, in Scottish historiography, the pivotal date is 1746 and the dismantling of 'the traditional society of the Highlands' that followed in the wake of Culloden (Hunter 2000: 43). This, then, is the period in which that other famous native of Badenoch, James Macpherson, assembled, translated and augmented his *Fragments of Ancient Poetry, collected in the Highlands of Scotland* (1760), transforming the remnants of a bardic oral tradition into a literary form. As is wellknown, Macpherson's collections, particularly *The Works of Ossian* (1765), were hugely popular with cosmopolitan audiences and inspired the first waves of what might feasibly be termed 'heritage tourism' in the Scottish Highlands: crammed with ethnological and antiquarian anecdotes, Pennant's *A Tour in Scotland* (1771), Johnson's *Journey to the Western Islands of Scotland* (1775), and Boswell's *Journal of a Tour to the Hebrides with Samuel Johnson* (1786) are merely the most famous of the many published accounts (see Stafford 1988; Andrews 1990; Gold and Gold 1995). Other evidence of the historicisation of the Highlands at this time may be found in the establishment of the Highland Society in London in 1778, the avowed intention of which was the 'preservation of ancient Highland tradition' (Devine 1999: 234), the founding of the Society of Antiquaries of Scotland in 1780, and in the steady growth of the Highlandist discourse associated with Scott, which would culminate in the 'King's Jaunt' to Edinburgh in 1822 (see Chapters 1 and 4).

Whilst these various publications, institutions and ceremonial events may all be understood as *lieux de mémoire*, the most material manifestations of this new historical consciousness are those memorials erected to commemorate the Highland past: those, for instance, at Glencoe, Glenfinnan and Culloden. Culloden is particularly interesting in this context, not only because the battle is so iconic a turning point in Highland history, but particularly because of the way in which the battlefield has evolved over the last 250 years as a complex memorial text – a process which has seen the name of the battle displace the name of the land over which it was fought (Drumossie Moor has thus become Culloden Moor). It was not until the 1880s that a monument was actually raised on the site, and, indeed, as Colin McArthur notes, prior to the 1850s, Culloden was marked by its 'discursive invisibility' in Scotland (1994: 106). Thus in the cumulative index to the *Inverness Courier* (the *Inverness Journal* until 1817), only one reference is found to Culloden before 1825; in the period 1825 to 1841, there are only four entries; and it is not until the centenary of the battle, in 1846, that it rises more prominently in local consciousness. After two abandoned attempts to erect a memorial in the 1850s, Culloden was finally 'landscaped' as a commemorative site in 1881 by Duncan Forbes, the landowner of the time. As well as the 20-foot high cairn (Figure 7.1), Forbes had erected a series of stones marking the supposed burial places of the clansmen who fell in the battle. The 'Culloden Memorials', as they became known, were scheduled as Ancient Monuments in 1925,

Figure 7.1 The Culloden memorial cairn erected in 1881 (Paul Basu)

and the battlefield site itself passed into the ownership of the National Trust for Scotland, in somewhat piecemeal fashion, between 1937 and 1989. Throughout this period the site has undergone considerable transformation (the cutting down of a forestry plantation, the re-routing of roads, reinstatement of dykes, etc.), and new components of the memorial site have been added including various commemorative stones, a visitor centre, on-site interpretation panels and a viewing platform. As reported by the respondents to my questionnaire, and noted by Ray (2001: 134, 179), a visit to Culloden is an important part of many roots tourists' homecomings. The following comments, posted to the Homecomings discussion list, demonstrate that such visits are often particularly emotional experiences:

> I went to Culloden a few years ago. I am glad that I finally went but don't think I want to go again. I stood beside the Campbell gravestone and it was one of the eeriest feelings I have had. It was as if the whole place was steeped in sadness. (DK, Texas, USA)

> We went to Culloden after the anniversary of the battle and saw all the flowers and plaques left by the descendants of those who died there: how could you not feel the past? It slaps you in the face. I was overwhelmed by sadness. (DH, New Mexico, USA)

> I stood on the edge of the field and I was filled with such a sense of loneliness and desolation. I was a child and yet the place caught me and held me as if it were cold and raining on that bright shining day. I wanted to cry and I did not know why. (NY, Washington, USA)

Such sites of memory are evidently also 'sites of mourning' (Winter 1995), the 'sacred centres' of a nation or ethnie's 'moral geography' (A. D. Smith 1991: 16): places which, in a Highland context, mark the passing of a (mythical) golden age of tradition, of certainty, of a 'simpler' way of life.

As we have seen, in popular Scottish diasporic consciousness, this 'passing' is in fact understood as a 'destruction' – a destruction which can be narrated, thanks largely to the popular historian John Prebble, in three parts, beginning with the 1692 Massacre of Glencoe, reaching its climax at Culloden, and ending with the Highland Clearances. Thus, in his foreword to *Glencoe*, Prebble explains, 'I have written this book because its story is, in a sense, a beginning to what I have already written about Culloden and the Clearances – the destruction of the Highland people and their way of life' (1968: 9). Whilst the first two acts of this morality play are 'performed' at the commemorative sites of Glencoe and Culloden, no similar 'intentional' monument exists to commemorate the Clearances (although, as we shall see in Chapter 9, there was recently a campaign to erect such a monument in Sutherland).

The absence of a single memorial site to focus the 'recollection' of the Clearances has the effect of charging the whole Highland landscape with the 'memory' of these events. Thus, Rob Gibson, in his self-published *Highland Clearances Trail*, writes, 'from Gleann Mor to Beinn a' Bhragaidh the bare hills tell their own story of unfinished business' (1996a: 2). Elsewhere I have examined in some detail the mnemonic landscapes of the Clearances, and how the ruins of croft houses and the cairn-like remains of old settlement clusters that one frequently encounters in the Highlands, are often interpreted as evidence of the Clearances regardless of their age or the specific circumstances of their desertion (Basu 1997; 2000). In the Scottish Highlands, the ruined croft, I have argued, stands in metonymic relationship to the Clearances, such that the whole Clearance narrative is told in every ruin (Figure 7.2). This can be illustrated with reference to a page entitled 'Where to "see" the Highland Clearances and Diaspora' on the personal web site of an informant from Pennsylvania. He explains that,

> Evidence of the Clearances (*Na Fuadaichean*) can be seen *everywhere* in the Highlands and Islands. The evidence is there in the form of thousands of ruined and/or overgrown villages and homesteads. But only a few sites are identified in any way. (www.geovisualbusinessmaps.com/diaspora.htm; emphasis in original)

Unlike the intentional monuments erected at Glencoe, Glenfinnan and Culloden, such ruins may be understood as 'unintentional monuments'. Thus, while the art historian Alois Riegl, in his 1903 essay 'The Modern Cult of Monuments', defines an intentional monument as a 'human creation, erected for the specific purpose of keeping single human deeds or events ... alive in the minds of future generations' (1982: 21), unintentional monuments may be said to have *acquired* commemorative value, even though this was 'not their original purpose and significance' (ibid.: 23). Of course, unintentional monuments, such as the remains of 'overgrown villages and homesteads', may become intentional monuments in so far as their mnemonic potential may be appropriated and they may be reconstructed to recall a specific set of events. This process is most apparent when such sites are developed into heritage attractions and provisioned with interpretative panels and such like: thus, a growing number of 'Clearance villages' may be found throughout the Highlands (examples include Rosal and Achinlochy in Sutherland, Badbae in Caithness, Leitir Fura on Skye, and Milton of Glen Banchor in Badenoch) (Figure 7.3).

This transition from ruin to monument, *milieu de mémoire* to *lieu de mémoire*, is not, however, always so intrusively effected. Thus, the aforementioned *Highland Clearances Trail* by Rob Gibson (1996a) and a leaflet entitled 'In the footsteps of the Clearances' produced by the Skye and Lochalsh Museum Service (1998) narrate these landscapes without materially altering the landscapes themselves – they merely alter their meanings

Figure 7.2 The uninterpreted ruins of Broubster in Caithness. Such unintentional monuments remain 'open emblems' and, though often of a later period, are often regarded as 'evidence' of the Highland Clearances (Paul Basu)

Figure 7.3 Through interpretation, the mnemonic potential of deserted settlement sites such as Rosal in Sutherland is appropriated and the unintentional monument is remade as an intentional monument commemorating the Clearances (Paul Basu)

(by the very attribution of meaning). The 'In the footsteps of the Clearances' leaflet, one of a series produced by the museum service, is itself a fascinating memorial text, juxtaposing explanatory prose with archive images of an inhabited and cultivated crofting landscape, 'eyewitness' accounts of the Clearances, photographs of the now-deserted and ruinous settlements, brief histories of each site and maps showing walking routes that encourage visitors to explore the sites for themselves.

These sites do much more than merely arouse curiosity. 'The deserted place "remembers" and grows lonely', writes Kathleen Stewart (1996: 156). It is as if the landscape itself 'holds' the memory of its past and tells its own story, quite separate from the subject who perceives it. Thus Neil Gunn writes of the Sutherland clanlands of the MacKeamish Gunns, cleared in 1813–14,

> In Kildonan there is today a shadow, a chill, of which any sensitive mind would, I am convinced, be vaguely aware, though possessing no knowledge of the clearances. We are affected strangely by any place from which the tide of life has ebbed. (1987: 32)

The 'sense of place' may therefore be experienced as if it is emitted from or dwells in place itself, an *animus loci*. Yet, of course, such a sense is derived from the experiencing subject, or, more precisely, from the juxtaposition of subject, place and the specific circumstances of the encounter (weather conditions, season, prior knowledge, etc.). We do not, after all, experience place naïvely: as Casey notes, knowledge of place is not 'subsequent to perception' but is 'ingredient in perception itself' (1996: 18). The landscape is never inert, never a material *tabula rasa* awaiting inscription, but is always already embedded within webs of personal and cultural narratives, memories and associations (Tilley 1994).

But just as the past may be objectified or externalised in the landscape as sites of memory, so the sites of memory – and thus the past they seem to embody – become internalised through individual engagement and encounter with them. Bourdieu characteristically describes this process as the *'dialectic of the internalization of externality and the externalization of internality'* (1977: 72; italics in original). This dialectic has the effect of 'reflecting back' the emotions that a visitor unconsciously invests in a site, mystifying as well as magnifying the poignancy of the experience. As Young cogently argues, 'by themselves, monuments are of little value, mere stones in the landscape' (1993: 2): how and what we remember in their company 'depends very much on who we are, why we care to remember, and how we see' (ibid.: xii). For the returning 'exiles' who feel the presence of their ancestors at Culloden or sense them among the tumbled down ruins of an old croft house, the *lieux de mémoire* of the Scottish Highlands have a very particular resonance.

But to begin to understand the depth of feeling engendered in home-comers at these sites, we again need to return to Nora. The *lieux de mémoire*, he explains, 'are fundamentally remains, the ultimate embodiments of a memorial consciousness that has barely survived in a historical age that calls out for memory because it has abandoned it' (1989: 11). 'The passage from memory to history', he continues, 'has required every social group to redefine its identity through the revitalisation of its own history' (ibid.: 15); there is, he suggests, a concern among such groups that without this 'commemorative vigilance, history would soon sweep them away' (ibid.: 12). But neither is this concern restricted to institutions of the state, ethnic groups or other collectivities: the obligation to remember falls as keenly on the individual (ibid.: 15). The sites of memory effectively become 'bastions' upon which we 'buttress our identities', bastions that would be uncalled-for 'if what they defended were not threatened' (ibid.: 12). Individual memories thus 'surface at the interstices of broken collective memories', and it is 'amidst the remnants of the collective memories of family, church, and nation [that] the individual forges his identity by historicizing his own memory' (Hutton 1993: 151). Nowhere is this more apparent than in the practices of genealogical research, in which everyone is quite literally called to be 'his own historian' (Nora 1989: 15).

'What is being remembered?' Nora asks. 'In a sense', he suggests, 'it is memory itself' (ibid.: 16). We may come to the same conclusion when considering the phenomenon of roots tourism in the Scottish Highlands, and these journeys may indeed be understood as being driven by an absence of memory and a need to somehow re-establish continuity with a past ruptured by successive migrations and the forgetfulness of assimilation. Time and again, this compulsion to remember the past in order to relocate the self in time and space – in history – is articulated by my informants in their adherence to the adage that 'in order to know who one is and where one is going, one must know where one has come from':

> I am deeply interested in my origins and roots. Without this interest I would consider myself an eternal refugee. / Family history is a great help to orientate oneself in the world. / I am the product of my ancestors. Knowing them helps me understand myself. / How can one fully know one's identity if one doesn't know from whence he/she came? / To understand my heritage and where I come from helps to understand myself and my place in the world. / Understanding my roots helps me to know who I am and why I am who I am! / Knowing my family origins tells me who I am. / It is important to know who my family was so that I can better understand who I am. / It gives me a better understanding of who I am and what my place in the world is. / To know who one is, one must know their ancestors. / It's easier to figure where you are going if you know where you come from: cliché but true. / Knowledge of one's origins is a basis for a sense of self worth. / You have to know where you came from in order to know where you are going.

Such is the 'mantra' of the family historian.

This spatialisation of memory – knowing *where* one has come from – is, of course, intrinsic to a more fundamental metaphorical logic through which we communicate abstractions, but in a context in which the past is perceived quite literally as a country that has become foreign, the possibility of physically visiting that past invests the practice of roots tourism with a powerfully symbolic aura. It will be abundantly evident from the above oft-repeated comments that these journeys to the past are also journeys of self-understanding and self-knowledge, and, thus, in a fusion of the metaphorical, the metaphysical and the mundane, the sites of memory, which are their destinations, become hugely significant. This is true of the sites of *collective* memory such as Culloden and even the diffuse unintentional monuments of the Clearances, but especially so of those sites that speak directly to the individual. Is it any wonder, then, that the sight of an ancestor's initials, scratched, prior to emigrating, into a stone in the now ruinous walls of an old family croft should induce a tumult of mixed emotions in the 'returning' descendant? (Figure 7.4). Through such affective processes the sites of memory become 'sources of identity': originary places from which the identity of the self is perceived to derive, and to which the self, thirsting for identity, may resort for sustenance.

Figure 7.4 'H M' – the initials of Henry Macdonald scratched into a stone in the wall of the family croft house at Upper Lappan, Dunbeath, prior to his emigration to Australia in the 1920s. Several of Henry's descendants have made the journey back to visit the old home and see the initials (Paul Basu)

8 Homecomings

Self-seeking in late modernity

'Identity', argues psychologist Dan McAdams, 'is the problem of unity and purpose in human life' (1997: 60). Because of a 'confluence of disorientating factors such as wars, campaigns of genocide, rapid technological and ideological change, the breakdown of moral authority, and the saturation of the mass media', the self can no longer be thought of as a unitary entity (McAdams 1997: 48). Instead we have witnessed what Berger *et al.* call a 'pluralization of the lifeworld' (1973: 64) and the rise of a 'protean' self (Lifton 1993). As McAdams explains,

> Like the Greek god Proteus, one takes on whatever forms and qualities that a particular life situation demands. One juggles multiple roles, tries on different hats, different lives, forging selves whose unity is at best tentative and provisional, selves waiting to be dissolved into new combinations or even discarded for brand new editions when life changes and new challenges arise. (1997: 48).

Whilst proteanism represents an adaptive model for how to live amid a world of perceived mobility and fragmentation, McAdams claims that it has left the individual feeling 'few connections to the past and little faith in the future' (ibid.; Lasch 1991: 68). This results in an inability in people to make meaningful and long-term commitments to each other, to institutions and 'to the more enduring aspects of selfhood that may reside beneath the surface of everyday role-playing' (McAdams 1997: 48). The self for which the modern individual thus thirsts is a deeper, more unified, more enduring, and more meaningful one.

As self-identity has become 'increasingly open-ended, transitory [and] liable to on-going change' (Berger *et al.* 1973: 78), it has simultaneously been called upon to fill a 'value gap' resulting from the decline in traditional 'value bases' such as family, church and community (Baumeister 1997: 199). Thus, the 'subjective realm of identity' has also become 'the individual's main foothold in reality' (Berger *et al.* 1973: 78) and the self has acquired a new moral value: 'more than just the agent who decides how to implement moral principles and other obligations . . . it is now the source of those moral principles and obligations' (Baumeister 1997: 201; Taylor 1989). Consequently, the need to 'know' the self has become one of life's imperatives, whilst, at the same time, the nature of the self (its 'knowability') has become increasingly complex and problematised. The pursuit of self-knowledge has therefore 'come to be regarded as an important, large and difficult task' (Baumeister 1997: 204).

The self may thus be regarded as a 'reflexive project' (Giddens 1991: 75), requiring 'a concerted examination of the modern person's rich inner life, where it is assumed, some form of truth or meaning may be discerned' (McAdams 1997: 62). Whilst this 'hermeneutics of the self' (Foucault 1988: 46) implies the divination of something present but obscure within the self, in fact the project is not reconstructive, but constructive in nature. The process of 'selfing', most explicit in the practices of psychoanalysis and self-realisation therapies, should not, Donald Spence argues, be understood as an archaeological project in which the 'true self' is excavated from the recesses of suppressed memory, so much as a creative project in which the self constructs a narrative of itself which is, above all, 'true' to its own logic (1984). The object of a self-narrative is not its 'fit' to some hidden reality, but rather its 'external and internal *coherence, livability,* and *adequacy*' (Polonoff cited by J. Bruner 1990: 112). 'We achieve our personal identities and self-concept through the use of . . . narrative configuration, and make our existence into a whole by understanding it as an expression of a single unfolding and developing story' (Polkinghorne cited by J. Bruner 1990: 115–16) – which is to say, that self-narration is not only a descriptive act, but also a *generative* act through which the self emerges (Kerby 1991: 4).

This is not, however, to suggest that there are not constraints on an individual's self-constructions. The 'narrating subject' is, after all, also a 'narrated subject', and is, furthermore, limited in its auto-creativity by the possibilities of its particular habitus. As Anthony Kerby explains,

> It should be clear that such narratives are considerably influenced by the social milieu in which the human subject functions. The stories we tell of ourselves are determined not only by how other people narrate us but also by our language and the genres of storytelling inherited from our traditions. Indeed, much of our self-narrating is a matter of becoming conscious of the narratives that we already live with and in. . . . It seems true to say that we have already been narrated from a third-person perspective prior to our even gaining competence for self-narration. Such external narratives will understandably set up expectations and constraints on our personal self-descriptions, and they significantly contribute to the material from which our own narratives are derived. (1991: 6)

A pertinent elaboration of this notion of 'narrative heritage' may be found in the work of the Scottish moral philosopher, Alasdair MacIntyre, who himself emigrated to the USA in 1970:

> I inherit from the past of my family, my city, my tribe, my nation, a variety of debts, inheritances, rightful expectations and obligations. These constitute the given of my life, my moral starting point. . . . The story of my life is always embedded in the story of those communities from which I derive my identity. . . . What I am, therefore, is in key part what I inherit, a specific past that is present to some degree in my present. I find myself part of a history and that is generally to say, whether I like it or not, whether I recognise it or not, one of the bearers of a tradition. (1981: 205–6)

It may, therefore, be more correct to say that a dialectical tension exists between the 'narrating self' and the 'narrated self' (Lambek and Antze 1996: xviii), and that the 'life story is jointly authored by the person and his or her defining culture or cultures' (McAdams 1997: 63).

The relationship between 'self-determination' and 'external determination' is not, however, simply a contest between choice and constraint. As Mary Waters has explored in her analysis of the 'ethnic options' open to white, middle-class American citizens, there is a large degree of choice available to individuals of mixed 'ethnicity' in their negotiations of identity (evinced, for example, in that fact that her informants' self-defined ethnic identities changed over time and in different contexts (1990: 16)). However, Waters also makes clear that this choice is determined by a range of external factors such as knowledge of ancestors, surname, physical appearance and the relative 'ranking' of different ethnic groups, and is therefore not entirely 'free' (or, indeed, free from prejudice) (ibid.: 57). Furthermore 'choice' is rarely understood as such, and ethnicity continues to be perceived as a fixed, biological attribute of the individual, an 'objective fact' and not a social construct or a symbolic resource (ibid.: 18, 167). This is certainly evident in my own informants' comments, and, indeed, it is the proclaimed absence of choice that is striking in many of their statements. Scottish identity is thus frequently described as being 'in the blood', 'in the marrow of my bones', and so forth. As an informant from Ontario explains, 'For me, being Scottish is not a choice, it's in the blood. It is something which has no name, but yet lingers there within me'.

This genetic connection with an ancestral identity is often also extended to places associated with these ancestors. Thus a profound 'resonance' is felt at certain sites: something strange and affecting, which is rationalised (or, perhaps, further mystified) as a 'race memory', 'ancestral memory' or 'genetic memory'. An informant from Washington speculates,

Do we have a genetically inherited memory for places? Is this the real secret of 'déjà vu'? Is this why we bite back the tears of sorrow at the sound of the bagpipes? Are we responding to memories that we have, but have no understanding of?

Another, from Victoria, Australia, ponders on the exact nature of her inheritance from her Ayrshire ancestors,

> Something of those early Strachans does remain – it's buried in me and all those other Strachan descendants now scattered all over the world. We all share a genetic inheritance derived from those generations of Ayrshire coal mining families. And I hope it is an inheritance that affects more than the colour of our skin, hair and eyes.

Interested in Jungian psychology, this informant felt that her journey to Scotland was also a journey into the 'Scottish psyche' and, ultimately, a journey into herself: 'I come from those people, I share that psyche, therefore journeying into it is a journey into myself'.

In seeking ontological security in an era of existential anxiety, Giddens argues that the self creates coherence and continuity, through narrative, by situating itself on a 'trajectory' from the remembered past to an anticipated future. In this reflexive project, he explains, 'we are, not what we are, but what we make of ourselves', and, to these ends, 'the individual appropriates his past by sifting through it in the light of what is anticipated for an (organised) future' (1991: 75). The self thus creatively 'reworks' the past to suit its future-orientated present (ibid.: 85). Crucially, however, I suggest that, in order to provide that ontological security, the constructive nature of this project must remain obscure and must, instead, be misrecognised by the subject as a *re*constructive process. The narrating self may, I contend, effectively *choose* to reject choice, and continue to believe in a '"real", inner, essential [self] that lives behind the public presentation of self' (McAdams 1997: 64). From the roots tourist's perspective, for example, the revelation that 'we are what we make of ourselves' provides little consolation; what is sought is not a deconstruction of the myth of self, but rather its revitalisation. Thus, to answer those insistent questions of late modernity – 'What to do? How to act? *Who to be?*' (Giddens 1991: 75; emphasis added) – the genealogist turns to the supposedly indubitable inheritance of the blood, and intuits there a vague memory of 'home'. As an informant from Pennsylvania explains, 'it's like having the Highland soil coursing through my veins, having dreams of a land I've never seen and love for a family I've never known'.

The grail

In his influential work *After Virtue*, MacIntyre explores the idea that the contemporary search for self may be understood as a 'quest', that life itself can be defined as a journey of self-discovery (1981: 203–4). The heroic quest narrative has long been used to allegorise the trials and tribulations of the 'journey of life', but what attracts MacIntyre to this metaphor is the particular nature of its destination. There is, for example, the very positing of a destination or 'final *telos*', which motivates the quest in the first place; more significant, however, is the fact that this anticipated destination remains essentially indeterminate. The quest is a journey to an unknown destination. 'It is clear', MacIntyre writes, 'the medieval conception of a quest is not at all that of a search for something already adequately characterised', but, rather, it is only through the process of questing that 'the goal of the quest is finally to be understood' (1981: 204). The quest is therefore 'always an education both as to the character of that which is sought and in self-knowledge' (ibid.). The 'mysterious object' at the heart of the quest – something that remains abstruse, inadequately defined, but which is nevertheless intuited and glimpsed obliquely – is, I suggest, also an essential aspect of the 'mystical homecoming' that is roots tourism.

'Root metaphors' such as 'quest', 'homecoming', and 'pilgrimage' (and they are, of course, also 'route metaphors') not only provide a heuristic framework for the 'etic' interpretation of these contemporary travel practices (Ortner 1973; Lakoff and Johnson 1980). They are also commonly used by roots tourists themselves to describe and characterise their journeys, and therefore provide an insight into the 'emic' interpretation of these practices (see Basu 2004b). Thus, Sarida, an informant from Texas, draws upon ideas of pilgrimage and quest to explain the homecoming experience:

> A Diasporic Scot returning to the ancestral lands is more of a traveler or pilgrim than a tourist. He or she is not necessarily going to the major tourist centers or popular destinations of Scotland. Usually there is a quest involved here, a quest for ancestors or the lands where the family originated. A quest for lost memories and traditions, a hunger for identity and belonging, a reaching for connections from something severed long ago. Like the quest for the Grail itself, it is a complex, convoluted and perilous journey and perhaps the Grail of our selves is unobtainable.

Another informant, Frank, from Colorado, goes further, drawing out other correspondences between the genealogical journey to Scotland and the 'archetypal' grail quest, including its associations between the health of the land and the health of the person, and the healing potential of the journey itself.

In the old Grail myths there is a sense that the holy object can simultaneously heal the king of his wound, as well as the land itself . . . Like many other instances of Celtic sovereignty, in the old Grail tales the king is connected to the land. What happens to the king happens to the land. So, in this context, the Arthurian tales speak of the land falling into a wounded state because of the wounded king.

The knights are sent out on a quest for the only object that can restore the king and the land: the Grail. In the tales there is a guiding question that if answered truly will result in the seeker finding the true grail. The question? What ails thee?

So, not to discount the line of inquiry re: are we tourists?, but whether one is a Homeland or a Diaspora Scot I think another question to ask alongside this is: what ails thee?

How does participating in the dynamism of the Scottish landscape assist you in that ailment? What was wounded in the first place, and is that wound related to the Scottish landscape itself?

In my own participation with the Scottish landscape, and my own family's relationship to our place of origin (Argyll, the Isles and the Orkneys), the premise of the Arthurian and other Celtic tales seems to suggest a formula of sorts.

There is an old saying, 'The healing of the wound must come from the blood of the wound itself'. This denotes the biological reality that it is largely the blood of the wound that cleanses the wound. If the blood is our ancestry and cultural heritage as well as the landscape and the wound is a ripping up of foundation, a severing of connectedness, the formula suggests that it is precisely by revisiting the landscape that we begin to participate 'in the quest' for our healing and reconnection.

Whilst some may find the New Age tone unpalatable, Frank articulates what remains implicit or at best vaguely intuited in many roots tourists' journeys. Although rarely stated as such, for many the homecoming journey *is* a therapeutic act. And if, as this informant suggests, the journey provides the cure through reconnecting the roots tourists with the 'bloodlines' of their ancestry and cultural heritage, then it is left for us to extrapolate the ailment: the loss of 'memories and traditions', 'a hunger for identity and belonging', a sense of being 'severed' from one's roots?

The wasteland motif of the grail quest is also significant in the context of the Scottish diaspora. Wandering around those areas of the Scottish Highlands affected by the Clearances or subsequent depopulations – landscapes of ruins and deserted settlements – one is left with the impression that the 'land' has indeed fared ill. Similarly, from an ecological perspective, Frank Fraser Darling has written that, due to deforestation and generations of environmental mismanagement, 'the Highlands are a devastated countryside', and that this 'man-made devastation is no environment for psychological health in a people' (quoted in Hunter 1995: 151). The 'struggle' for and with the land is key to contemporary Highland identity in both homeland and diaspora. As we shall see in Chapter 9, the Clearance narrative in particular provides the diaspora with its traumatic 'origin myth' and leaves many roots tourists in no doubt that their ancestors were *pushed* from the land, torn away from their foundations, rather than *pulled* by the prospect of opportunity in the New World, severers of their own roots.

Regardless of whether, in the majority of cases, this claim of being an exiled people, separated from the land which confers their identity, withstands serious scrutiny, the narrative is internalised and is central to many individuals' senses of what it means to be descended from Highland Scots. The 'memory-myth' is transmogrified over generations, incited by periodic jingoism and mobilised in the arena of a global identity politics. Little wonder, then, that at an individual level the 'exile's return' is an often poignant and restorative experience.

Drawing upon three North American examples, I should now like to explore the nature of these homecoming journeys in more detail. Here, then, I switch register and, making extensive use of interview material, tell three stories of three journeys.

Sounding the stones: Bonnie and Pat – Uig, Lewis

Bonnie, 56, and Pat, 54, are sisters. Both live in the state of Washington, USA. Bonnie is an education outreach manager, Pat an environmental project manager. Their great-grandparents, Malcolm Matheson and Margaret Buchanan, emigrated from the Isle of Lewis in Scotland's Outer Hebrides to Canada in 1870. This would be Bonnie's second visit to Lewis, Pat's third, but their first journey to the island together. Indeed both felt it was very important for them to make this trip 'as sisters'. In addition to five days on Lewis, Bonnie was also enjoying a walking holiday in the Highlands with her partner, while Pat had spent three days on Iona, a place sacred to both the early church and the contemporary 'Celtic spirituality' movement.

Pat's first visit to Lewis, in 1996, was very much a 'first pass', without the time or sufficient information to make much progress establishing family connections with either people or places. It was, however, a powerful experience with memorable visits to Callanish stones and to places associated with the broader Clan Matheson: 'I was the first of our family to actually go to Scotland. It changed my life and connected me with that part of my heritage'.

On returning home, Pat compiled a scrapbook about the trip, including accounts of places that she and her husband had visited, photographs they had taken, notes on Matheson clan history, copies of tourist leaflets and excerpts from a Canadian local history which included a biographical section about her pioneer great-grandfather. These she copied and distributed to family members as Christmas presents, encouraging them to make the journey themselves and add their own discoveries to the book. What especially surprised Pat in that first visit was a feeling of connectedness to her *female* ancestors:

> As the boat approached Lewis, I could almost 'see' years of Scottish women on the shores and bogs. I got my first real sense of the female side of the Scots (it had been a very male based, bagpipe playing, Scotch drinking part of my US upbringing) and I suddenly felt like I acquired a lineage of strong Scots women that was not available to me in our male clan family mythology.

This is a significant observation, not least for the academic study of the Scottish diaspora, which also inevitably focuses on that most visible aspect of 'Highland' identity: the masculine myth of clanship with its patronyms and parades, its games and gatherings (see Ray 2005). Thus, rather than the specificities of a particular family's story, Bonnie and Pat had been raised with a more generic sense of 'Scottishness':

BONNIE: What we were brought up on was what a 'true Scot' was.
PAT: 'The clan.'
BONNIE: The clan, the family, the sense of honour, the integrity, the loyalty . . . that you stuck together and took care of your own, that you were honourable and honest and hard-working . . . hard-drinking probably too!
PAT: It was very male.

Considering this gendered bias, I asked whether their father had any interest in visiting Lewis himself.

BONNIE: I think Dad is one of those Scots who would never come back, regardless of what his health was or circumstances, because he would not have wanted the reality to be any different from the dream. He's been the quintessential Scot all my life, I mean we've had the tartans up in the house, and he's taught himself to play the pipes, and most of his closest friends are Scots – of Scottish heritage – and he's kept alive in his heart and in his mind his image of what Lewis and the Highlands were. And I don't think he would ever have wanted that to have been challenged.
PAT: I certainly encouraged him to go – before I'd been here – and I think other people had. You know, it was 'Why don't you go?' The direct answer always was, 'Oh no, it's just a bunch of big cities now . . . it's not like Scotland was'. He sort of ended up taking the easy way out.

Here the fascinating, and familiar, complexity of diasporic identity is apparent: the binary opposition between the urban/inauthentic/uprooted present of the diaspora and the rural/authentic/rooted past of the homeland. But there is also a reflexive awareness that such a view is a myth, or likely to be so, and Bonnie and Pat's father engages in a willing suspension of disbelief. He prefers to live with the myth rather than to risk exploding it by discovering that Scotland, too, has entered the twenty-first century. The sisters were disappointed that he couldn't be persuaded, especially after they themselves had taken the chance. Bonnie explained that when Pat returned from her first trip, 'the image that she brought back wasn't just as good as what the dream was, it was better'.

As we visited places associated with the family history – burial grounds, the sites of deserted townships, the beach near the village where their great-grandfather was born and lived before emigrating – I wondered whether Bonnie and Pat also had a sense of travelling back in time, of visiting the past in this 'other' country.

> PAT: I think part of the excitement has been that when we got to come and see these places, we know that they look relatively like they did at the time of the ancestors that we're finding out about. There hasn't been a lot of change, and so you get to see it with those eyes and go, my God! this is what it looked like 150 years ago! . . . this is what the beach at Aird looked like when our great-grandfather decided to leave . . . I don't think you get that chance too often.

Of course such an opportunity does not exist – not, at least, to the same extent – for those roots tourists who trace their ancestors to Scotland's cities or those areas that have been more heavily developed. But, nevertheless, rural Lewis *has* entered the twenty-first century: I asked Bonnie and Pat whether they were slightly disappointed that their old country 'cousins' were living with all the comforts and conveniences of any modern North American suburban home?

> BONNIE: No, I don't think I expected everyone to still live in blackhouses. I think what amazes me is that, as difficult as it must be to make a living in this area, the people are affluent enough to almost take for granted double-glass windows, heating systems in separate rooms, not just mod cons, but high quality, very modern, state-of-the-art conveniences.

There are, of course, others for whom the idea of a dishwasher and watching CNN on satellite television does not accord with their image of the homeland, and we found advertising leaflets for the nearby 'Gearrannan Blackhouse Village' appealing to this market. Here is 'a cluster of thatched, drystone buildings overlook[ing] the Atlantic Ocean';

self-catering cottages, where you can 'immerse yourself in the ancient culture of the West Side of Lewis' and find 'a haven of peace and tranquillity' in the 'traditional setting'. Needless to say, the 'traditional setting' does not extend to the inconvenience of sleeping on lice-infested straw mattresses, cooking on a smoky peat fire, or surviving a week without running water and a flush toilet.

After Pat's original visit, Bonnie took on the role of family historian and made contact with the Harris-based genealogist, Bill Lawson. Lawson was able to produce a basic family-tree chart and sufficient information for Bonnie to plan an 'ancestor-hunting' trip more precisely. Thus, when Bonnie made her first visit to Lewis in 1998, she had some knowledge of the region her ancestors had lived in. Serendipity played its part too, however, when Bonnie found herself staying at a hostel, 'which turns out to have been the manse just above the old cemetery where all our people had been buried for hundreds of years'. The hostel manager, not a Lewisman himself, suggested Bonnie contact a member of the local historical society: 'once I'd made contact with her, it was just like doors opening'.

Bonnie soon found herself being invited to tea at the house of 90-year-old Malcolm Og and his sister, Peggy Ann, with whom, she was told, she shared a nineteenth-century ancestor. This was to be a very significant meeting for Bonnie.

> Malcolm was special to me because he was the first person who could tell me what life had been like, and he was the first person who could say to me, 'Well, yes, I'm directly related to you,' you know, 'We have the same blood, the same genes, and this is where your family was from. This is your home country. This is your home soil, and, yes, where you are is where your ancestors have been buried'. It was very much like being at the nexus of all my questions at that time, and it was like suddenly having discovered this phenomenal resource.

Malcolm was well known locally for his great knowledge of genealogy and he had many stories to tell Bonnie of their common ancestors. Alas, he could throw no light on why Bonnie's great-grandfather was the only one of nine siblings to leave Lewis for Canada. Bonnie had hoped to introduce Pat to Malcolm Og during their current visit, but it was with sadness that she learnt of his death a few months before they were due to leave.

What had begun in Pat's visit only two years previously as a general interest in the Matheson clan, its history and lands, had now become a very particular quest. The generic clan identity, so important in the sisters' 'Scottish upbringing', seemed to have become almost irrelevant in the context of new, more personally relevant intrigues: Why did Bonnie and Pat's great-grandparents leave Lewis? Why did Malcolm say that their great-great-grandfather, born in the early nineteenth century, was not a 'true' Matheson? He seems to have been adopted by the family, but what were the circumstances? And what about the story of their Buchanan ancestor who had to be carried across Uig Sands when the family home was 'cleared'? These were some of the questions the sisters had in mind as they visited and enjoyed the hospitality of other sets of distant cousins Bonnie had subsequently discovered: Mathesons, Buchanans, MacAulays, Mackays, all still living in close proximity to one another.

The contrast between the communities the sisters found on Lewis and those among which they lived in the USA was marked, 'I mean, I barely know my neighbours on both sides', remarked Bonnie. The experience was sufficient to alter the way in which she perceived herself:

> I feel 'webbed' for the first time . . . I tend to be a pretty visual person, and if I were to have drawn my family before, we would have looked at a circle, and then there would have been five dots or whatever inside the circle. After having been here, if I were to draw my family again, we are then looking at a central circle, but [with] all sorts of overlapping designs and arms shooting out with circles on them in each area based on which family connection we happen to be investigating at a time . . . It just expands, not only my vision of who those individual people are, and that knowing them enriches my life, but it expands in some way my perception of who I am myself, because it connects me to all these other people.

But if this homecoming was more 'people centred' than many such journeys, Bonnie and Pat's hosts were also keen to show their 'American cousins' the land. Here, then, were the remains of the blackhouse that the sisters' great-great-great-great-aunt once occupied at Bostadh on Bernera. The village had been abandoned in the 1870s, but the MacAulays who guided them knew exactly which of its several ruins had been the family home. They were told that stones from the houses had been used to build the nearby cemetery walls. They were also shown the remains of a recently excavated Iron Age settlement: 'this could have been the home of an ancient MacAulay', someone joked. But the joke was only partly in jest. Spread before Bonnie and Pat was at least 2,000 years of Bostadh's history – and they were part of that history.

Journeying from the impersonal masculine clan myth evoked in castles and feuds, tartans and tales of clan chiefs, Bonnie and Pat had found their own personal heritage in the intricacies of their genealogical charts, in the stories of Malcolm Og and other new-found relatives, in an outline of turf-covered stones that mark the place of an abandoned home. But ultimately the process is not one of extracting the individual family story from a broader social or cultural history. On the contrary, it is through the family narrative, made tangible in the homecoming journey, that the grand narratives of history may be understood in their true human dimensions.

The 'history' in which Bonnie and Pat's own story could now be placed was not about clans and tartans, but about the struggle of a rural community undergoing structural change. We were taken to see a cairn erected to commemorate the 'Bernera Riot' of 1874 (Figure 8.1).[1] The 'riot', a demonstration of resistance and solidarity among the small tenant farmers against the unrestrained power of their landlords, represents for many a turning point in the Highland 'land war', the beginning of a process that eventually led to far-reaching agrarian reform (Buchanan 1996: 25). It was in the context of this struggle that Bonnie and Pat's great-grandparents left Lewis.

Neither is the struggle over; it continues in more insidious form. 'This is a dying place', one elderly relation told us. 'I could take you to the place where my grandfather's house was, but it's been taken away. Its walls were up when I was a boy ... The gravel was more important than the house, so the house lost out'. Whilst accepting the inevitability of change, there is still an understated resistance to the notion that the economic benefits of a quarry, for instance, should necessarily take precedence over the rich store of memory and symbolism represented by the crumbling ruins of a house.

This same relation described how his great-grandfather (Bonnie and Pat's great-great-great-great-grandfather) had been cleared from the township of Carnish to marginal land at Aird in 1849. He explained that until recently there were ten houses at Aird, 'now there are six, and of the six three are occupied ... and not a young soul among them'. Thus the struggle for the land continues, the irony observed in many regions of the Highlands and Islands being that once the battle against rampant landlordism was won, there was a far greater adversary to contend with: the desire of the young to leave the region and seek opportunities elsewhere.

Both Bonnie and Pat felt a particular affinity for Uig Sands. This was the bay across which, according to Malcolm Og's story, their Buchanan ancestor had to be carried when he, too, was cleared from the family home at Carnish, this time to Crowlista on the opposite side; this was also the location of the ancient burial ground at Balnakeil that Bonnie discovered on her first trip.

> I'm tied to Uig Sands. I don't know why ... Balnakeil just represents sort of the centre of the historical universe for me, and it is a particularly beautiful setting, and for me, if I were to picture my historic home then it's going to be some place on Uig Sands, whether its Carnish that sits on one side or Crowlista on the other side. That bay is sort of 'ground zero' for me. It's strange that it didn't turn out to be Aird, but Aird to me is always a sort of removal place, some place that we went after we left the homeland.

'Homeland', then, which once may have been defined by Bonnie and Pat as Scotland as a whole, and only later as Lewis, was now identified not

Figure 8.1 Bonnie and Pat visiting the Bernera Riot Cairn (Paul Basu)

even as the parish of Uig or as Aird, the village of ten houses where their great-grandfather (the one who emigrated to Canada) was born, but to what they understand to be their great-grandfather's own ancestral home two or three miles away.

For Bonnie, especially, the connection to place extended to the people of that place: descendants of those same ancestors, the ones who have stayed in the area.

> Whereas our ancestors were cleared off Carnish and moved from their ancestral home into a multitude of other small villages, there was always a remnant that [stayed] in the area, and their being in this area made it currently relevant to me. That I intellectually like knowing that they'd been here for hundreds of years, but it was important to me emotionally that they were still here. I think Americans, and particularly someone whose life history has been as nomadic as mine has been, suffer from that lack of sense of place, and for me it wasn't just the natural surroundings, but my sense of place includes the people.

Bonnie and Pat were welcomed into the homes of strangers as cousins. 'So you're a Matheson *and* a Buchanan? – Yes, I can see it now', said one distant relation. 'We're two of a kind', said another. Bonnie was conscious of an irony that after just two visits to Uig, totalling perhaps no more than seven days, she somehow belonged to the place and its people in a way that incomers who may have lived in the area for decades could not. She referred to the owner of the hostel she had stayed at on her first visit.

> As Richard at the inn there says, he will never be an insider in this culture. It doesn't matter that he's lived here for twenty years and he's raised his kids here, he will never have the same status in the community as I do. And I haven't lived here at all! But the connections, that unseen Scottish chemistry, the blood and sinew and bone, whatever, that somehow is shared in some respect, however dilute, between the people who live here and those of us who come back looking for our roots separate us from the English people who come to the island, from the Germans who come to the island.

The issue is not whether Bonnie is correct in her assessment of the local politics of belonging, but rather that she perceives her relationship to Uig, its people, places and culture, in these terms. Here, at 'ground zero', Bonnie found herself to be part of a web that extended beyond herself both spatially and temporally.

Such a search for connections as incontrovertible as those conferred by the 'blood, sinew and bone' of kinship was not always a part of Bonnie's self-conception, but rather an aspect of maturity, an evaluation of her 'true nature' after the self-forging ambitions of youth had subsided.

BONNIE: I think part of it is maturity. We didn't think seriously about coming here when we were much younger. I think you reach a certain age and you begin to want to place yourself in the stream. Instead of the young person's approach to life, which is kind of adventuresome and 'do everything' and 'no boundaries', I think maturity is beginning to understand that there are limits on experience and there are limits on life, and there's a structure and a pattern in your life, and that you can see where you fit . . . and, for want of anything else, this visit is a matter of 'fit' for me.

It takes me back to the 'Scottish Soldier' song – do you [Pat] remember listening to that over and over? – I think there's a line in it somewhere that 'they aren't the hills of home' . . . you know, it's being supposedly sung by a fellow who's somewhere else, he's off fighting somewhere else and, 'the hills are beautiful and the hills are green, but they aren't the hills of home'.[2] And what it makes me think of is that you can understand why Scots have been adventuresome and travellers for hundreds of years, but there tends to be a need to come back and refuel, to refresh . . . and go out again. It doesn't mean that after you've been gone for a while, that you're somehow empty and you go home and you go home to stay, but that you can refresh yourself spiritually or emotionally or however it is that you need to tap into that energy that comes from the place you belong . . . and then you go again.

PAT: I keep thinking of the phrase you [Bonnie] and I talked about a long time ago. It doesn't have anything to do with Scotland – but it does to me now . . . It was something that had resonated literally with each of us, this process of a sculptor, how he sounds a stone. He sounds it, and it's by sounding it that he kind of figures out internally where it's dense and what resonates and what shape he could pull out of that. And Bonnie and I have done some talking about that, that we feel like a lot of our life has been about sounding stone and figuring out what rings true, what resonates internally.

BONNIE: Where the cracks are and what slabs chip off under pressure . . . and it's finding the shape underneath.

PAT: Part of this journey is a tap on that rock and we know whether it's true and real . . .

BONNIE: We're sounding the stone . . . we're sounding the stone.

For Bonnie and Pat, then, the journey to their ancestral homeland – Scotland, Lewis, Uig, the burial ground at Balnakeil – is about searching for their own 'shape', it is about self-knowledge. But, importantly, the shape is not determined (not, at least, perceived to be determined) by the self itself, but by a 'pattern' external to the self. The sisters needed to travel to a place outside their routine experience, a symbolic 'home from home', a far country into which they somehow 'fitted' and which represents the opportunity for personal renewal. Bonnie and Pat had 'sounded the stone' of their homeland and discovered in its web of intermingled histories, landscapes and genealogies something of themselves.

The last of the clan: Don – Strathnaver, Sutherland

Don is 74, a retired carpenter from Ohio. He has harboured an ambition to visit Scotland since childhood. At last the dream has come true thanks to his wife, Gladys, who has encouraged him to make the trip and who bought their air tickets as a 50th wedding anniversary present. After a week in the Highlands, visiting the 'Mackay country' of Strathnaver in Sutherland, Don and Gladys intend to spend a week in Edinburgh.

Don explained to me that he had been brought up to be proud of his Scottish heritage:

> I was raised a *proud* Mackay, and as a proud Scotsman. And my father used to say, 'Ahm a Heelan' Scot an' damned proud of it!' and I was raised that way. Oh yes, I've gotten into some pretty good fist fights over the fact that I was a Scotsman . . . *and I won 'em all*!

Yet, despite this bravado, he actually knows very little about his Scottish family history. Don had been very close to his grandfather, but

> Grandad didn't talk much. I really didn't know enough then to ask him. Didn't have sense enough to ask him about all that stuff. So, as far as his people and where they came from, I got very little of it. They did say something about one of them being born in Edinburgh, now I'm not sure about whether they were talking about my great-grand-mother or great-grandfather or somebody totally unrelated.

Indeed, Don's grandfather had led a colourful life. According to an old obituary Don showed me, he was born in England in 1860 and was brought to the USA at the age of eight when his parents emigrated. He was orphaned soon after and went to sea as a cabin boy working on the 'square riggers' plying between Liverpool and New York. He then jumped ship in New Orleans and worked his way up to Canada driving ox carts in lumber camps; he became a Pony Express rider carrying mail through Death Valley between Las Vegas and Fresno; and in 1876 he became an Indian scout in Custer's Seventh Cavalry. It is hardly surprising, then, that as a child Don was more than satisfied to hear about his grandfather's all-American adventures and wasn't particularly interested in the more distant past.

Don appeared to be used to narrating his own life adventures too. He had a repertoire of stories that he retold frequently, often repeating the exact phrasing. Many of these were quite brutal stories concerning the acquisition of what he identified as Scottish values and traits: loyalty, pride, self-reliance. For instance, there is one story of his grandfather telling Don he had no intention of leaving him any inheritance, 'firstly because I don't suppose I'll have anything to leave you, secondly, because if I did you'd only piss it away'. 'Instead', his grandfather explained, 'I'm going to leave you a trade, because, with a trade, a man will never go hungry'. Then there is the story of his father threatening to beat him if he caught him running away from the neighbourhood bullies; he made Don confront them, and 'from that day on I have never run from a man, I don't care how big he is: I'm seventy-four and I'll still stand and fight'. It was through such 'lessons' and the masculine posturing of his father and grandfather that Don learnt what it was to be a Scot in his neighbourhood in the 1930s:

> When I was a boy there were three Scottish families in a German and Italian neighbourhood: the McIntyres, the McLeods and the Mackays. Aside from being looked on as foreigners, my grandfather didn't help much by playing the pipes every night at nine o'clock. In the summer you could hear doors slamming for blocks around. He would pipe three pieces, one of which was the 'White Banner of Mackay', then he would go to bed and things would return to normal. Sometimes when I am sitting alone I can still hear him pipe.

Since his childhood Don has pursued a casual interest in Scottish culture – 'I've been pickin' up a little here, pickin' up a little there, a little Scots history, a little clan history' – but it was only when he damaged his back and was temporarily bed-bound a few years ago that the opportunity presented itself for him to look into his heritage more seriously: 'I decided to do what I had never had time to do before, find out who I was and where I came from'.

Don's research has mainly been conducted via the internet and has been focused on the Clan Mackay. Thus Don has read voraciously all he can find on Mackay genealogy: a genealogy of kings, chiefs and warriors spanning the centuries. Don's objective has been to connect his own family history to this exalted clan history:

> My great-grandfather is the missing link . . . If I can connect my great-grandfather to what I've got now, then I'm done. I've got it all . . . all the way back to Macbeth. Otherwise, I'm back to the 1830s, as far as I can go back.

Alas, he has been unable to locate any further information concerning his great-grandparents beyond their names on their son's death certificate, that vague reference to Edinburgh, an assumption that they were born in the 1830s, and a belief that the family were Mackays from Strathnaver in Sutherland.

Don had hoped that a meeting with the Highland Council's genealogist, Alistair Macleod, during the trip would help, but there were too few clues to go on. I asked Don whether he was disappointed at not being able to establish this link:

> Well, no, not really. Naturally I was expecting to find some definite, solid proof of my great-grandfather, but it's really evident that I'm not going to, not right now anyway. And I didn't come over here with the idea that I was absolutely going to find him, I came over with the idea that I was going to look.

To be honest, Don was expecting rather a lot of his elusive great-grandfather: a blood link with the characters of this clan mytho-history in which Don had steeped himself. He would have to contend himself with a working-class man and woman who appear to have lived in the north of England in the 1860s, emigrating with their child to North America before disappearing from the records and leaving Don's grandfather an orphan with a Highland surname and a sense of Scottish pride. And, like so many nineteenth-century immigrants, Don's grandfather epitomised the 'self-made man' ideal of the American dream: a wanderer without roots, an opportunist and a survivor.

Despite having failed to establish this link, Don still styles himself as 'the last of the clan':[3] 'I realised that I was the oldest living member of my branch of the Mackay clan. Then it hit me like a brick, when I go there will be no one old enough to remember'. And thus he set himself the task of 'writing' a book for the benefit of later generations of his family – particularly the male line. The volume, somewhat grandly entitled *The Book of Mackay*, is to have three parts: 'History of the House of Mackay', 'The House of Mackay' and 'Bits and Pieces from My Life'. The first two sections, which concern the clan, its history and genealogy, are comprised more or less entirely of print-outs from various Scottish-interest web sites. The final part is a compilation of autobiographical notes. Don hopes that this book will form a kind of family chronicle that his son, grandson and great-grandson will take forward after him.

> It ought to, when they get it, give 'em a pretty good insight of the clan from the beginning, all the way through, right up to their day – you know what I mean? – to right now. Then [my son] will add to it, then, when he goes, his son will add his bit to it, then my great-grandson will read that and he'll add his little bit to it.

It struck me that Don wanted to bequeath to his great-grandson what his own great-grandfather had not been able to bequeath to him: a past. I asked Don what 'bits and pieces' of his life he was including in the auto-biographical section.

I'll tell them the story that I just told you about Dad teaching me not to run. About my grandfather and what he said about ever leaving me anything other than a trade, stories like that that they have no other way of knowing, and I know they'd be interested in . . . I know I would, if I was a kid and I was sitting at somebody's knee and they were telling me stories like that, I'd be interested in them.

Don's book seemed to compensate for a regret for stories untold.

As we drove through the Highlands to North-West Sutherland, the Strathnaver homeland of the Mackays, Don advised me that he was not inclined to get emotional or indulge in daydreams and speculation, and that he believed there was more to Scotland than 'piles of stones and old graveyards'. He was responding to those messages posted to the Homecomings email discussion list, to which he subscribed, in which roots tourists described profound, even supernatural, experiences at ruins and burial grounds associated with their ancestors. Given his desire to play down the personal significance of such places, I asked Don why he felt compelled to make this journey to the clan homeland himself.

Because this is where I'm from. Not physically. I didn't physically come from here, I wasn't physically born here, but *this is where I'm from*, if you can understand that. Before, I was proud of being a Scot, because my father was a Scot, my grandfather was a Scot, my

Figure 8.2 Don overlooking the Kyle of Tongue, Sutherland (Paul Basu)

aunts, uncles, all of them were Scots. I was a Scot. I was proud of that. But this gives all that meaning . . . so that not only am I proud of being a Scot because of my family, but I'm proud of being a Scot because of this. This is where they lived. Because of the battles and that kind of thing that the clan had fought. I'm part of that clan. That's who I am.

That the experience of visiting a deserted township site near Bettyhill, or the Strathnaver Museum, housed in the old parish church at Farr and surrounded by its graveyard, did affect Don was evident despite his resistance to the idea. He counted fifteen or twenty gravestones which bore his own name or those of known relatives and marvelled that he might be standing among kin. Indeed, he seemed to forget that he hadn't actually substantiated any direct family connection to the area and that his great-grandfather apparently died (or, at least, disappeared) after emigrating to the USA:

> I looked at those stones and I thought now, by golly, that could be my great-grandfather buried there, because I know he came from this area, the Strathnaver area. That's where I was, and being in that area gave me the feeling like, well, hey, my great-grandad used to run around here. Now here I am standing where he at one time stood.

In effect, Don's 'history' began when his eight-year-old grandfather was brought to the USA in 1868. He was unable to find the missing link that connected him incontrovertibly with the more ancient cultural heritage represented by the far country of Strathnaver. Whilst denying any inclination to speculate, it appeared, however, that Don had unconsciously 'forged' that link. This extended to internalising the Clearance narrative and using it to explain his own family's plight. In a posting to the Homecomings list, Don claimed that he came 'from a family that at one time was cleared from Strathnaver'; and even that his grandfather was shamefully aware of repeating history in his own actions, implicated as he was in the 'clearance' of native Americans from their lands to make way for European settlers:

> My grandfather was an Indian scout for General Armstrong Custer's 7th Cavalry. In later years he made mention of the fact that he was not too proud of the fact that he had been a part of the same actions that had brought his family to [the United States]. His father was a child when they were forced from their home and he felt he was betraying the family by being a part of yet another eviction.

This despite admitting in another email, 'to be true about the whole issue of the Clearances all I really know about it is from writings by Ian Grimble and John Prebble'.[4] But identity is not contingent on the 'facts' of history or the family tree, and, as such, the 'fact' that Don has been unable to ascertain that his family came from Strathnaver, let alone that they were affected by the infamous Sutherland clearances of the early nineteenth century, is of secondary importance. Of primary importance is that, consciously or not, Don chooses to identify with the tragedy myth of a once noble people reduced to exile.

In the Strathnaver Museum, Don was struck by the fact that the clan armorials and insignia that decorated the 'Mackay Room' were, indeed, the same as those he had made in his workshop and hung on what he called his 'heritage wall' at home in Ohio: 'I'm saying to myself, hey, I've got those! And since they're in the museum here, they've got to be authentic'. The images in the museum display validated Don's sense of membership: he bore the appropriate badge.

But Don was insistent that he was not just interested in the past or seeing places associated with clan history, he wanted to know what the people of Scotland were like today. There was little opportunity of acquiring such knowledge within the few days of the trip, but he and Gladys particularly enjoyed meeting and talking with some acquaintances of mine in the locality when we stopped in for a cup of tea.

> They live different than we do, yet they live the same. By that I mean you don't find everybody running around in kilts and tootin' on pipes. The people live basically the same as we do, day-to-day: normal household duties, normal work duties, but that's the thing I'm interested in as opposed to all the gift shops and all the tourist attractions and all that kind of stuff.

Don distanced himself from both the 'average tourists' who he characterised as enjoying rather superficial experiences, and from other homecomers whom he felt had rather overactive imaginations and were obsessively interested in those piles of stones and old graveyards. No, in this respect, Don was keen to make connection at a decidedly domestic level: home(land) at its most humdrum. When he was sure my tape recorder was switched off, he quietly confided in me, 'I feel right at home here. I don't feel out of place at all'.

Two worlds, two minds, I live them both: Brenda – Strathaird, Skye

Brenda, 41, is a youth counsellor. She was born in Halifax, Nova Scotia, but has lived most of her life in Ontario. When Brenda made her first trip to Scotland in 1998, she vowed to herself that she would return every other year for the rest of her life. I began corresponding with Brenda a few months before her second visit, in 2000, after she completed the online questionnaire that featured on my research web site. Brenda's answers were particularly full, amounting to several thousand words of comment about what she called her 'Scotland feelings', and they deserve more thorough discussion than space allows here. I should, however, like to mention just one or two aspects of Brenda's experiences.

As with many other informants, Brenda's journey had long been anticipated:

> My love and sense of belonging to Scotland has always been intense since childhood. I knew (no wondering, but knew) at the age of 14 that I would be there someday. It wasn't a promise to myself nor a dreamed commitment – it was just the way it was. I would be in Scotland someday.

Although her parents had moved to Ontario when she was just two, Brenda was aware of an 'undercurrent' of Scottishness in her upbringing, especially during summer holidays back in Cape Breton,

> We'd stop and see all the relatives and we'd spend weeks there . . . I can remember Sydney Forks, you know, was Uncle George, Uncle Charlie and Grandma's house, right next door to each other . . . You were just all together, all of us all together . . . that kind of closeness.

The family was musical and Brenda remembers family gatherings 'with the combinations of fiddles, spoons, guitars and whisky'. At the time, Brenda thought of this simply as a 'down east' style, 'but now knowing some Scottish music', she realises, 'it's the same thing'.

The destination of Brenda's initial quest was very much Scotland as a whole. It was a 'place' she had inhabited in her imagination for many years based on her avid consumption of Scottish books, web sites, music and so forth: a place of 'powerful beauty in nature, misty rains, remote kirkyards, miles of walking in solitude'. When Brenda finally visited, it would appear that she projected her imagined Scotland onto the actual Scottish landscape. Unsurprisingly, she derived some satisfaction from apparently discovering what she had hoped to find.

> Each moment, each experience, each mile of travel I felt and saw what I had anticipated. I truly felt at home, and never once felt lost. It continually amazed and comforted me. To simply awaken with the dawn, walk or hop on a train not knowing where I would lay my head that night and feeling comfort in that. I felt continually humbled and comforted by all around me. Each kirkyard wandered was remote and beautiful . . . Each evening I found water that flowed the same as it always did throughout any turbulent history it saw. That was always emotional – to walk in my bare feet alone . . .

waiting for the setting sun, my footsteps washed away forever when I left but merged with thousands of others who walked there before me.

In her choice of language and imagery, Brenda articulates a desire to relinquish control, to give herself up to 'Scotland', to merge with her homeland and with the generations that had gone before, to be part of a timeless landscape – a desire which is expressed most literally in her wish to eventually have her ashes scattered there.

Elsewhere in her questionnaire Brenda described the violent emotions she experienced during a kind of catharsis when first encountering the grandeur of Glencoe. Regaining some composure as the episode abated, she found herself standing beside a mountain stream.

> I stepped into the pool knowing what I had to do. Both feet in the freezing water I let go of my dress letting it soak up the water. I reached down and placed my hands into the water . . . I washed that water over my face with my hands. Oh it was so fresh! Then, compelled, without even a thought, I cupped the water again and drank from it. I felt inside the cool and I felt settled. Scotland was now in me, coursing through me, filling me.

The incident suggests a baptism: Brenda's rebirth as a Scot, with 'Scotland' entering her as some kind of holy spirit. Indeed, there is no doubt that Brenda felt this to be a 'spiritual' experience: 'I realise that I have never, ever felt this whole in my life. I feel as if a part of my soul is filled and I am content, I am whole finally'.

The objective of Brenda's second journey to Scotland was to visit those areas associated with her MacKinnon clan: regions of the isles of Mull, Skye, South Uist and Barra. I joined Brenda for part of this two-week trip, exploring with her the MacKinnon strongholds of Castel Moil and Dun Ringill, along with numerous other sites in the Strathaird region of Skye (Figure 8.3). Brenda remarked at the 'power' she sensed at the dun and castle, but it was an old burial ground at Kilmarie that left the greatest impression on her. She placed pebbles on the MacKinnon graves and lingered over a row of older uninscribed stones, one in particular that she felt seemed 'small and all alone'.

Many roots tourists collect stones and other souvenirs from ancestral sites to take home. They function as relics acquired at religious shrines, fragments of the sacred introduced into the mundane: in this case fragments of the ancestral homeland introduced into the domestic home space where the roots tourist ordinarily resides. Brenda had many such stones which, with her books and CDs, she used to transport her to Scotland when she was in Canada. But Brenda was also keen to leave something of herself behind in Scotland. Thus I observed her depositing a ring in the

Figure 8.3 Brenda at Castel Moil, Kyleakin, Skye (Paul Basu)

massive walls of the ancient Dun Ringill. She wrote to me later, explaining why she did this.

> By putting my cheap ring inside the walls, I felt I was giving a humble offering, asking, almost begging to be part of it forever . . . I wanted to leave a part of 'me' there. I did not know this before that moment, nor had I planned to do so. But when I did it, I felt extremely good, extremely relieved.

Again, obvious parallels may be drawn with the practice of pilgrims leaving *ex votos* at shrines. Such objects represent metonymically those who have travelled to seek a cure and are left at the shrine after they have departed to suggest a continued presence.

Brenda had not yet discovered the identity of her MacKinnon ancestor who emigrated to Canada, and therefore didn't know where the old family home had actually been. She had not pursued her family history rigorously but was confident that the facts would emerge at the appropriate time.[5] For now she was content to let fate guide her and enjoy this 'communion' with MacKinnon lands. Indeed, Brenda identified herself strongly as a MacKinnon, but she seemed not to be referring here to a clan or family identity so much as a sense of personal integrity. She was conscious of losing this integrity as she grew older, married, became a mother and took on other responsibilities. Part of her journey to Scotland and to these MacKinnon lands was an attempt to recover for herself this primary identity aside from subsequent roles.

BRENDA: Over in Canada, I don't feel that world right now. I haven't thought of [my daughter] all morning. And that's so bizarre for me. I'm here, I'm me. I'm alone, I'm me.

PAUL: Do you mean, in some senses, you're not 'you' when you're back home in Canada?

BRENDA: Yeah, yeah. I'm not. I don't have all those hats on my head. All those different people. I'm just me right here.

PAUL: So what are those 'hats' that stop you being you?

BRENDA: Oh, well . . . motherhood, responsibility. You know when you're a wife you think of others, and I'm working with high-risk children: you're on the outside always relaxed, but on the inside always thinking and formulating things for other people to get through their problems and that . . .

I just feel so lucky to be here. And this is the real me. At home, I mean of course that's the real me – don't get me wrong – and I love my family and my life and I'm very proud of my life at home. But this is where . . . I don't want to say this is where my heart is. It goes deeper. My heart is with my child and my husband and my MacKinnons at home. My *soul* is here. It's deeper. It's like no one can take that away.

When I'm at home you can't feel it, but when you're here, the skies give you permission to feel it. It's beautiful.

Returning to the far country of the MacKinnons, it seems Brenda was also able to return to the secure identity of her youth, an identity lost with the acquisition of adult responsibilities and her husband's surname. It was important for Brenda to make the journey alone to find her 'real' self – not as wife, mother, professional child counsellor or other possible identity, but as 'Brenda MacKinnon', her essential self, her 'soul'.

But there was clearly also a tension here. I sensed Brenda felt guilty that the reality of her Canadian home seemed to diminish as she became immersed in this alternative reality represented by Scotland, that she had to leave behind her husband and daughter in order to feel 'whole'. She described her mixed emotions when, returning from her first trip, her husband met her at the airport.

> When I arrived in Canada and saw my husband and he said, 'Well, what was it like?' as he hugged me, I cried immediately and said that I have to go back and then I told him to let me cry and I couldn't talk yet. I think returning to Canada caused me to suddenly realise that in my soul, I had actually left my true country (Scotland) and I wasn't feeling happiness to be home in Canada.

Brenda sent me a poem that she felt expressed her feelings. She didn't know who had written it but explained, 'it's the closest I have ever seen in print of how I feel each day of my life here in Canada'.

> Of days winter and cold, I watch from sunbleached sands
> And look beyond the sky's edge toward this other land
> Pride flows hot in this eager blood born onto this place
> But to the past I would follow away from this time and space
> Thoughts create reflection of thistle and tartan splendour
> Old worlds renewed like the lover's kiss, I crave the rampant tender
> One foot leading to the future, the other in yesteryear
> Many generations have left her shores, yet still I must travel there
> And born far away I hear the call, my feelings forever roam
> Two worlds, two minds, I live them both, this new land
> And Scotland . . . my homes.[6]

Pilgrims to the far country

> This far country was the country that he had hoped one day to see.
> And the day had come.
>
> Neil M. Gunn, *Highland River*

It was Brenda who stated in her questionnaire, 'I am not and never will be a tourist in Scotland' (see page 2). In the above three narratives, I hope to have demonstrated that, in this instance, 'pilgrimage' is not merely an anthropological analogy, but a genre of travel invoked by certain visitors to Scotland – and, no doubt, to a greater or lesser extent, certain visitors to other 'old countries' too – to distinguish and define the purpose and meaning of their visits (Basu 2004b). Pat had been given a book by her daughter to read during her journey to Lewis, a personal-development manual entitled *The Art of Pilgrimage: The Seeker's Guide to Making Travel Sacred* (Cousineau 1999). Pat had copied some quotes from the text into the back of the volume. For example, she wrote:

> 'Personal answers to ultimate questions. That is what we seek' – Alexander Eliot
> 'Footprints of the Ancestors'
> 'Songlines' – Bruce Chatwin
> 'Our lives are woven from a melody of calls that draw us out and help us to define ourselves – David Spangler
> 'We must find our touchstones where we can' – John Bunyan

These few excerpts, divorced from their original contexts, delineate the nature of these homecoming journeys with some precision. These quests are, without doubt, personal responses to the insistent questions of our narcissistic late modern age: 'Who am I?' 'Where do I belong?' (Giddens 1991). They are also characterised by attitudes of devotion, respect and mystical reverence towards place informed, I suggest, by a growing aware-ness of native American and Australian conceptions of ancestral landscapes and origin myths: might we not find in these 'Celtic odysseys' some parallel to the Aboriginal 'Songlines' described by Chatwin: a modern, urban, Western quest for the 'Aborigine within' (Rolls 1998)?

Spangler's 'melody of calls' reminds us, however, that modern identity, even when self-defined, is plural and dynamic: some roots tourists select discriminatingly which of their several possible ancestral heritages to pursue, others combine elements from each in strange and creative ways. Finally, in the quote from Bunyan, is the acknowledgement that identity *is* a constructive project of the self in which the self is also at liberty to act as arbitrator: it may 'sound the stones' until it finds one that rings, not 'true', but according to its wishes.

Homeland Scots sometimes respond to the sentiments expressed by their diasporic cousins with embarrassed incredulity. Another informant, from British Columbia, found their attitude 'disparaging' and offensive: 'with the Scottish people', she explained, 'it seems that you are some sort of emotional cripple if you are trying to make a link to the old country'. Yet, indeed, one of the key motivations for setting out on pilgrimage is to seek a cure. I did not directly ask my informants 'what ails thee?' as my informant from Colorado suggested, but I did attempt to understand what 'salvation' each found in the Scottish homelands they encountered. The senses of connection, depth, resonance, 'fit', authenticity, belonging and being 'in place' which Scotland seemed to confer have, ultimately, little to do with Scotland itself. The homeland, rather, is a product of the diasporic imagination, a far country onto which, as with the bones of saints, a capacity for working miracles is projected – even a salve for the ills of modernity. Daniel, an informant from New Mexico, articulates it so well:

> Being disenfranchised, unattached to my heritage, going to Scotland was becoming connected to an origin that had never before existed. Whether the Scots themselves or anyone else acknowledged it or not, it was my connection. It was sacred to me because it was something of my soul, that part that you don't share with anyone, can't share with anyone. My 'self' has changed since that pilgrimage, whether anyone believes, acknowledges, validates or confirms it or not. Yes to me it was sacred. I now know that my ancestors came from somewhere, and I've been there, I've breathed the same air and touched the same ground as they did. Perhaps a little esoteric? I guess you have to be an American and 'generic' all your life to understand.

9 Exiles and emigrants

Negotiating the moralities of migrant family histories

> However ambiguous or polysemous our discourse may be, we are still able to bring our meanings into the public domain and negotiate them there. That is to say, we live publicly by public meanings and by shared procedures of interpretation and negotiation. Interpretation, however 'thick' it may become, must be publicly accessible or the culture falls into disarray and the individual members with it.
>
> Jerome Bruner, *Acts of Meaning*

Given the distinctions in the way Scottish heritage is enacted across both geographic and social space, the variety of forms of roots tourism, the different anxieties and desires which motivate an interest in genealogy, and the contingencies of each individual family history, it is evident that these homecoming journeys can have no singular meaning. It is also evident, however, that in bringing meaning to these disparate acts, much of this potential for polysemy is lost. Meaning, after all, is not implicit in actions and events, an essence awaiting discovery, but rather emerges in relation to other existing discourses and practices. As Jerome Bruner argues, the 'symbolic systems' that individuals use in constructing meaning are systems that are 'already in place, already "there", deeply entrenched in culture and language' (1990: 11).

Cultural dynamics are affected not only by the spatial movement of people and things, but also by the movement of meanings and discourses across and between groups that may or may not be spatially distinct. Thus, in a context defined by historical migration, indeed, in which migration has become foregrounded in the politics of identity (by which I mean to suggest that it had previously formed only a background), I should like to examine, in turn, a 'semantic migration' concerning notions of diaspora, and a 'discursive migration' concerning notions of indigenousness. At the centre of such migrations is the interpreting subject – the homecomer – and the relationship between the homecomer and the homeland. The meaning of homecoming is, I suggest, contingent on the meaning of the homeland (re)visited which is, in turn, contingent on the perceived circumstances of separation of homecomer from homeland. In other words, the relationship between diaspora and homeland (and therefore the significance of 'return') is at least partly defined by the circumstances through which the diaspora is understood to have been created. Knowledge of these circumstances may appear to be incontrovertible, but, particularly in situations such as that with which I am concerned, where the separation from homeland is a matter of family history and not personal experience, such knowledge is constructed from diverse sources of variable reliability: a matter of interpretation and, therefore, contestation.

Benedict Anderson has argued that 'all profound changes . . . bring with them characteristic amnesias', and that 'out of such oblivions . . . spring narratives' (1991: 204; *cf.* Lambek 1996: 241). In the absence of specific knowledges of what caused their ancestors' migrations, the interpretative procedures through which homecomers make sense of these dispersions tend to become polarised around two dominant cultural narratives concerning the dispersal of Scots from Scotland: one predicated on exile and banishment, the other on emigration and expansion. In the postcolonial era, these each imply very different moral connotations: 'exiles' as innocent victims of displacement, more sinned against than sinning, and thus exempt from responsibility; 'emigrants' as agents of colonialism, implicated in the displacement of others. In what follows I hope to demonstrate how these alternative 'public meanings' come to eclipse and act as substitutes for the particularities of personal family narratives, and how such meanings are negotiated and internalised, becoming central to individuals' senses of self. The construction of a meaningful and morally defensible family history may thus been seen as an ingredient of that broader 'project of the self' (its prehistory, as it were): something which has everything to do with contemporary values and predicaments, and arguably little to do with the past it appropriates and presses into its service (Giddens 1991: 75).

1 – EXILES

A child of the Clearances?

The first – semantic – migration with which I am concerned may be introduced by an examination of the comments of an informant named Christina, a 49-year-old business woman, born and residing in Vancouver. Although also of Irish and Scottish Lowland descent, Christina describes her cultural identity as a 'Highlander' of the MacInnes clan. It was her paternal grandparents who emigrated, separately, from Skye and Sutherland to Canada in the early years of the twentieth century. Christina articulates the sense of problematised belonging in the New World described by other informants in Chapter 3, contrasting the shallowness of her settler roots with the deep-rootedness of native populations:

I think there is a place on this earth that has the collective history of your people in the very ground you walk upon. If you live in North America you understand that you have only a very tenuous hold on the geography. There has to be a place to which you have a stronger connection, that tells the myths and legends of your ancestors, not someone else's. In this country we will always be immigrants not really belonging in that very primal way.

In search of such 'primal' connections, Christina has made two visits to Scotland and intends to make another with her daughter. She describes being strongly affected by the Highland landscape, particularly by its emptiness and her encounters with the remains of deserted settlements, which, as we have seen, are quite prevalent in certain areas. She attributes this emptiness to the Highland Clearances. As I have already discussed, the Clearances are often evoked as the completion of a process that began in the aftermath of Culloden, involving the eradication of the Highlanders and their culture from their 'native glens' in order to open the land up for intensive sheep farming. The narrative of the Clearances has *become* well known among Scottish heritage communities throughout the world, particularly through the work of popular historians and novelists (see Gouriévidis 1993; Basu 1997). John Prebble, for example, in the most popular of the popular Clearance histories, begins,

> This book . . . is the story of how the Highlanders were *deserted* and then *betrayed*. It concerns itself with people, how sheep were preferred to them, and how bayonet, truncheon and fire were used to *drive them from their homes*. It has been said that the Clearances are now far enough away from us to be decently forgotten. But *the hills are still empty*. . . . It is worth remembering, too, that while the rest of Scotland was permitting the expulsion of its Highland people it was also forming that romantic attachment to kilt and tartan that scarcely compensates for the *disappearance of a race* to whom such things were once a commonplace reality. The chiefs remain, in Edinburgh and London, but *the people are gone*. (1969: 8; emphases added)

Christina's descriptions of her visits to the Highlands demonstrate how, in her very vocabulary, she has internalised this powerful cultural narrative:

> I had been brought up on very positive stories about Scotland and Celticness. When I first went to Scotland I was ready to enjoy the country, and to have some fun looking up all the places that I had heard about. When I got there and as I traveled north my thoughts began to change. *The place was empty, everyone was gone.* There were no places to see that I had heard so much about. No one even knew where they might be. *We weren't missed!* This had been *an ethnic*

cleansing. If anyone remembered that it had taken place at all, their attitude was that its was really a benefit to the evicted! I also saw the remnants of *broken cottages*, the *remains of runrigs* up the mountains, the *empty glens that used to be full of people*. All of this had an impact on me that I truly wasn't expecting. *The land is still full of ghosts* and *no one is telling their tale*.

She goes on,

I find it hard to believe that *my people were so unwanted in their own land*, and especially hard to believe that nothing has ever been done about it. Maybe it is the fact that we come from Canada where past injustices are expected to be rectified before moving on into the future that we had these views. *We really didn't see that much difference between what happened in the Highlands to the Gaels and what happened in North America to the Native Indian population. Except that the Indians were not actually expelled from the continent.*

Christina was struck by the apparent lack of understanding or care of the Scots she met during her visit.

It seemed very moving to me and yet oddly surreal, because nobody there seemed to acknowledge or even be aware of the feelings it engendered in someone like myself who is *a child of the outcasts*. I guess I don't understand the *silence* about the whole issue both here and in Scotland. They mostly seem indifferent.

Finally she states,

I have never understood the way that Scotland ignores its sons and daughters all over the globe. The Irish are not so foolish neither are the Jews. ... I don't think Scotland will ever be completely whole until the question of the clearances is put to rest. Don't forget, *we, on this side of the pond, were not wanted, and made to leave*, so maybe we are starting from a feeling of inferiority that makes us very sensitive. On the other hand, there is, in the *exiles*, a strong feeling of belonging to the land, what is needed maybe is a link to the people. That is really what I think the Irish and the Israelis have done. (Emphases added)

Christina's comments reflect convictions that are widespread among people of Highland descent overseas, but a number of important points should be kept in mind. First, knowledge of these 'past injustices' is rarely derived from stories passed down within the family – as Christina explains, she had been brought up hearing 'very positive stories about

Scotland'. Such knowledge is instead most often acquired from popular history books (Christina herself cites the work of John Prebble) and historical fiction, as well as at web sites and heritage-centre displays that are often drawn from the same sources and which perpetuate their genocidal rhetoric (Figure 9.1). Second, the equation of Clearance with expulsion overseas is, generally speaking, unfounded. The Clearances occurred at a time of huge social and economic transformation throughout the British Isles (and much of Europe), which included the general shift of populations from rural areas to the industrialising urban centres as well as the first waves of mass emigration – migrations driven as much by the so-called 'pull factors' of the New World (land, opportunity, the prospect of wealth, etc.) as by the 'push factors' of rural poverty, famine and, indeed, avaricious landlords.[1] Finally, it should be noted that Christina's grandparents emigrated from Scotland in the early twentieth century, at least fifty and ninety years after the Clearances that occurred in Skye and Sutherland respectively. In others words, Christina's grandparents were not exiles, outcasts, or the victims of an ethnic cleansing. It is more likely that they left Scotland voluntarily, hoping, with so many millions of other European migrants, to 'better their fortunes' in America.

Figure 9.1 One of many web sites 'dedicated to the remembrance' of the Highland
   Clearances. On its homepage, this one features a detail from Thomas Faed's
   painting 'Oh, Why Left I My Hame?' (1886) depicting a homesick
   Highlander sitting dejectedly on the shore of Lake Ontario, Canada.

My intention in citing Christina is not to insensibly challenge the veracity of the stories she and many other informants have constructed around their families' pasts, so much as to examine the circumstances through which this particular narrative has come to dominate and shape a new exilic imagination. I suggest that one explanation for this may be found in the rubric of 'diaspora' and 'homeland' itself. It has been said that 'there is a will to power in nomenclature' (Hassan quoted by Tölölyan 1996: 4), and I am here concerned with the nomenclature of diaspora in a Scottish, and particularly Highland, context.

The nomenclature of diaspora

As outlined in Chapter 1, there has been much debate among academics regarding the correct use of the term 'diaspora' and it is perhaps worth reiterating the key points of the discussion here. Tölölyan, for example, argues that the term is in danger of losing its power to evoke because it has become a 'promiscuously capacious category that is taken to include all the adjacent phenomena to which it is linked but from which it actually differs in ways that are constitutive' (phenomena such as expatriate communities, immigrant communities, ethnic and racial minorities) (1996: 8). He asks how and why is it that, at the end of the twentieth century, 'a term once saturated with the meanings of exile, loss, dislocation, power-lessness and plain pain' becomes a 'useful' and even 'desirable' way to describe such a wide range of dispersions? (ibid.: 9). Some believe that, if the term is to retain any discrete significance, its use ought to be limited to describing the dispersion and exile of the Jews from their historic homeland and that its use in other contexts must remain metaphorical, 'in much the same way', suggests Safran, 'that "ghetto" has come to desig-nate all kinds of crowded, constricted, and disprivileged urban environments, and "holocaust" has come to be applied to all kinds of mass murder' (1991: 83). Whilst many accept that this Jewish paradigm may be applied to the experience of other victimised peoples, there is some consensus that 'diasporic populations do not come from elsewhere in the same way that "immigrants" do', and that the term, even if it is to be applied more broadly, is still a category of *subaltern* identification (Clifford 1997: 250).

This interpretation is challenged by those who believe it is necessary to transcend the Jewish tradition and return instead to the etymological roots of the word, the Greek 'to sow over' or 'scatter', and its earliest usage in relation to human dispersion, referring to expansionism not forced exile. Such a tactic permits Robin Cohen, for instance, to recognise the multiple causes of population dispersal and assemble his ideal typology of diaspora, which includes not only victim diasporas, but also trade diasporas, impe-rial diasporas, labour diasporas, and so forth (1997). As discussed in Chapter 1, within this inclusive and flexible framework, it is certainly possible to posit the existence of a Scottish diaspora and to demonstrate how it displays characteristics of these various types.

This contest over the appropriate use of 'diaspora' in academic discourse is made possible because there is a semantic instability around the term. This might be understood as a tension between the denotative and connotative meanings of the word. Put simply, denotation is the primary, direct or literal meaning of a given text, whereas connotation includes its metaphorical, symbolic or secondary meanings. Roland Barthes explores this distinction in his book *S/Z*. 'Definitionally', he writes, connotation 'is a determination, a relation, an anaphora, a feature which has the power to relate itself to anterior, ulterior, or exterior mentions, to other sites of the text (or of another text)' (1990: 8). If we accept Cohen's argument, the primary or denotative meaning of diaspora is its original meaning, a neutral term which might be appropriately employed to describe (voluntary) emigration as much as (involuntary) exile. We must, however, also accept that one cannot divorce the denotative meaning of a term from its connotations. Thus, in referring to a Scottish diaspora, one cannot help but imply an association or relationship with the Jewish diaspora. We might therefore agree with Jonathan Boyarin when he writes, 'It is important to insist, not on the centrality of the Jewish diaspora nor on its *logical priority* within comparative diaspora studies, yet still on the need to refer to . . . Jewish diaspora history within the contemporary diasporic rubric' (quoted in R. Cohen 1997: 3).

This, then, is the first semantic migration that affects what may be understood when invoking a Scottish diaspora. But within academic discourse this is somewhat incidental, since the term is rarely used without some qualification as to what exactly is meant. A more serious slippage occurs when the notion of a Scottish diaspora enters popular consciousness, which, without doubt, it has. And here it is necessary to return to Barthes, because, in *this* migration, the hierarchy of denotation and connotation is reversed. What is, in academic discourse, the connotative or secondary meaning becomes, in popular discourse, the denotative or primary meaning. Barthes writes that actually,

> denotation is not the first meaning, but pretends to be so; under this illusion, it is ultimately no more than the *last* of the connotations, . . . the superior myth by which the text pretends to return to the nature of language, to language as nature (1990: 8).

In other words, outside the close readings of academic discourse, it goes without saying that 'diaspora' means victimisation, enforced exile and all the other associations of the Jewish paradigm. Thus it is that, in the popular Scottish diasporic imagination, a moral rhetoric of exile comes to dominate a morally ambiguous history of emigration and colonisation.

A rhetoric of exile

This rhetoric of exile is particularly conspicuous in that most democratic of media: the internet. 'We're the children of the clearances' go the lyrics of one song which circulates on Scottish-interest email lists:

> We're the children of the clearances the wanderers old and young
> And a heart and soul in Scotland just like you
> So when you sing of the great white sheep this you must also know
> While Scotland mourns her tragedy it was us that had to go
> In exile now far away from the land of our race's birth
> We're the living flag of Andrew scattered all across the Earth.[2]

And from an essay published on the internet entitled 'Cries of the Never Born' by an American-Scot living in Florida:

> In the last 270 years, more than a quarter of a million indigenous people were forced off their ancestral lands, burned out of their homes, sold into slavery, and forcibly assimilated into a foreign culture. But these were not Native Americans, or black Africans, or Jews; these were the white residents of the Scottish Highlands. Their crime: Occupying land others coveted. (www.coyotegulch.com/bookart/sym00006.html)

Note how the crimes against the Highlanders have now escalated to include slavery and forced assimilation. At the end of the article, the author encourages readers to contact an Arkansas-based 'Highland Clearances Memorial Fund', a non-profit organisation established, according to its founder, 'to raise awareness of the Clearances and their aftermath in both Scotland and the US' (Steve Blamires pers. comm.). Such are the 'webs of retrospective indignation' Richards describes, through which 'the uninhibited passions and prejudices of a worldwide network of Highland sympathizers' are orchestrated (2000: 3).

The hyperbole is not, however, restricted exclusively to the diaspora. In May 2000, for instance, the letters pages of the Scottish broadsheet *The Herald* were buoyed up with angst for weeks in response to comments made by the historian and columnist Michael Fry, who was accused of issuing 'utterances on the Clearances reminiscent of the Holocaust denial of David Irving' (Macaskill 2000). Thus, one letter-writer, Dennis MacLeod of Easter Ross, leading a campaign to erect a Clearances memorial and study centre in Helmsdale, promulgates the popular misconception that to be descended from Highlands Scots is necessarily to be descended from the victims of the Clearances when he writes,

> The descendants of the cleared people are measured today in only tens of thousands in the Highlands of Scotland. But throughout the world

they comprise tens of millions. The project, therefore, belongs not just to today's Highlanders but as much if not more to all of Highland descent, be they from the Lowlands of Scotland, England, USA, Canada, New Zealand, Australia, Africa, or elsewhere.

It is hoped that such descendants will embrace and support this project as their own. It will be an opportunity for millions of people, scattered to the far reaches of the earth, to focus in one location their long-held quest for the recognition of their unique history, culture, and heritage. (MacLeod 2000)

Another letter-writer, again conflating Clearance and emigration, equates the plight of Highland emigrants in Canada with that of the biblical exile of the Jews:

I remind [Michael Fry] of two exiles who wrote of the agony of being driven from their homeland. The first, the Psalmist, wrote, 'How could we sing the Lord's song in a strange foreign land? If I forget you, O Jerusalem, let my right hand wither away'. The second was written by John Galt . . . 'From the lone shieling of the misty island, Mountains divide us and the waste of the seas; Yet still the blood is strong, the heart is Highland, And we in dreams behold the Hebrides'. (McDermid 2000)[3]

Such explicit parallels between Jewish and Highland experiences are not particularly new. Andrew Matheson, a somewhat overlooked land-reform agitator, whose father had been evicted from Kildonan in Sutherland, and he himself from Dunbeath in Caithness, published a booklet in 1870 entitled *The British Looking Glass* which is peppered with biblical references, providing precedents for his arguments that his readers would no doubt be familiar with. Thus, the 'British landlord' by his practice of rack-renting is placed 'in full position parallel with the Egyptian bondage (Exodus 1: 11–14)', while the tenants have become 'white slaves . . . a step lower than the Hebrews were under Pharaoh (Exodus 5: 7–19)' (Matheson 1993: 31–2). Even the 'Assyrians, who put the Jews to the sword and took them prisoners of war' were not as evil as the clearing landlords because they 'would not remove them from their places in Samaria till they provided for them in Assyria (2 Kings 17: 6)' (ibid.: 39).[4] Alas, Matheson was also a man of his time and he apparently did not perceive the inconsistencies in his argument when, with missionary zeal, he justifies the forcible appropriation, colonisation and exploitation of other people's lands:

Idolatry and abuse of their land talents are the justifiable causes which entitle and warrant Britain to make war upon heathen countries, such as Australia &c., for making their lands, by artificial industries, more fruitful and useful by the yields of both mines and crops to support mankind, and making their inhabitants tributaries (Deut. 20: 11 and 15). (Matheson 1993: 46)

But neither are these parallels limited to the *biblical* history of the Jews: much popular writing on the Clearances today is laced with hyperbolic references to the Holocaust and other modern genocides (Table 9.1). Indeed, even the aforementioned proposal for a Highland Clearances memorial at Helmsdale arguably draws from the mnemonic architecture of many Holocaust memorials and museums, with its 120-foot high bronze statue, its processional pathway marked with 'standing stones' inscribed with Clearance history, its 'Wall of Descendants', and its anticipated collections of oral testimonies and other records housed in a dedicated 'Clearances Centre' (Highland Clearances Memorial Centre project brief, March 2001) (Figure 9.2).[5]

Furthermore, the influence of a global post-colonial 'politics of reconciliation' (evinced in the Australian Council for Aboriginal Reconciliation Act of 1991, the South African Truth and Reconciliation Commission of 1995, etc.) is apparent in a motion brought before the Scottish Parliament by Jamie Stone, Liberal Democrat MSP for Caithness, Sutherland and Easter Ross, in September 2000:

Figure 9.2 Artist's impression of the proposed 'Highland Clearances Memorial' above Helmsdale (Highland Clearances Memorial Centre)

Table 9.1 The Highland Clearances as Holocaust – excerpts from popular histories (1962–2000)

- the victims of the Clearances [were] objects of intense hatred such as the gypsies and the Jews were to experience under the Nazis and other groups in the Western World (Thompson 1974: 61)
- like the shipping-off of the Polish and other Jews in cattle trucks (Craig 1990: 72)
- Sellar's crimes against the people of Strathnaver, [Grimble] said, were to be ranked with those of Heydrich, the man who perpetrated unspeakable acts against the Jews in Prague in the Second World War (Richards 2000: 10, discussing Grimble)
- *Na Hitleran breun Breatannach* Those stinking British Hitlers
  A mhurt mo thìr mu thuath Who murdered my northern land
  Gu Lebensraum do chaoraich To make *Lebensraum* for sheep,
  Is na daoine sgiùrs' thar chuan Who scourged the people across the ocean
  (Murchadh MacPhàrlain quoted by Newton 2000: 73)
- She had been to Auschwitz concentration camp but there was no statue to Hitler. Back home she felt that the 1st Duke of Sutherland had dealt in genocide . . . (Gibson 1996b: 41, discussing Winnie Ewing MEP)
- Highland Holocaust (Gibson 1996b: 6, 38, 40)
- a planned *blitzkrieg* against the Gaelic civilisation (Craig 1990: 76)
- Sutherland's managers kept records of their shipments of people with the obsessional thoroughness of an Eichmann (Craig 1990: 129)
- The policy of genocide could scarcely have been carried out further (Grimble 1968: 23)
- a diaspora which has many recent counterpars . . . that of the Jews from Germany and Poland (Craig 1990: 3)
- the 1st Duke ranked with Hitler and Stalin (Gibson 1996b: 22, discussing the views of Councillor Sandy Lindsay)
- the cultural genocide of the Highlands (Newton 2000: 281)
- the Gaels were, and indeed are today, in no way different from the Red Indians, the Jews, the Eskimoes and the vanishing tribes of the Amazon River (Thompson 1974: 62)
- akin to genocide (Grimble 1962)

That the Parliament expresses its deepest regret for the occurrence of the Highland Clearances and extends its hand in friendship and welcome to the descendants of the cleared people who reside outwith our shores. (Scottish Parliament 2000: Col 700)

Among many similar contributions to the ensuing 'debate', Fergus Ewing, Scottish National Party MSP for Inverness East, Nairn and Lochaber, supported Stone's motion, reiterated familiar sentiments regarding confronting the past in order to move forward, and again drew parallels between the 'Highland diaspora', Native Americans and Australian Aborigines:

> In other countries, the genocide and ethnic cleansing that has taken place, against the Indians in America and the Aborigines in Australia, was acknowledged long ago. Today, the time to acknowledge what happened to those who were cleared from the Highlands has come. We can now acknowledge and regret what happened and perhaps then move on. (Scottish Executive 2000: Col 703)

Despite the implicit invocation of a 'Truth Commission', Stone and Ewing seem less concerned with interrogating the 'truth' of the Clearance narrative, so much as asserting a supposedly self-evident equivalence of this particular cultural trauma with other less equivocal instances of 'genocide'.

As I have suggested, the experience of the majority of my informants is characterised by a sense of discontinuity with the past, particularly with the past prior to their ancestors' emigrations. Few have grown up knowing just how, when and why their ancestors emigrated, or even necessarily knowing from which country or countries. This lacuna of knowledge partly motivates their current interest in family history research, but it also makes them vulnerable to this vivid cultural narrative that seems to explain their fate. Thus, in popular Scottish diasporic discourse, and according to Robin Cohen's heuristic framework, the Highland Clearances come to constitute the traumatic event which caused the dispersal of their ancestors from an original centre and which provides the diaspora with a 'folk memory' – albeit a recently acquired one – of the great historic injustice which binds the group together *as* a diaspora (1997: 23). The strength of this narrative displaces Cohen's second proposition, which, in fact, accounts for the vast majority of emigration from Scotland: i.e. 'the expansion from a homeland in search of work, in pursuit of trade or to further colonial ambitions' (ibid.: 26).

Homecomings for homeless minds

This claim may be seen in the context of what has been described as the 'new white ethnic movement': the desire of white, suburban, middle-class, assimilated citizens to effectively dissimilate themselves and recover a more distinctive, particular ethnic identity (Waters 1990). Individuals thus turn to their family histories and choose which of their various ancestors' ethnicities to identify with: generally-speaking, the more 'ethnic' and the more persecuted the better (ibid.: 150–5). This may seem a rather cynical suggestion but the trend is certainly evident in the comments of my informants, and, of course, the phenomenon is not restricted to the descendants of Scottish Highlanders. In a recent book exploring the emergence in the

1960s of a Holocaust-centred Jewish-American identity, Peter Novick identifies the concurrent rise of a more general 'culture of victimization'. He describes a state of 'Holocaust envy' in which different groups, each with its own atrocity to commemorate, compete to be 'America's number one victim community' (Novick 1999: 190).

One explanation for this may be found in the desire to maintain a positive or moral self-image in which it is more acceptable to consciously or unconsciously identify with the oppressed rather than with the oppressors. However, it is also tempting to find some analogy between this social phenomenon and the psychological phenomenon of false memory syndrome, where an identifiable – even though imagined – traumatic episode is believed to account for the symptoms of trauma, the true causes of which remain obscure. Thus, perhaps this sense of exile evinced by many of my informants is less a result of any historical trauma than that consequence of modernity described by Berger *et al.* as 'a metaphysical loss of "home"' (1973: 82; see discussion in Chapter 1). Despite Rapport and Dawson's recent critique of the homeless mind theory, there seems to be much to support it in the field of genealogy and roots tourism, practices which may be seen as further instances of that demodernising impulse, in which the alienated individual so evidently hungers to belong and seeks to connect itself spatially, temporally and socially with something *beyond* itself, but authentically *of* itself.

Drawing equally from psychoanalytic theories and historiography, a more recent exploration of these themes may be found in the work of Dominick LaCapra. In *Writing History, Writing Trauma*, LaCapra contrasts 'structural trauma' with 'historical trauma'. Structural trauma is described as an 'anxiety producing condition' to which 'everyone' is subject and is associated with absence (for instance, the 'absence of an absolute') (2001: 82). Absence is transhistorical in so far as it 'is not an event and does not imply tenses (past, present or future)' (ibid.: 49), and so the source of anxiety or trauma remains elusive. As part of the cognitive process, however, absence becomes narrativised and is typically misrecognised as loss. 'The conversion of absence into loss,' writes LaCapra, 'gives anxiety an identifiable object – the lost object – and generates the hope that anxiety may be eliminated or overcome' (i.e. through recovering the 'lost object') (ibid.: 57). Structural trauma thus becomes converted into an historical trauma: an identifiable, datable event, 'the scene of losses that may be narrated as well as of specific possibilities that may conceivably be reactivated, reconfigured, and transformed in the present or the future' (ibid.: 49). Put simply, through this process, the perplexing and irresolvable state of 'paradise absent' is transformed into 'paradise lost', and with this is implied both 'the notion of a fall from a putative state of grace, at-homeness, unity, or community' and the possibility that this golden age might be regained. One consequence of this misrecognition of structural trauma as historical trauma is the emergence, as noted by Novick, of a generalised 'wound culture' based on false memory and 'surrogate victimage' (Novick 1999: 40). Thus, according to LaCapra, the conflation of absence and loss facilitates 'the appropriation of particular traumas by those who did not experience them, typically in a movement of identity formation which makes invidious and ideological use of traumatic series of events in foundational ways or as symbolic capital' (2001: 65).[6]

In LaCapra's terms, I suggest that the Highland Clearances emerge as the historical trauma through which the existential anxieties of people of Scottish or part-Scottish descent dispersed throughout the world may be acted out, narrated and brought into the public domain. The Clearances are thus misidentified as the foundational trauma of the Scottish diaspora, a myth in which the Highlanders (who, as we have seen, come to stand for all Scots) suffered a genocide, were expelled from their ancestral homeland, and were forced to live in slavery and exile overseas. According to the mythic structure, prior to this 'Highland Holocaust', was a paradisical Golden Age of 'at-homeness, unity [and] community' – an idealisation of all that is perceived to be absent in the postlapsarian modern world of the diaspora. But, as LaCapra argues, 'Paradise absent is different from paradise lost' and, as absence is transformed to loss, there is also created the potential for redemption and return: a (not im)possible homecoming for the homeless mind (ibid.: 57).

So it is that, at the beginning of the twenty-first century, 'a term once saturated with the meanings of exile, loss, dislocation, powerless and plain pain' comes to be a useful and even desirable form of self-identification by a group for whom such connotations would seem to be largely inappropriate (Tölölyan 1996: 9).[7] 'Diaspora', then, provides a language through which such individuals can both articulate generalised senses of personal alienation and recover a sense of belonging to a historical community. The process reaches its zenith in the journey 'home' – to the ancestral homeland where Berger's metaphorical and metaphysical home is made material and where a paradise, of sorts, may at last be regained.

2 – EMIGRANTS

A rhetoric of equivalence?

The relationship between 'indigenous' Scottish Highlanders and the indigenous populations of North America and Australasia has been characterised both as one of similarity and of difference according to who is making the comparison and to what ends. Writing in the first quarter of the nineteenth century, for instance, Patrick Sellar, the factor-cum-sheep farmer from Morayshire still demonised throughout the Highlands for his part in the notorious Sutherland Clearances, epitomises the pejorative view of the internal colonist when he finds equivalence between the natives of

Sutherland and the natives of America in their remoteness from what *he* defines as civilisation:

> Their seclusion places them, with relation to the enlightened nations of Europe, not very different from that betwixt the American Colonists and the Aborigines of that Country. The one are the Aborigines of Britain, shut out from the general stream of knowledge and cultivation, flowing in upon the Commonwealth of Europe from the remotest fountain of antiquity. The other are the Aborigines of America, equally shut out from this stream: both live in turf cabins in common with the brutes. (quoted by Grimble 1996: 25)

This is, of course, the inverse of that contemporaneous discourse of both Highland Scotland and colonial America: that of the 'noble savage'. Thus, Alexander Mackenzie dedicates his 1883 *History of the Highland Clearances* to John Mackay whom he describes as 'a native of Sutherland, a true Highlander, and *one of Nature's Noblemen*' (1883; emphasis added). And, in his 1877 account of the depopulation of Aberarder in Badenoch, Charles Fraser-Mackintosh writes, 'since the introduction of sheep into the Highlands, and before rapacious Lowland sheep farmers, the people disappear as surely as the Red Indians from the advance of the Whites' (1877: 418).

Such historical sources are employed tendentiously by present-day cultural revivalists to construct the Highlanders as an indigenous population, akin to other native peoples, in opposition to the dominating colonising culture with its barbarous ethnocentrisms. Through such oppositional logic, Highland settlers thus become excluded from participation in the violence of colonial appropriations and, instead, are typically portrayed as intermarrying and living peaceably with their indigenous 'kinsfolk' (e.g. Hunter 1996). Michael Newton, for example, writes that 'Native Americans often felt an affinity for Highland custom and costume. Some tribes adapted the tartan into their own native clothing, wore the feathered bonnet, and shared a disdain for breeches' (2001: 197). In contrast to this cosy coexistence, he refers only to the 'racial ideologies' of the 'Anglo-Saxon order' or the 'Teutonic-Gothic peoples of England and the Scottish Lowlands' to explain the prejudices which underpinned the 'Anglo-British Empire' (2000: 281; 2001: 216–19). Such prejudices, he argues, could not exist naturally in the Celtic mind, and if Highlanders were implicated in the colonial project this was surely 'a consequence of the Faustian bargain of incorporation into greater England' (2001: 232).

Similarly, Newton's collection of Gaelic verse composed in the USA is entitled, *We're Indians Sure Enough*, a phrase translated from a Gaelic lullaby that articulates the Gaels' sense of identification with the dispossessed Native Americans. It is ironic, therefore, that Newton also quotes an earlier version of the lyric, in which the phrase *Tha sinn 'nar n-Innseanaich* (*We* are Indians) is instead *Tha sibh 'nur n-Innseanaich* (*You* are Indians), and in fact the earlier lyric is sung from the point of view of a Highland soldier fighting *against* the Indians in America, and is addressed, disdainfully, to rebel colonists who have effectively 'gone native' and abandoned their European habits and customs (Newton 2001: 4, 175–8, 239; J. L. Campbell 1999: 59–61). The song's evolution tells a fascinating story of changing attitudes and identifications, but what is problematic is Newton's privileging of one interpretation over another in order to characterise the 'Legacy of the Scottish Highlanders in the United States' as a benign one according to current sensibilities. It should be remembered that the Highland regiments distinguished themselves in numerous British colonial conflicts throughout the later eighteenth and the nineteenth centuries, and, indeed, elsewhere in his volume, Newton quotes an eighteenth-century song in praise of the 43rd Regiment (the 'Black Watch'). It is significant that he chose not to select the title of his book from the following lines (Newton 2001: 111–12):

'N America gum b' àraidh iad	They were distinguished in America
Gun dealachadh ri'n àbhaisteachd:	And did not depart from their custom:
Bha eireachdas 's buaidh-làrach orr'	They were spectacular and victorious,
Gu guineach teinneach, sàr-bhuilleach	Fierce, fiery, dealing expert blows,
Gu lasrach, sradach, tàirneineach	Full of flames, sparks and lightning,
Le luaidh is fùdar gràinneach	With lead and gunpowder,
Cur Innseanach air aithreachas	Making the Indians repentant,
Mar chuireadh grian le làthaireachd	Just as the presence of the sun
An dealt de bharr an fheòir.	Makes dew disappear from the grass.

In the nineteenth century, similarly contradictory discourses are apparent in the context of the colonisation of Australia and New Zealand. In the excerpt from Andrew Matheson's *The British Looking Glass* quoted earlier in this chapter, it will already be apparent that at least some Highlanders – land reform activists included – considered the forcible colonisation of 'heathen countries' such as Australia and the subjugation of their people to be justified and warranted on the grounds of sound theological reasoning (Matheson 1993: 46). An alternative impression might be formed, however, when considering the establishment of *An Comunn na Feinne* (the Fingalian Society) of Geelong, Victoria in 1856. Although this society was formed by Highland migrants 'for the cultivation and preservation of ... the Gaelic language and Highland nationality' and 'to embrace ... all that is entitled to our respect and admiration on the patriotic spirit, manners and customs of our ancestors' (Wood n.d.: 4), its charitable activities were soon expanded to include the welfare of the wider community: both settler and native. As Cliff Cumming notes, 'A feature of the Comunn na Feinne from its initiation ... was the participation by local Aboriginal groups, both as recipients of material goods and by their involvement in games and through displays of their traditional skills' (1996: n.p.). The society had a most remarkable badge which featured a Scottish Highlander and an Australian Aborigine standing either side of the Scottish royal crest, each clothed in their 'tribal' apparel, the Highlander carrying broadsword and targe, the Aborigine, boomerang and spear (Figure 9.3).

The temptation is to thus imagine Highlander and Aborigine standing on equal footing, united in a brotherhood of *noblesse sauvage*, and to forget that the Wathaurong tribe, which, it is estimated, had occupied the *iDjillongi*/Geelong region for twenty-five millennia, was, within fifty years of European settlement, on the verge of extinction (Lane 1988; I. D. Clark 1990) – displaced, not least, by the heroic 'Fingalians' among the thousands who flocked to '*fearann an òir*' to seek their fortunes in the gold diggings of 1852 or in the no less lucrative woollen industry of which Geelong became the capital (Richards 1985b).

As Ann Curthoys points out, 'the past is hotly contested territory in Australia', particularly so since the 'Great Australian Silence' concerning the 'fatal collisions' between settlers and indigenous populations has only relatively recently been broken (Stanner 1979: 207; Curthoys 1999: 1). Since the 1960s, however, much has been written on the violent realities of frontier life and we can be in little doubt regarding the truths that such euphemisms as subduing 'the land' conceal (see, for example, Reynolds

Figure 9.3 The Geelong Comunn na Feinne badge (Geelong Historical Society)

1996; Foster *et al.* 2001). There is now an alternative narrative to the heroic pioneering legends of White Australia, one which tells a 'profoundly discomforting story of invasion, colonisation, dispossession, exploitation, institutionalisation, and attempted genocide' (Curthoys 1999: 1). My main concern in the second half of this chapter is therefore to explore how Australians of Scottish Highland descent negotiate this less heroic narrative, particularly through their articulation of the discourse of 'indigeneity' itself. First, however, it is necessary to remind ourselves that not all sectors of Australia's settler society are equally perturbed by these unsettling histories (Stasiulis and Yuval-Davis 1995).

White settlers/black natives

An assertion of equivalence between native Highlanders and native Australians is apparent in the use of the pejorative term 'white settlers' in the Highlands to refer to English and Scottish Lowland incomers to the region (Jedrej and Nuttall 1996). Such incomers are often perceived as colonisers of the Highlands, who displace the 'traditional' values and lifestyles of the locals – the 'black natives' (ibid.: 15) – by bringing with them the urban attitudes and practices they typically seek to escape. The term is used by one informant, a fifth-generation Australian from Melbourne, to describe the 'strangers' who now occupy Strathaird House, once the property of his ancestors on Skye (a property he is determined, somehow, to reacquire):

> I must at least get this position back. It calls me constantly. My soul roots are homeless. I must relive (*sic*) there again, my ancestors command it. I also want to turn part of Strathaird House into a Macalister/Mackinnon Clan Centre. ... I will turn it over to the Highlands and Islands Board if I am able to reclaim or repurchase Strathaird House again. This way Strathaird will never be lost again or pulled down or desecrated by white settlers.

Note, especially, how, in this informant's opinion, the presence of incomers constitutes a violation of the *sanctity* of his ancestral home.

It is ironic that my informant's Macalister ancestor actually purchased Strathaird House and its estate (previously a MacKinnon holding) in 1789 after inheriting a sizeable fortune amassed by his brother while he was serving as an officer in the East India Company. That is to say, my informant's inalienable ancestral home was purchased with the proceeds of colonial enterprise. As a large family on a relatively small estate, the Macalisters' male offspring pursued professional and military careers, and continued to engage in colonial interests in British Guyana and, especially, in New South Wales. Lachlan Macalister was the first of the family to settle in Australia: serving as an ensign with the 48th Regiment, he had been posted to New South Wales in 1817 and, in 1824, had received an 810-hectare grant of land there. Lachlan was to prosper as a sheep farmer, and by 1838, now joined by a number of his brothers and their families (among them my informant's great-great-great-grandfather), he had become one of the major landowners in New South Wales. As the family's fortunes were expanding in Australia, they were, however, declining at Strathaird, and, in 1883, its entitlement to the estate was contested and possession passed to a distant cousin then residing in France. My informant believes this was an act of skulduggery, in which this French cousin and his Scottish solicitors conspired to trick his great-grandfather into signing 'a document of disentailment, disinheriting himself and his family and succeeding generations to their roots and lands of Strathaird'. He explains that he feels 'like young James Balfour', the hero of Stevenson's novel, *Kidnapped*, who was cheated out of his inheritance, and he describes the powerful emotions he experienced on his 'return', 'carry[ing] the past six generations of [his] ancestors within [him]':

> Since 1991, I have made three trips back to Skye and Strathaird. Some of my ancestors are buried there. I feel as if my life has not really started until I am finally there. Home!! Back to where we left in 1817. My soul cannot rest until I reclaim my ancestors' ghosts. When I visited Strathaird House in 1991 the hair was prickly on the back of my neck. I cannot find the words to properly explain the peculiar feelings which were flowing through me. I had a magnificent feeling of being at ease, at undisturbed peace. I wandered around and over Strathaird with mixed feelings of being somewhat lost but yet as if I seemed to know where I was, as each newly discovered bend, and turn, and glen, and burn revealed itself to me. I discovered my ancestors' partially lost and forgotten tomb after two attempts to find it. I now carry some of that soil in a gold acorn around my neck. I am never without Skye. Its soil touches me every day.

With such a profound feeling of connection with the soil of Strathaird, his sense of injury caused by the 'wrongs done to [his] ancestors', his belief that his ancestral home had been 'desecrated' by 'white settlers', and his 'quest' to return to Strathaird and restore it to its 'rightful' owners, I asked my informant whether he had some sympathy for the cause of Aboriginal land rights in Australia. His reply was forthright:

> As to my thoughts regarding the aboriginals, etc. I don't have any sympathy for them or their so called cause. The recent land rights grants has done nothing but further bugger up this country . . .
> Paul, when this country was first settled in 1788, and funny enough, it was 1789 when my ancestor purchased Strathaird in Skye,

there was a history of continual skirmishes with the aboriginals up until the 1850s. In fact an ancestor of mine, Ronald Macalister, was speared in the back and killed in 1843 during the exploring and discovery of Gippsland. His hands were cut off and later found being worn around an aboriginal's neck. His kidney fat was hacked out as evidently this was a prized trophy to be eaten, etc. As a result of this murder my ancestors from Skye formed a party and rode out and hunted down some 150 aboriginals. This event happened here in Gippsland in 1843. We never had any more trouble with the aboriginals after that.

This shocking incident is discussed at some length by the Melbourne historian, Don Watson, in his book *Caledonia Australis*, and, although there are conflicting accounts, it appears that the murder that provoked what is known as the Warrigal Creek Massacre was itself an act of revenge for the killing of an Aboriginal boy, either at the hands of Ronald Macalister or a stockman in his employ named John Morrison (Watson 1984: 165–6). The party responsible for the massacre was organised by Angus McMillan, a native of Skye and Lachlan Macalister's son-in-law, who is regarded as the 'discoverer' of Gippsland, and who, ironically, was to become 'Protector of Aborigines' for that territory in the 1860s (ibid.: 185). The posse was known as the 'Highland Brigade' since it was comprised more or less exclusively of Highland settlers of the region (ibid.: 167).[8]

The atrocities committed by the Highland Brigade ought to stand as an unambiguous refutation of the often-made assertion that the Highland emigrants were innocents caught up in an evil English colonial project. Yet, even in the face of such damning evidence of Celtic complicity, excuses are found and the familiar victimological exile myth is invoked. Thus, in an email discussion list exchange concerning the Warrigal Creek Massacre, a local secondary school history teacher spuriously explains, 'The Scots settlers' own ancestors were hunted down like animals in the Highlands by the English only 100 years before – is it any wonder that they behaved the way they did?' (posting to aus-vic-gippsland-l@rootsweb.com, 20-Feb-99). The likes of Macalister and McMillan were ambitious colonialists, they were not the victims of an equivocal genocide, but the perpetrators of an unequivocal one.

Complicating belonging

My informant's almost proud recollection of his ancestor's part in the 'dispersal' – i.e. shooting – of native populations in Victoria demonstrates that colonialist ideologies have not been wholly displaced by post-colonial sensibilities. Accepting this caveat, there has, however, undoubtedly been a 'tectonic shift' in attitudes concerning Aboriginality in a large proportion of the white Australian population since the late 1960s (Davis *et al.* 1998:

vii). This shift gained 'official' expression in the early 1990s with the passing of the Council for Aboriginal Reconciliation Act, the precedent-setting 'Mabo judgment', and the then-prime minister Paul Keating's willingness to accept responsibility, on behalf of white Australia, for the injustices of the country's colonial past:

> We took the traditional lands and smashed the traditional way of life. We brought the disasters. The alcohol. We committed the murders. We took the children from their mothers. We practiced discrimination and exclusion. (Keating quoted by Davis *et al.* 1998: vii)

To acknowledge such responsibility is, as Curthoys suggests, 'profoundly discomforting', especially for those whose identity has been constructed around the moral certitude of being the victims, not the perpetrators, of dispossession. Indeed, she suggests that this has provoked among the descendants of eighteenth- and nineteenth-century settlers a new fear of displacement, 'of being cast out, exiled, expelled, made homeless again, after two centuries of securing a new home far away from home' (1999: 17). She adds, 'if we fully recognise Indigenous claims to the land, if we have a sense of living in someone else's country, we are, in a metaphorical if not a literal sense, perhaps in danger of homelessness again, of having to suffer yet again the original expulsion' (ibid.: 18). This problematising of identity based on the moral ambiguities of migrant family histories is expressed by Anna, another informant from Melbourne:

> I have noticed the similarities between what happened to the Highlanders in the Clearances and what happened to the Australian Aborigines, i.e. a whole load of men in red coats arrive and say 'Get off the land, we want to put sheep here!' Unfortunately, I'm not sure this made my pioneer ancestors any more sympathetic to the local Aborigines. It seems to have been a case of 'what's done to you, you do to others'. But I do think that for us in the diaspora, especially third or fourth generation like me, our idea of 'homeland' is inextricably linked to the place we live in now. And I sometimes wonder if part of the longing for a homeland is a longing for a place of uncomplicated belonging, especially in the current Australian climate, where a lot of conscience examining is going on. It's hard to claim a place here without being aware of who is being displaced by that claim. . . . The idea of a place where my ancestors belonged for thousands of years is very appealing. In Australia nobody except the Aborigines has been here for more than about two hundred years. There simply can't be the same sense of continuity without reference to ancestors somewhere else. And there is something mystical about belonging to a particular place on the earth.

Here Anna both invokes the Clearance narrative in accounting for the displacement of her ancestors and acknowledges that her displaced ancestors were implicated in the displacement of others in the process of settling their New Country. Anna's great-great grandparents had emigrated to South Australia under the auspices of the Highland and Island Emigration Society in 1855. After several years working in Adelaide they took up a land selection at Belalie in the north of the colony. Visiting the ruins of the farmhouse they built there, Anna explains that she was shocked to discover that there were 'gun slits in the walls' and to learn that the farmhouse was called 'The Fort', 'because it was fortified against the local Aborigines'. If Anna's ancestors were the innocent victims of 'forcible removal' in their old country, Anna is fully cognisant of that fact that 'they are not innocent by the time they get to Australia'. 'Belonging', Anna suggests, 'is problematic in some sense for all Australians' – 'for all white Australians and for indigenous Australians, whose belonging has been made very problematic'.

What I find particularly interesting in Anna's comments, however, and what I should like to concentrate on in the remainder of this chapter, is the way in which she negotiates these ambiguities through considering the possibility of her own 'aboriginality'. Thus, Anna expresses a desire to find 'a place of uncomplicated belonging', which she defines as a place that her own ancestors have occupied for thousands of years, a place in which she is effectively the Aboriginal. This assertion, along with her reference to a 'mystical' relationship between land, ancestry and identity, suggests that her own negotiations of belonging have been influenced by discourses of Australian Aboriginality which have become prominent in middle-class, urban, white Australian society. This, then, is the second 'migration' to which I referred in my introduction to this chapter: the migration of popular discourses of aboriginality from one context to another. Whilst I shall focus on Australian examples, a similar process is also apparent in North America and New Zealand, although with different emphases which reflect differing notions of indigenousness and the varying prominence of such notions in mainstream popular culture (King 1985; Cornell 1988; Dominy 1995; Nagel 1995; Havemann 1999).

In Australia, changing social attitudes towards Aboriginality are reflected in recent census statistics, the analysis of which has demonstrated an increasing propensity for individuals, particularly those with mixed indigenous and non-indigenous origins, to identify themselves as indigenous (Australian Bureau of Statistics 2001a). Thus, between 1986 and 1996, the indigenous population in Australia increased by some 55 per cent, compared with only a 12 per cent increase in non-indigenous populations, a figure which far exceeds 'natural growth' (Australian Bureau of Statistics 2000).[9] This changing propensity for individuals to choose to identify themselves as indigenous or Aboriginal is not an isolated phenomenon and should be seen in the context of other, largely urban, cosmopolitan social trends: the growing disenchantment with secular materialism, the increasing interest in non-Western and New Age religions, the ecological movement, arguably all further examples of the 'demodernization impulse' (Berger *et al.* 1973; Tacey 1998, 2000; Heelas 1996).

Although, as we have seen, it is by no means shared unanimously across Australian society, the inclination to take responsibility and even to feel guilt for the treatment of indigenous populations in the colonisation of Australia further polarises distinctions between 'settler' and 'Aboriginal' culture in a post-colonial reversal of colonial values. Settler culture thus becomes associated with excessive materialism, spiritual impoverishment, moral corruption, and a sense of being lost in uncertainty; whereas Aboriginal culture comes to embody all that is authentic, rich and wholesome (e.g. Hammond 1991; Tacey 1998, 2000) (Table 9.2). Needless to say, this view is based upon a romanticisation of Aboriginal culture, which is in fact a more accurate reflection of the aspirations of the settler culture in crisis.

David Tacey, a Melbourne-based academic and prominent commentator on such issues, writes, 'I think white Australians would agree more readily today with the Aboriginal accusation that we have no spiritual culture. . . . There is a realisation of our spiritual emptiness beside the spiritual richness of traditional Aboriginal culture. . . . Aboriginality remains a symbol of spirituality in the Australian mind' (2000: 42–3). As the colonial commoditisation of landscape becomes increasingly marginalised in this new value system, Tacey suggests that white Australians are experiencing a kind of 'colonisation in reverse': 'after two hundred years of white colonial arrogance, where we believed that we "conquered" the land and imposed European images and practices upon it, this land is now conquering us' (ibid.: 99).

Thus, what was once considered by colonists and settlers as *terra nullius* is now perceived as a landscape dense with the spirits and dreamings of a people who have occupied it for tens of thousands of years. The consequence, as Curthoys argues, is yet another displacement as the settlers' ontological and epistemological bearings are again cut adrift. This is forcefully articulated by the Australian historian Manning Clark in a speech of 1988, in which he recognises the incompatibility of his Western, historical modes of thought and the 'Aboriginal' landscape he attempts to apprehend.

> Sometimes when I stand in the Australian bush on a clear windless day, I am visited with strange thoughts: am I living in a country where history has not begun, or where history is all over? I wonder whether I belong. I am not alone in such thoughts. I am ready, and so are others, to understand the Aboriginal view that no human being can ever know heart's ease in a foreign land, because in a foreign land there live foreign ancestral spirits. We white people are condemned to live in a foreign country where we have no ancestral spirits. The conqueror has become the eternal outsider, the eternal alien. We must either become assimilated or live the empty life of a people exiled from their source of spiritual strength. (1997: 144)

Table 9.2 Post-colonial re-evaluation of 'Settler' and 'Aboriginal' cultures

Settler	Aboriginal
Superficial	Deep
Young	Old
Modern	Traditional
Secular	Spiritual
Uprooted	Rooted
Unconnected to land	Connected to land
Immoral DESIRE	Moral
Complicated belonging	Uncomplicated belonging
Victimisers	Victimised
Dominant	Minority
Discontinuity	Continuity
Uncertainty	Certainty
Culture	Nature
Rational	Intuitive
Extension in context of 'British' roots	
Anglo-Saxon	Celtic
English	Scottish
Lowlander	Highlander

Clark characterises the alternatives facing the descendants of settlers as being either a new exile or assimilation to an *Aboriginal* Australia. A third response is, however, possible: one in which white Australians turn to their *own* ancestral connections to find some 'answering image' to that represented by traditional Aboriginal culture (Tacey 2000: 142).

Roots tourists in the Scottish Highlands and Islands are not only interested in visiting the ruins of croft houses, deserted settlements and graveyards with which they have established some documented connection, they are also often drawn to prehistoric monuments in the areas in which they have traced their ancestors (Figure 9.4). Part of this attraction no doubt reflects a more general contemporary 'megalithomania' (Mitchell 1982): archaeological tourism has, for instance, become the mainstay of the Orkney Islands' tourist economy and is rigorously promoted in other regions of the Highlands and Islands. I suggest, however, that, for roots tourists, in addition to this general interest, such places have other more particular meanings and connotations, and that they are in some way equivalent to the sacred sites of indigenous populations in the New World, sites from which settler populations feel excluded. At these standing stones, henges and tombs, roots tourists are permitted a profound sense of connection – these, they believe, are the sacred sites of their own ancestors and they approach them with attitudes of reverence.

Figure 9.4 A Canadian homecomer at Clach na h-Annait, near Torrin, Isle of Skye
(Paul Basu)

A Celtic Dreaming

Figure 9.5 shows Janet, an informant from Geelong, and Elspeth, her sister
from Melbourne, during their visit to their ancestral home in the Outer
Hebrides in 1999. It is an enlarged photograph of this standing stone on
Berneray in the Sound of Harris, with her ancestral island of Pabbay in the
background, which is framed on Janet's kitchen wall. Whilst the visit to
Pabbay itself – its old burial ground, the ruins of the township where the
sisters' ancestors are recorded in the 1841 census – was an understandably
profound experience, this stone had a special significance for Janet.
Similarly, when we discovered what appeared to be a prehistoric midden
eroding out of the island's sandy cliffs, Janet remarked that she had come
across similar remains along the coast where she lived in Australia:
Aboriginal middens. Conscious of the debates in Australia concerning the
ownership of the past and the complexities surrounding archaeological
excavation at Aboriginal sites, she expressed reservations when I asked how
she felt about excavation in these islands: 'That's *our* stuff', she stressed.

Janet explained her sense of belonging in the islands in two ways. First,
there was a rational sense of equivalence:

Figure 9.5 Australian homecomers, Janet and Elspeth, photographing a standing
stone on Berneray in the Sound of Harris. Their ancestral island of Pabbay
can be seen in the distance (Paul Basu)

> I've sort of been interested in Aboriginal culture, but I've never felt a
> connection with it. So, if you find an Aboriginal midden – and I've
> found several on the coast that I live on – it's not part of you, it's sort
> of part of Australia, but it's not connected with me. And so it's quite
> different finding a midden in the place where your ancestors had been,
> possibly for thousands of years.

This, then, was her own prehistoric heritage, but she also explained that
her attitude towards these sites was influenced by her spiritual beliefs,
which she described as being pagan and animistic, more akin to Aboriginal
belief systems as she understood them. Familiar with indigenous land title
legislation in Australia, Janet half-jokingly – but only *half*-jokingly –
mooted the idea of making an indigenous land claim on Pabbay. She said
that in Australia, 'The commonly accepted criteria for determining
Aboriginality are that the person identifies themselves as Aboriginal, that
the Aboriginal community they claim to be part of accepts them, and that
they are descended from Aboriginal people'. In these terms, despite also
having Lowland, English and Polish roots, she felt that she qualified as
being indigenous to Pabbay, a conviction that was confirmed to her when
local people accepted her as such.

> I certainly saw my visit to the now empty Isle of Pabbay as returning
> to my native land, and was thrilled about how, once I had established

my credentials by quoting my lineage, I was immediately accepted and introduced to others in the Isles as a *Pabbaich* [i.e. someone who belongs to Pabbay].

Australians, such as those of Scottish Highland descent, who claim a Celtic heritage have an especially powerful 'answering image' to Aboriginality at their disposal. The Celt, in a British context, is to the Anglo-Saxon what the Aboriginal, in the Australian context, is to the settler. Displaced by the invader and forced to the margins, before being forced into exile overseas, the Celt is perceived to be the British – or even the European – aboriginal.[10] For the person of Scottish Highland descent living in Australia, for example, and so inclined, to have Celtic roots is to demonstrate that one also has a rich, tribal heritage, rooted deeply within a landscape that is both mystical and mythical. And, indeed, the Celtic spirituality books nestle closely with those concerned with the Aboriginal Dreamtime on the shelves of the 'Esoteric' and 'New Age' sections of bookshops from San Francisco to Sydney . . . to Boulder, Colorado.

I mention Boulder because this is the home of Frank, an informant I quoted in the last chapter, who describes himself as 'a poet, ecopsychologist and visionary teacher in the Celtic spiritual traditions', and who leads 'pilgrimages' to the Scottish Highlands to promote what he terms 'Highland cultural soul retrieval'. Frank claims to have spent twelve years studying with Native American teachers before participating in the Sun Dance ceremony of the Lakota people: a transformative experience which started him on his exploration of his own Celtic heritage. He explained to me,

> I see great difficulty in the fact that a Native American born in downtown Tulsa is perceived by his or her own people as someone who could easily go on to become a medicine person or healer or shaman – despite being a city Indian – but a person of Scottish or Welsh descent born in Powys, Fife or Virginia, let's say, is simply seen as a cultureless individual, not to mention that we don't see them as a potential Druid, healer, etc. without a great deal of suspicion, scepticism and so forth.

'What happened to our indigenous self?' he asks. Incidentally, his second, as yet unpublished, volume of poetry is entitled *Moss Roof, Stone Pillow: Poems of the Celtic Dreamtime*.

The discursive migration that results in this melding of American, Australian and Celtic notions of aboriginality is, of course, not always so pronounced. Roots tourists often keep journals during their visits and sometimes they adapt these into short stories which they self-publish and distribute within their families and to members of family history societies. In one Australian example, the author describes her Dreamtime trail as the 'Low Road' or 'Fairy Way' along which the spirits of dead exiles would return to Scotland. She writes,

I'm a fourth generation Australian but I know that the thread reaching back to the obscure past has never been broken. The process of evolution has failed to break the translucent thread that's mysteriously joined to the Isle of Skye.

I cannot explain some of my experiences, or why I wanted to go to the Hebridean Isles long before I knew some of my forebears came from there. My only explanation is that the spirits of my ancestors kept calling me back. (Rooks n.d.: 2)

A significant characteristic of this informant's narrative is that it is not she, the homecomer/author, who is calling to her ancestors as a way of negotiating the complexities of belonging in contemporary Australia, but rather her ancestors who are calling to her. Here, again, is the subtle influence of an alien discourse, reversing the logic whereby individuals typically possess a heritage, such that the individual becomes the possession of her ancestors. Thus, the author's home may be in New South Wales, but it is to Skye that she belongs.

Ultimately the appeal of aboriginality is the appeal of autochthony. In an era in which senses of belonging are complicated by an acute awareness of the historical injustices of invasion and colonisation, the merging of land, ancestors and identity evoked in Aboriginal origin myths represent an ideal of uncomplicated territorial belonging. As discussed in Chapter 6, the popular diasporic perception of the Scottish Highland clans, inseparable from their territories, evokes something similar. Thus, as we have seen, we can talk of the MacKay country of Strathnaver or Macpherson country in Badenoch. According to antiquarian writers and folklorists, this close association between clan and territory is a survival of a much more ancient tradition with autochthonic overtones, something which also surfaces in much fairy lore (Newton 2000: 207–20; Henderson and Cowan 2001). Thus, in his collection of *Celtic Manners as Preserved among the Highlanders*, first published in 1831, James Logan records that,

Particular clans had certain hills to which the spirit of their departed friends had a peculiar attachment. *Tom Mòr* was that appropriated to the house of Garva, a branch of Clan Pherson; and *Orc*, another hill, was regarded by the house of Crubin, of the same clan, as their place of meeting in a future state, and their summits were supernaturally illuminated when any member of the families died. (1867: 354)

Seton Gordon, referring to this latter hill (actually *An Torc*, 'The Boar of Badenoch'), notes simply that it was considered 'by the Macphersons of Crubin to be their supernatural home' (1995: 213 fn; see also Alexander Macpherson 1893: 348, 357).

The anthropologist, W. E. H. Stanner's Aboriginal informant memorably explained to him that,

White man got no dreaming,
Him go 'nother way.
White man, him go different
Him got road belong himself. (Stanner 1979: 24)

Journeying to Creag Dhubh or An Torc, the Australian roots tourist with a few Macpherson ancestors in her family tree, might justifiably reply that, whilst hers is indeed a different road, she has a Dreaming of her own.

But lest this begin to appear rather cosy, there is a further movement in this discursive migration. It may come as some surprise to learn that the 'prehistoric' stone circle pictured in Figure 9.6 was in fact only erected in 1991, and is not in Scotland, but in a place with a Scottish name: Glen Innes in New South Wales. According to Ian MacDiarmid, president of the Australian Standing Stones Management Board,

> They were erected as a national monument to commemorate the many thousands of immigrants who, over more than 200 years, have come from Cornwall, Ireland, the Isle of Man, Scotland, Wales, Brittany and other Celtic areas of Europe, to make Australia their home. The collective contribution of these highly talented incomers is immeasurable. Suffice to say that had they not come, Australia today would be a much lesser country than it is. (pers. comm.)

Figure 9.6 The Australian Standing Stones, Glen Innes, New South Wales (John Tregurtha)

Thus the new Celtic Dreaming comes to colonise the Australian landscape. I asked MacDiarmid whether he felt Aboriginal systems of thought regarding the landscape had influenced Celtic-Australian attitudes and he replied, 'Not at all in my opinion, except to make everyone, Celtic or non-Celtic, aware of the constant possibility of land claims. These appear often to be lodged for political purposes, and their authenticity is sometimes questionable'. He assured me that no Aboriginal site had been affected by the erection of the stones, and besides, 'the present-day Aboriginal population of the Glen Innes district are largely later arrivals with no tribal affinity to the area' – unlike the Celts, one is tempted to add, who hold their annual festival there.

10 Heuristic journeys

> He that cannot live as he desires at home, listens to the tale of fortunate
> islands, and happy regions, where every man may have land of his own . . .
> Samuel Johnson, *A Journey to the Western Islands of Scotland*

From a perspective at the beginning of the twenty-first century, a paradox
is apparent in this short excerpt from Johnson's 1775 account of his tour,
with Boswell, through the Hebrides. This has to do with changing perceptions of 'home' and its 'elsewheres'. In the 1770s, would-be emigrants
listened to the tales of 'fortunate islands and happy regions' embodied in
the idea of America – *the New World*. Such people sought escape from the
drudgery of poverty and the narrow prospects of home in an uncharted
future. Two hundred and thirty years later, many descendants of those
emigrants find that they cannot live as they desire in the homes their ancestors built in that new world and, for them, the tales to which they are now
prone concern the fortunate islands and happy regions of a past of imagined certainty and stability embodied in the idea of Scotland – *the Old
Country*. For the critic, there is no doubt that such regions, whether of the
future or of the past, are constructs of the imagination: mirror opposites,
reflections of the inadequacies of the 'here and now'. To merely dismiss
such imagined worlds as utopian would, however, be careless, and our
objective should instead be to seek to understand what aspirations these
imaginings conceal.

Just as we may speak of the various push and pull factors that acted
upon Scottish migrants in the eighteenth, nineteenth and twentieth
centuries, and which therefore contributed to the creation of a Scottish
diaspora, so we might consider what push and pull factors now act upon
their descendants in their quests to 'hunt down home'. For the middle-
class, cosmopolitan Americans, Australians, Canadians and New
Zealanders who make up the majority of my informants, these are, of
course, no longer matters of material welfare, and the desires that drive
these more temporary migrations are concerned rather with the welfare of
the 'spirit' or the 'soul'. Based on the comments of my informants, it
appears that among those factors pushing the roots tourists from the New

World are a discontentment with modernity with its rampant consumerism, superficiality, rootless mobility and excessive individualism; a problematisation of belonging in regions to which they have no ancient claim; and a corresponding sense of existential homelessness. Among those factors pulling the roots tourists to Scotland – to the Highlands – is, above all, its deeply mythologised, romanticised and emotion-laden landscape and culture, to which is added the possibility of a more profound belonging and the promise of finding there an aboriginal land of their own: 'a place', in Christina's words, 'that tells the myths and legends of [their] own ancestors, not someone else's'. For those who by dint of fortune may claim a Scottish heritage (and, one might add, by dint of having all the things that modernity offers), the fortunate islands and happy regions of the Highlands thus represent an 'other landscape' where each may find a 'true homeland' of her or his own. But 'homeland', no less than 'Highland', is surely no more than a euphemism for a more obscure 'region of the heart': a 'secret place' – and, I suggest, a sacred place – to the research of which the roots tourist is devoted (Dumont 1993: 94).

Shrines of self – defining the sacred in the homecoming journey

As we have seen, one of the dominant metaphors used by roots tourists to define their journeys is that of pilgrimage. Aside from the broad structure of the journey from 'an accustomed place towards a place or state that is held to embody ideals of importance' and back again, and the simultaneity of its 'outward and inward' trajectories (Morinis 1992: ix, 10), roots tourism and pilgrimage share many characteristics. Not least among these is the practice of collecting souvenirs or relics from ancestral places: as discussed in Chapter 3, such items typically include stones, pebbles, pieces of driftwood, sprigs of heather, pottery sherds and, as in the case of the Arizonans I mentioned in my Prologue, even flasks of water drawn from lochs, rivers and wells. Like purported fragments of the 'real cross' or ampullae of holy water hawked outside medieval cathedrals, such objects contain the 'sacred substance' of the ancestral home, which roots tourists can then carry back to the diaspora and display on mantelpieces, book-shelves and other household shrines devoted to Scottish memorabilia. Conversely, intimate objects such as finger rings and brooches representing the homecomer or others unable to travel (elderly parents, for example) are sometimes left at ancestral places like *ex votos* at the shrines of saints.

The homologies between roots tourism and pilgrimage are also noted by Celeste Ray in her study of the Scottish heritage community in North Carolina. Discussing tours to Scotland organised by clan societies, she explains, 'I interchange the term pilgrim with heritage tourist, because community members describe their own travels as pilgrimage, and also because their travels are structured by and have meaning as pilgrimage' (2001: 134). The structure to which Ray refers is Turner's notion of 'ritual process' – the passage between 'structure' (ordinary, profane) and 'anti-structure' (non-ordinary, sacred) (Turner 1974) – and, particularly, the application of this process to touristic practices (MacCannell 1976; Graburn 1989; E. Cohen 1992). Thus, according to Graburn, because the touristic journey 'lies in the nonordinary sphere of existence', its goal is 'symbolically sacred and morally on a higher plane than the regards of the ordinary workaday world' (1989: 28). Pursuing this Turnerian orthodoxy, Ray explains that the 'commemorative activities' performed by 'heritage pilgrims' during these tours 'have ritualistic and religious qualities' (2001: 134) and she draws attention to the sense of *communitas* achieved among clansfolk during such events (2001: 133). I have certainly found much to support this argument in my own research with roots tourists in the Scottish Highlands. Indeed, as roots tourists leave behind the 'ordinary' world of their diasporic homes and enter the 'non-ordinary' sphere of the ancestral homeland, they do appear to enter a 'liminal' zone where they often report supernatural occurrences and altered states of mind (feeling ancestral presences, having premonitory dreams, etc.). Such other-worldly experiences add to the transformative potential of these rites of passage, and roots tourists may return to their ordinary homes significantly changed, sometimes experiencing difficulties readjusting to domestic routines and commitments or else determined to resolve outstanding problems.

In these terms, roots tourism may undoubtedly be conceptualised as a kind of ritual process or secular pilgrimage (Reader and Walter 1993), but I am not convinced that this wholly explains the sense of 'sacredness' that animates these journeys, nor fully explores the metaphor of the roots tourist as pilgrim. Understanding roots tourism specifically as a *social* drama (Turner 1974), Ray argues that 'heritage pilgrimage' is 'not the individual pilgrimage of finding oneself, but that of finding one's "people" and one's "place"' (2001: 133). I contend, however, that, in these journeys, a more complex dialectic exists between this integrative social identity and a more 'self-centred' individual/individuated identity. 'It is the "soul" that yearns to return to its own land and return to its own people', explains an Australian informant, 'it is the "soul" that needs to regain its sense of self at the grass roots'. 'In finding our ancestors', remarks another, 'we somehow find ourselves'.[1] I suggest that what empowers these transformative journeys of discovery, what imbues them with an aura of the sacred, is this very convergence of socialising and personalising trajectories: a quasi-mystical finding of oneself in others and others in oneself. In a transcendental epiphany of 'connectedness', the apparent contrariness of oneself *as another* and oneself *as being other* (Ricoeur 1992) is thus resolved, and the 'sites of memory' and 'sources of identity', which are the destinations of these journeys, ultimately also become 'shrines of self'.

In this respect, I am not unmindful of the post-structuralist critique of the sacred that has characterised much anthropological writing on pilgrimage since John Eade and Michael Sallnow's *Contesting the Sacred* (1991). It goes without saying that the 'spiritual magnetism' (Preston 1992) which empowers the particular 'sacred centres' of roots tourism, is highly selective in its influence, drawing only those who seek it. As such, it would be foolish to suggest that there is anything inherently sacred about these destinations outside the emotional, intellectual and physical journeys through which their sacredness is constructed; or to doubt that they are, if not exactly 'voids', then certainly 'vessels' into which roots tourists 'devoutly pour their hopes, prayers and aspirations' (Eade and Sallnow 1991: 15). However, like Rapport and Dawson's contestation of the rootedness of identity, such deconstructions prioritise 'etic' over 'emic' interpretations, and therefore do not fully engage with the subjective realities of the experiences of those we are studying. Thus, just as the practices of roots tourism demonstrate that modern individuals continue to 'centre themselves' in a notion of home that is itself centred on the specific spatial and temporal coordinates of homeland, so they attest to the resilience of a concept of the sacred that is perceived to emanate from particular places rather than merely being projected onto such places according to the needs of each subject (cf. Eliade 1958: 369). This is surely crucial if we are to attempt to understand not only how certain places come to be regarded as sacred, but also how they acquire the capacity to effect *real* personal transformations in the individuals who experience them as such.

By taking seriously the metaphorical practices of roots tourists, we discover not the formulation of 'ever more vacuous' generalisations of the sacred (Eade and Sallnow 1991: 9), but evidence for the reconfiguration of the sacred in the context of what has been characterised as a 'post-secular' age (Tacey 2000). Whether these post-secular pilgrimages are rooted in the routes of more ancient pilgrims' ways, as in the contemporary reanimation of the Camino de Santiago (Frey 1998), in New Age meccas such as Glastonbury or Sedona (Ivakhiv 2001) or, indeed, in the moral geographies of an ancestral homeland, they succeed in remapping the sacred in terrains both physical and metaphysical, thus re-enchanting a world perceived to be dulled by secular rationalism with transcendent mystery. Metaphorically translated into pilgrims, roots tourists are thus called to cross 'the boundaries of their familiar territory' and set off 'in search of the earthly home of their god' (Morinis 1992: 1). And, if it is not God in any orthodox sense that they seek, then the question remains: to what ideals incarnate are these contemporary spiritual odysseys directed?

A clue may be found in the guidebooks that such pilgrims carry with them on their journeys: not the *Codex Calixtinus* of old, but 'personal growth' manuals such as Phil Cousineau's *The Art of Pilgrimage: The Seeker's Guide to Making Travel Sacred* (1999), John O'Donohue's *Eternal Echoes: Exploring Our Hunger to Belong* (1998), and Frank MacEowen's

The Mist-Filled Path: Celtic Wisdom for Exiles, Wanderers and Seekers (2002). As Nancy Frey notes of the motives that draw post-secular *peregrinos* to Santiago, 'the spiritual shares the stage with a wide variety of esoteric, cultic, or individualized religious practices characteristic of Western religious and New Age movements' (1998: 34). Such alternative spiritual callings often entail a rejection of religious orthodoxies in favour of 'more vaguely defined personal searches or inner journeys of transformation' (ibid.: 33). Thus these pilgrimages become 'personal therapeutic acts' (Morinis 1992: 9), influenced as much by popular psychology as more institutionalised ritual practices – active responses to the perceived 'relative dearth of effective rites of passage' in the secular world of the West (LaCapra 2001: 76).

In this New Age canon, we find a familiar assertion of opposition between the alienating, urban world of (post)modernity and the prospect of home and wholeness represented by some inner spiritual realm that may, nevertheless, have its material counterpart in nature and, particularly, in the 'Celtic' homelands. The Connemara-based John O'Donohue, for example, borrows Berger *et al.*'s phrase, 'the homeless mind', to characterise this 'postmodern' malaise (1998: 233):

> In this post-modern world the hunger to belong has rarely been more intense, more urgent. With many of the ancient, traditional shelters now in ruins, it is as if society has lost the art of fostering community. Consumerism propels us towards an ever-more lonely and isolated existence. . . . And although technology pretends to unite us, more often than not all it delivers are simulated images that distance us from our lives. The 'global village' has no roads or neighbours; it is a faceless, impersonal landscape from which all individuality has been erased. (Ibid.: xvii–xviii)

Frank MacEowen reiterates these sentiments when he explains, 'We are not at home in our homes, because we are not at home in ourselves. . . . We are not at home in our minds' (2002: xxi). He continues, 'We have become exiles from one another, exiles from the lives we yearn to live; we have become disenfranchised from our dreams, strangers to our own inner faces, wandering like hungry ghosts for some sense of belonging' (ibid.: xxii). 'My wish for you', he states, in outlining the objectives of his book, 'is a homecoming in this life' (ibid.: xxiii).

Such a homecoming is made possible through practices that enable the individual to reconnect with an inherited wisdom which is described as lying dormant *within* the self. MacEowen explains this as awakening the 'sleeping lineage' of one's ancestors (ibid.: 95); O'Donohue as recognising the 'stream of ancestry' (and, therefore, ancestral wisdom) 'that flows within us' (1998: 38). 'Blood is one of the most ancient and wisest streams in the universe', O'Donohue writes, and thus by heading upstream, as it were, to the source, the 'seeker' can draw on that wisdom in his or her 'pilgrimage of discovery' (ibid.). The pilgrim's way in this context is portrayed by MacEowen as 'The Hearth Way', the hearth being 'the heart of the Celtic home' (2002: 190). In another New Age text, David Whyte's *Crossing the Unknown Sea*, this journey 'to the centre of identity' is described as 'the holiest of pilgrimages' (2001: dustjacket). This liturgy of soul searching and the sacralisation of ancestral identity reaches its culmination for O'Donohue in a 'philosophy of *Dúcas*' (the Irish equivalent of the Scottish Gaelic *dùthchas* discussed in Chapter 6). O'Donohue explains that this untranslatable concept succeeds in capturing something of the 'many deep and penumbral layers to the way we belong in the world' and argues that, in Irish, 'the phrase "*ag fillead ar do dúcas*" means returning to your native place and also *the rediscovery of who you are*' (1998: 259; emphasis added).

> The return home is also the retrieval and reawakening of a hidden and forgotten treasury of identity and soul. To come home to where you belong is to come into your own, to become what you are, to awaken and develop your latent spiritual heritage. . . . *Dúcas* also refers to a person's deepest nature. It probes beneath the surface images and impressions of a life and reaches into that which flows naturally from the deepest well in the clay of the soul. It refers in this sense to that whole intuitive and quickness of longing in us that tells us immediately how to think and act; we call this instinct. (1998: 259–60)

Invoking the victimological narrative of an indigenous people 'forcibly relocated from the[ir] homelands', MacEowen portrays this 'deep longing for home' as a particularly Celtic (and, more specifically, Celtic diasporic) predisposition (2002: 54). After being 'separated from the ancestral lands by several generations', he writes, 'the Celtic soul has sprung up again from the moist roots of our past, and the spirit of longing now travels like a restless ghost seeking embodiment, expression and manifestation' (ibid.). Whilst MacEowen's 'Celtocentrism' blinds him to the 'spirit of longing' that surely haunts those who identify with other 'ethnic' heritages (and with none), there can be no doubt that roots tourists who do share in this Celtic Dreaming find such 'embodiment, expression and manifestation' in their encounters with the Scottish landscape.

Although the New Age is notoriously eclectic in its borrowings and appropriations, many of its primary influences are drawn from Jungian and transpersonal psychology. In a recent commentary on psychology as a religion, G. William Barnard argues that religion and psychology now largely 'fulfill similar, if not identical, roles and functions': both may be understood as vehicles for the 'exploration of the depths of reality and consciousness', both enable healing and fulfilment 'via a dynamic, experi-

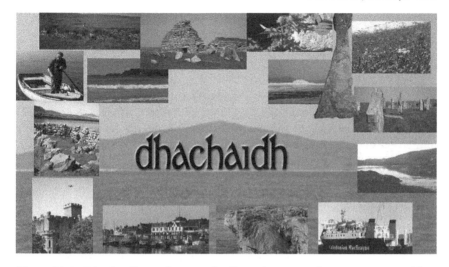

Figure 10.1 'Dhachaidh' – 'a home, a dwelling place'. A collage-poster created by an Australian informant recalling her homecoming journey to the Hebrides

ential, living contact with a cosmic "more"' (2001: 297). In this context, it is interesting to note that at the culmination of his genealogical journey in *Roots*, Alex Haley uses the term 'the peak experience' to describe his homecoming to Juffure, the Gambian village to which he has supposedly traced his eighteenth-century ancestor (1991: 676). The phrase is borrowed from the founding father of transpersonal psychology, Abraham Maslow, who used it to characterise the 'dramatic, if short-lived openings of consciousness leading to feelings of awe, a sense of wholeness and connection or even union with the natural world' (Barnard 2001: 309). Maslow sought to disassociate such 'mystical illuminations', which he believed were the 'intrinsic core' of all religions, from institutional religious structures and instead incorporate them within a new naturalistic faith based on personal experience (ibid.). Along with Jungian theory, transpersonal psychology 'stresses the need to unfold the innate potentials hidden within each person', but it also emphasises those 'aspects of the human psyche that seem to transcend personal boundaries' (ibid.). Combined with the ascendant discourse of 'genetic essentialism' associated with the new genetic sciences (Strathern 1992, 1995; Sykes 1999; Nash 2004), this vision of cosmic connectedness in the very substance of the individual injects a potent new 'genealogical rhetoric' into the stolid, matter-of-fact world of family history research, transforming it into an atavistic mystery religion of sorts. The *'mysterium tremendum'* at its heart (that to which it makes its 'pilgrimage of discovery') is not, however, the ancestors themselves ('one's people'), nor 'their place', hallowed though that land may be, but is ultimately no more, and no less, than the self. The obfuscation is, of course, a necessary component of the *mysterium* – as Gerhard Tersteegen wrote, 'A God comprehended is no God' (quoted by Otto 1980: 25) – and the ineffable, non-rational, numinous 'peak experience' becomes an end in itself, 'something sought for its own sake' (Otto 1980: 33).

Roots tourists in the Scottish Highlands often report feeling especially drawn to a particular ancestor they have discovered in their genealogical research. For Sharon, an informant from New South Wales who I have quoted elsewhere in this book, this was her great-great-grandfather, Alexander, born in 1807. Sharon explains that Alexander was 'just a name' when she first found him on an 1881 census, but by the time of her homecoming in 1999, when she visited his grave and the various places in which he had lived, she felt she had come to know him and sensed his presence beside her on her explorations. She explained,

> I read somewhere that a person dies three times, once when the soul leaves the body, the second time is when they are interred in the grave, and the third time is when their name is spoken for the last time. . . . Until I 'found' him in 1997 his life had passed into history. I have to wonder who was the last person to speak of him before me and how many years he had lain in that kirkyard before I came to visit. . . . I sometimes feel he lives again through me.

Despite this strong sense of identification with an ancestral figure, it is apparent, however, that Sharon's genealogical quest was not only about the past, but was in fact more concerned with her present, about 'finding Sharon', as she put it. On her second visit to Scotland, as we wandered around the ruins of Auchabrack, the deserted township in which her ancestors once lived, Sharon elaborated on this sense of self-(re)discovery:

> When I grew up I was always Betty's daughter, and then I sort of went from home to married life, so I was David's wife, and then David, Andrew and Steven's mother, and somewhere in all that Sharon got lost. And then when I came here, I had this sense of freedom, you know, this is *mine*. . . . Yes. This is mine. But in this being mine, *this is finding out who I am*, so really it's nobody else's. Who else can you let in? I can tell you for a thousand years how I feel a sense of belonging to this area, but you can never know it because it's an emotion, not a tangible thing or something you can write on paper. There's no words to describe it, because it's in here [pointing to heart] and it's in here [pointing to head].

In this way genealogical research and heritage tourism may be understood as the 'outward and visible form to an inward and conceptual process'

Figure 10.2 Sharon laying flowers at Alexander's grave (Paul Basu)

(Turner 1991: 96): past- and place-orientated practices effecting personal transformations in the present.

Heuristic journeys

> Sweet is the lore which Nature brings;
> Our meddling intellect
> Mis-shapes the beauteous forms of things: –
> We murder to dissect.
>> William Wordsworth, 'The Tables Turned'

> The contemporary zeal for the project of interpretation is often prompted not by piety toward the troublesome text . . . but by an open aggressiveness, an overt contempt for appearances. . . . The modern style of interpretation excavates, and as it excavates, destroys; it digs 'behind' the text, to find a sub-text which is the true one.
>> Susan Sontag, 'Against Interpretation'

In an analogy familiar to anthropologists (e.g. Clifford 1997), Sontag argues that the task of interpretation is one of translation: 'The interpreter says, Look, don't you see that X is really – or, really means – A? That Y is really B? That Z is really C?' (1983: 97). The task is a problematic one since, in our eagerness to discern the As, Bs and Cs, we perhaps overlook the 'X-ness' of the Xs, the 'Y-ness' of the Ys, the 'Z-ness' of the Zs, and so impoverish the world we believe we are enriching. 'To interpret', writes Sontag, 'is . . . to deplete the world – in order to set up a shadow world of "meanings"' (ibid.: 98–9). In 'meddling' with the haecceity or 'thisness' of the phenomenon under the vivisector's blade, the archaeologist's trowel, the anthropologist's participatory observations, the interpreter does indeed commit a destructive act. For example, in deconstructing the myths and rituals we have constructed and by which we live, we undermine their effectiveness in fulfilling their particular function, their *raison d'être*. 'Away', rejoins Sontag, with these shadowy 'duplicates' of the world, these intellectualisations, until we are again able to experience the immediacy of the phenomenal world (ibid.: 99).

In her nostalgia for an uninterpreted reality, a reality unmediated by the intellect, Sontag is, of course, no less a romantic than Wordsworth. Neither can she (nor he) escape the metaphorical logic that lies not only at the heart of the academic endeavour of 'intellectuals', but also at the heart of the intellectual endeavour that is part of being human: the fact that we are cognitive as well as sentient beings. We are, then, 'self-interpreting animals' (Taylor 1985), who live by myths and metaphors, and through other symbolic systems (Lakoff and Johnson 1980; J. Bruner 1990; Samuel and Thompson 1990), each perpetually engaged in a hermeneutics of the self and of the world in which we live (Foucault 1988: 46) (a process whereby old myths are continually razed and new ones set up in their place). Our experience of the world is not merely enriched, but is *enabled* by the analogical faculty through which an 'X' (for instance, the project of interpretation) may be understood in terms of an 'A' (for instance, the process of archaeological excavation) – which is emphatically not to suggest that we should be uncritical of our interpretative procedures or unperturbed by their potential for destructiveness.

In the absence – the impossibility – of any grand unifying theory, 'interpretation' has, I hope, been implicit throughout this book in a form recommended by Clifford Geertz: that is, as a 'discussion sustained' with and between the various 'texts' that have emerged in the course of my research (1993: 29). Such discussions do not resolve into any singular 'conclusion', and thus I have given a title to this concluding chapter that reflects an ongoing dialogical process and not an end. The title, 'Heuristic journeys', also acknowledges that, prior to the reader, there are at least two key interpreting agents engaged in this conversation: the anthropologist and the informant. Thus, in one sense, the title alludes to the analytical schema through which I – as anthropologist – have proposed that we might understand the practices described in this book: a course navigated across a discursive landscape between homepages and homelands, mediascapes and clanscapes, sites of memory, sources of identity and shrines of self. In another sense, the title recognises that these practices are themselves agents for (self-)understanding for those – my informants – who participate in them, and that the homecoming journey may therefore be understood *as* a heuristic journey.

Derived from the Greek verb *heurisko* (to 'find' or 'come to know'), in logic, a heuristic device is regarded as something 'conducive to understanding, explanation or discovery; . . . a problem solving procedure that may fall short of providing a proof' (Honderich 1995). In maintaining that the 'problem' to which these journeys are directed is the sense of estrangement consequent upon the individual's experience of modernity, I certainly do not pretend to claim this as a 'proof'. In fact, roots tourism fails get to the 'root' of the problem; on the contrary, it provides escape from the 'real issue', representing, along with a host of other demodernising and reenchanting strategies (Tacey 2000), no more than a temporary salve, adequate for the moment. Thus, the sense of homelessness that lies at the heart of homecoming can only truly be solved when we have indeed 'disarmed the genealogical rhetoric of blood, property and frontiers' (Rapport and Dawson 1998: v and 22; Carter 1992: 8) and finally made ourselves 'at home' in our rootless and restless lives – but that, alas, remains no less a vision of utopia than a diaspora's nostalgia for its homeland.

In the meanwhile, then, exploiting the very globalising technologies it rebels against, genealogical tourism succeeds in providing 'some expressive relationship to the past', 'attachment to particular territorial locations' that act as 'nodes of association and continuity', and, answering the desire in many 'to be "at home" in the new and disorientating global space', it offers some ontological security to counter the existential anxieties of late modernity (Giddens 1991; Morley and Robins 1995: 87). So conducive, in fact, are the procedures of genealogical research to 'understanding, explanation and discovery', that the consequence of this burgeoning phenomenon is actually a proliferation of roots, each, to repeat the hackneyed pun, offering a route back home.

By focusing on the migrations of meanings and discourses, as well as of people and places, I hope I have been able to show something of how the complexities, multiplicities and ambiguities of modern identity may be 'made sense of' in relation to family history and its geographies. Home – as an ideal of uncomplicated belonging, as a site of memory, a source of identity, a shrine of self – is made material in homeland, and is thereby given specific temporal and spatial coordinates that can be pinpointed on a map and which permit the homecomer to say, with Morag in Laurence's *The Diviners*, 'There is such a place. It really exists' (1989: 313; cf. Salmond 1982: 85). As metaphor is made material, so it transcends language-bound cognitive processes, and thus the homecoming journey articulates that which cannot be voiced and 'speaks' directly to the heart and soul – and, I suggest, to the homeless mind too.

Recalling her homecoming to Auchabrack, Sharon explained to me,

> Sometimes there are just no words that adequately describe such emotions. As I sit here now, I ponder on what words I could use to put what I feel into a sentence to convey these feelings to you. There are none. The fact that you go to these places says it all – it says you recognise your links, you accept your links and that link is part of you. Physical acts, the walking, the touching, even the breaths you take, the aromas you inhale, the sounds you hear, says it all. The earth is the same, the sounds and aromas are the same, be it now in 1999 or in 1799. This is me and I have depth! This depth goes back generations, too far for me to trace, I am a seed of a man who walked on this very ground 200 years ago, maybe many many more . . .

She added, 'I know I changed on that trip, whether I grew up, or wider or deeper is hard to tell'.

Notes

Prologue: other landscapes

1 The 'Province of Cat' or 'Cait' is an earlier name for the region including Caithness and Sutherland, supposedly relating to a Pictish tribe for whom the cat was a totemic animal. The point being that the Canadian-Scot, Gus, has retained or acquired such arcane knowledge, while the Caithness-born brothers are unaware of it.

1 Introduction

1 The authenticity of Haley's evocation of his ancestral journey in *Roots* has been contested by several critics; see Lowenthal (1985: 228), Shoumatoff (1995: 219–24) and Ebron (2002: 189–212) for discussion.
2 According to STB statistics, between 1997 and 2001, an average of 438,000 Americans, 127,000 Canadians, 110,000 Australians, and 24,000 New Zealanders visited Scotland per annum. The USA is Scotland's largest overseas tourism market (Scottish Tourist Board 2002).
3 There is a vast historical literature on the subject of Scottish migration and settlement overseas (e.g. Bumsted 1982; Cage 1985; Prentis 1987; Hunter 1994 and 1996; Devine 2003; Harper 2003), a substantial body of 'ethnological' work dealing with Scottish Gaelic culture in migrant contexts (e.g. C. W. Dunn 1953; MacDonnell 1982; M. Bennett 1989 and 1998; J. L. Campbell 1999; Cardell and Cumming 1999; Newton 2001), and a growing interest among anthropologists and cultural geographers concerning the Scottish heritage 'revival' in North America (e.g. Ray 2001, Hague 2002). I do not pretend to offer anything like a summary of these literatures in the book.
4 Concerning the Irish diaspora and famine narrative see, for example, K. A. Miller (1985), Akenson (1996), Crawford 1997; for a discussion of genealogy and identity in the Irish diaspora see Nash (2002).
5 See Harper (2003) for a thorough exploration of the 'complex fusion' of motives and experiences which characterise Scottish emigration and settlement overseas.
6 The Scottish Highlands, as a 'culture region' (Withers 1988), generally includes the Islands. Encompassing areas with diverse histories, landscapes and resources, there is actually no homogenous 'culture' within this region. As Withers argues, the cultural geography of Highland Scotland ought instead to be understood in terms of 'diversity within unity' (1988: 3). In this book, such diversity is reflected in the individual case examples discussed, otherwise I refer to the Highlands in a looser, broadly inclusive manner.

7   See Devine (1999: 31–48) for a succinct summary of Jacobitism in Scotland. Often misunderstood in both homeland and diaspora as a struggle for Scottish independence from England, it would be more correct to describe the Jacobite Uprisings, which occurred in the period 1689 to 1746, as a civil war between supporters of the exiled Catholic Stuart dynasty and supporters of the Protestant succession (after 1714, the Hanoverians). Allegiances often shifted throughout this period, as did the exact nature of the cause being contested. Following the defeat of the 1745–46 Uprising at Culloden, pro-Jacobite areas of the Highlands were subjected to harsh reprisals, culminating in the Disarming Acts which sought to dismantle the militaristic basis of clan society and pacify the region once and for all.

8   See Harper (2005) for a recent collection of essays on the theme of return migration.

9   In his 1905 novel, *The Clansman*, Thomas Dixon describes the nineteenth-century Ku Klux Klan members as 'the reincarnated souls of the Clansmen of Old Scotland' (Hague 2002: 155, fn 12).

2   An itinerant anthropology

1   The exhibition, 'Home and away: Highland departures and returns', toured venues throughout the Highlands and Islands with an associated events programme in 2001 and has subsequently been displayed at the Ellis Island Immigration Museum in New York.

2   Small, family-run B&Bs (i.e. bed and breakfast accommodation) were preferred by roots tourists since they permitted more personal interaction with their local 'hosts' and allowed 'guests' to stay either in or closer to those places associated with their ancestors.

3   Mention should be made of the wider political and cultural context in which my fieldwork took place. In addition to the linguistic and cultural reinvigoration associated with the 'Gaelic Renaissance' (Macdonald 1997b) and the more diffuse Celtic revival (Harvey *et al.* 2002), the research coincided with a number of high profile events that have contributed to a period of unprecedented Scottish national confidence and international prominence. These include the release of a number of hugely popular historical feature films set in Scotland (most notably *Braveheart* in 1995) (Petrie 2000), the return of the Stone of Scone to Scotland in 1996 (Gerber 1997), the successful devolution referendum of 1997 (Paterson 1998), the opening of the Museum of Scotland in 1998 (Fladmark 2000), the reinstatement of the Scottish Parliament in 1999 (Lorimer 2002), and, not least – though, of course, not specifically Scottish – the Millennium celebrations of 1999/2000, which imbued otherwise ordinary events with an extraordinary quality.

3   Genealogy and heritage tourism in the Scottish diaspora

1   Recent examples dealing specifically with Scottish ancestry include Moody 1988; James 1995; Cory 1996; Irvine 1996; Holton and Winch 1997; Bigwood 1999.

4   Imagineering home

1   The neologism 'imagineer' was coined by Disney to describe the work of its theme park designers. The role of Disneyland imagineers is summarised by one of

Sharon Zukin's informants thus, 'what we create . . . is a "Disney realism", sort of Utopian in nature, where we carefully program out all the negative, unwanted elements and program in the positive elements' (1991: 222). Francaviglia describes Disneyland's 'imagineered heritage landscapes' as reflecting '*essence* rather than *reality*' (2000: 61). Both definitions have a resonance in the Scottish context. The representation of Scotland in the diasporic mediascape is utopian in the sense that it is both a distillation of an ideal, and, literally, a *nowhere* or *no-place* which may yet be projected onto an actual landscape (Carey 1999: xi).

2 The terms 'Highlandism' and 'tartanry' are often employed interchangeably to describe the stereotypical representation of Scotland. Here I use them differently and with discrete meanings to suggest that the representation of Scotland is not only based on stereotypes, but that these stereotypes are codified in particular ways. In my use of 'Highlandism' I intentionally infer a correspondence with Said's notion of Orientalism, i.e. 'a style of thought based upon an ontological and epistemological distinction between [the Highlands and the non-Highlands]' (see Said 1978: 2). 'Tartanry' I take merely to be a genre of Highlandist discourse – one often associated *in Scotland* with kitsch and bad taste. The discourse of the Highlands as unspoilt nature (including the Highlander living in harmony with nature) is, I suggest, another genre of Highlandism, equally ideological as tartanry, but (mis)recognised as being more 'authentic'.

3 Both 'locality' and 'authenticity' are problematic terms in this context. I use them merely to demonstrate the relative construction of the local and authentic against a variable non-local, non-authentic. My objective is not to interrogate the authenticity of the homeland imagined, so much as to interrogate the articulation of authenticity in the processes of imagining.

4 For the sake of consistency, except in quotation, I use the agency's established name, the Scottish Tourist Board (STB), rather than VisitScotland throughout the book and use the italicised *VisitScotland* only in reference to the STB's primary consumer web site.

5 The STB's £3million Spring 2002 Campaign, based on 'consumer branding research', includes TV and cinema advertisements, posters and direct marketing campaigns. A mission statement explains, 'the campaign will focus on the fact that Scotland is genuine, authentic, real and sensual' (www.scotexchange.net/ PromoteYourBusiness/spring-campaign2.htm).

6 Commenting on the membership of the National Trust for Scotland, for example, McCrone *et al.* report, 'We are able to identify a solidly bourgeois and conservative stratum in which cultural capital matters. While entrepreneurial strata are under-represented, those from professional, and especially educational, backgrounds are most conspicuous' (1995: 145).

5   Home spaces, homepages, homelands

1 According to a 'facts and statistics' page, the LDS *Family Search* site contains over a billion ancestral records in its searchable database (www.familysearch. com). See Shoumatoff (1995) for a discussion of the LDS doctrine of the 'Baptism of the dead', which underpins this vast and systematic collection of family history data. In 2002, after completing fieldwork, the *Scots Origins* web site was superseded by *ScotlandsPeople* (www.scotlandspeople.gov.uk), a partnership between the General Register Office for Scotland and the National Archives of Scotland.

2 '*Fear a'Bhata*' ('Oh My Boatman'), a traditional Gaelic song recorded by the Celtic band Capercaillie, released on their 1995 album *The Blood is Strong*.

3 The poster's name has been changed.

6 Clanlands

1 The same proverb is quoted elsewhere as *Lean gu dlùth ri cliù do shinnsre* (Newton 2000: 112), and is translated more 'poetically' as 'Follow closely the fame of your fathers' (Badenoch Centennial Committee 1967).
2 The ideological basis of clanship (the 'pretence' of common blood) is, of course, an orthodox anthropological view. As Durkheim writes in 1912, 'the individuals who comprise [a clan] consider themselves joined by a bond of kinship but a bond of a particular sort. This kinship does not arise from the fact that they have well-defined relations of common blood; they are kin solely because they bear the same name. They are not fathers, mothers, sons or daughters, uncles or nephews of one another in the sense we now give those terms; nevertheless they regard themselves as forming a single family . . . solely because they are collectively designated by the same word' (1995: 100). Among the contemporary Scottish heritage community, the totemic 'object' which collectively designates a group under the same name may be said to be its patronym.
3 Significantly, since completing fieldwork, both establishments have been 'rebranded' to downplay their clan identities in order to attract more mainstream tourists. The Clan Donald Centre has thus become 'Armadale Castle Gardens and Museum of the Isles', and 'Clanland', after narrowly avoiding closure, has become 'The Storehouse of Foulis'.
4 Glenfinnan and Culloden are both in the care of the National Trust for Scotland. Both are served by visitor centres, and both are marked by nineteenth-century monuments. The monument at Glenfinnan was built in 1815 by Alexander MacDonald of Glenaladale, 'to commemorate the generous zeal, the undaunted bravery and the inviolable fidelity of his forefathers and the rest of those who fought and bled in that arduous and unfortunate enterprise' (Sked 1991: 3). The massive cairn at Culloden was erected, along with a series of individual clan 'gravestones', in 1881 by Duncan Forbes and bears the inscription, 'The Battle of Culloden was fought on this moor / 16 April 1746 / The Graves of the Gallant Highlanders who fought for Scotland and Prince Charlie are marked by the names of their clans' (Sked 1997: 30).
5 The Memorial Cairn at Grandfather Mountain, North Carolina – the site of the largest annual Highland Games and 'Gathering of Scottish Clans' in the USA – provides an interesting 'inverse' to the Macpherson monument. The Grandfather Mountain cairn was dedicated at the Silver Anniversary Games held in 1980 and incorporates seventy-four polished stones, donated by different clans, mostly collected from their 'home hills and vales of Scotland' (Grandfather Mountain Highland Games Programme, 1986: 28–9; see also Ray 2001: 147).

7 Sites of memory, sources of identity

1 Note the consonance between Gunn's narrative and ethnographic accounts of storytelling practices in the landscape; for instance, Keith Basso's informant's description of Western Apache storytelling: 'They got to a good place and camped there. All day they gathered acorns. The women showed their daughters how to do it. Now they stopped working for a little while to eat and drink. . . . Then one of the women talked to the girls. "Do you see that mountain over there? I want you to look at it. Its name is Dzil ndeezé (Long Mountain). Remember it! Do you know what happened long ago close to that mountain? Well, now I'm going to tell you about it". Then she told them a story about what happened there. After she had finished she said, "Well, now you know

what happened at Long Mountain. What I have told you is true. I didn't make it up. I learned it from my grandmother. Look at that mountain and think about it! It will help to make you wise"' (Dudley Patterson quoted in Basso 1996: 67).

8   Homecomings

1   The inscription on the Bernera Riot cairn reads as follows: 'This cairn was erected by the people of Bernera and Tir Mor in 1992 to commemorate the participants in the Bernera Riot of 1874. This event was the first successful confrontation with authority leading eventually to the passing of the Crofters Act which gave Security of Tenure to all crofters. Stones from every croft in Bernera and Tir Mor are incorporated in the cairn. The coping stones are taken from the houses of the three men who stood trial'. Note the explicit narration of local identity contra centralised authority in this 'intentional monument', also the symbolic incorporation of the stones from the crofting lands themselves and the 'unintentional monuments' represented by the rioters' houses (Riegl 1982; Basu 1997 and 2000).

2   'Scottish Soldier', the popular folksinger Andy Stewart's version of 'The Green Hills of Tyrol':

> Because these green hills are not my highland hills
> Or the island hills, they're not my land hills
> And fair though these green foreign hills may be
> They are not the hills of home

3   Along with his later 'Oh Why Left I My Hame' (see Figure 9.1), Thomas Faed's painting 'The Last of the Clan' has become something of an icon of Highland defeat, clearance and exile. When first exhibited at the Royal Academy in London in 1865, the painting was accompanied by the following extract from an apocryphal 'Letter to a Kinsman in America': 'When the steamer had slowly backed out, and John MacAlpine had thrown off the hawser, we began to feel that our once powerful clan was now represented by a feeble old man and his granddaughter; who, together with some out-lying kith-an-kin, myself among the number, owned not a single blade of grass in the glen that was once all our own' (Royal Academy Catalogue 1865).

4   Ian Grimble's *The Trial of Patrick Sellar* (1962) and John Prebble's *The Highland Clearances* (1969).

5   Soon after returning to Canada, Brenda was to discover that it was her great-great-great-grandfather, Niall Alasdair MacKinnon from Allasdale, Barra, who emigrated to Canada in 1821. On subsequent visits, Brenda succeeded in locating and visiting Allasdale.

6   The poem 'Loch Lomond' is credited to Paul Watson on various diasporic Scots' web sites.

9   Exiles and emigrants

1   The 1851 Lochboisdale emigration aboard *The Admiral* is a notorious *exception* where there are considerable grounds for associating Clearance and forced emigration. Having agreed to accept assisted passage to Canada, a number of Gordon of Cluny's erstwhile tenants from South Uist and Barra absconded from their homes prior to embarkation. With police assistance, the absconders were pursued and those who were caught were handcuffed and forced onto the waiting ship (see Richards 2000: 219–24 and Harper 2003: 57–61 for discussion).

2 'Born Beyond the Border', lyrics by Maggie Innis, posted to gen-trivia-scotland@rootsweb.com, 3 May 1999.

3 See Kennedy (1999) for an examination of nineteenth-century emigrant discourse in Nova Scotia, and Womack (1989: 178–80) for analysis of 'The Canadian Boat Song'.

4 Earlier examples of this drawing of parallels between Scottish and biblical exile may be found in the context of the 'Covenanting Wars' of the mid-seventeenth century (see Murdoch 1999) and the Jacobite Uprisings of the late seventeenth and eighteenth centuries (see Ní Suaird 1999; Pittock 1991: 9–10). Kerby Miller has explored equivalent biblical motifs in the context of Irish exile and emigration (1985: 104).

5 In September 2003, plans for the monument were abandoned due, it was announced, to spiralling costs. Through numerous conversations with local people, however, it is clear that the monument did not have unanimous popular support.

6 A second consequence is the 'projection of blame for a putative loss onto identifiable others' (LaCapra 2001: 58): in a Scottish diasporic context, blame for the destruction of the Highland way of life is, as we have seen, typically projected onto the English.

7 This is not to deny the dislocative trauma of even voluntary economic migration, but it is to recognise a qualitative difference between those *forced to choose* emigration due to the paucity of viable alternatives and those forced to emigrate under the threat of physical violence.

8 The density of Highland settlement in Gippsland, envisioned by Angus McMillan as 'Caledonia Australis', is evident in the placenames of its mountains, rivers, lakes and estates. The names of the larger estates, for instance, included 'Boisdale', 'Glenfalloch', 'Glenmaggie', 'Glencoe', 'Armadale', 'Ensay' and 'Clydebank'. In addition to Macalister and McMillan, other major landowners included MacFarlanes, Campbells, MacDonalds, MacLeods and Thomsons (D. Watson 1984: 136).

9 This trend is also apparent in Canadian and New Zealand census data. Between 1991 and 1996, statistics across Australia, New Zealand and Canada show total population increases between 6 and 7 per cent, and indigenous population increases between 20 and 33 per cent (Australian Bureau of Statistics 2001b). See also Nagel (1995).

10 The construction of an 'ethnicised' British Iron Age as 'Celtic' is, of course, not unproblematic (see Jones and Grave-Brown 1996; Collis 1996), nor is the 'appropriation' by modern-day Celts of earlier megalithic monuments and artworks as Celtic (Chapman 1992). For a recent review of the construction of 'Celticity' in contemporary identity politics, see Harvey *et al.* (2002).

10 Heuristic journeys

1 This last comment echoes the words of a 'prose poem' that features on many family history web sites entitled 'The Storytellers'. It begins, 'We are the chosen. / My feelings are in each family there is one who seems called to find the ancestors. To put flesh on their bones and make them live again, to tell the family story and to feel that somehow they know and approve. To me, doing genealogy in not a cold gathering of facts but, instead, a breathing life into all who have gone before. We are the storytellers of the tribe. All tribes have one. We have been called as it were by our genes. Those who have gone before cry out to us: Tell our story. So, we do. / In finding them, we somehow find ourselves' (attributed to Tom Dunn).

Bibliography

Akenson, D. H. 1996. *The Irish Diaspora: A Primer*, Belfast: Institute for Irish Studies, Queens University of Belfast

Amit, V., ed., 2000. *Constructing the Field: Ethnographic Fieldwork in the Contemporary World*, London: Routledge

Anderson, B. 1991. *Imagined Communities: Reflections on the Origin and Spread of Nationalism*, London: Verso (first published 1983)

Andrews, M. 1990. *The Search for the Picturesque: Landscape Aesthetics and Tourism in Britain, 1760–1800*, Aldershot: Scolar Press

Appadurai, A. 1990. 'Disjuncture and Difference in the Global Cultural Economy', *Theory, Culture and Society*, 7(2–3): 295–310

—— 1991. 'Global Ethnoscapes: Notes and Queries for a Transnational Anthropology', in R. G. Fox, ed., *Recapturing Anthropology: Working in the Present*, Sante Fe: School of American Research Press

Aspinwall, B. 1985. 'The Scots in the United States', in R. A. Cage, ed., *The Scots Abroad*, London: Croom Helm

Australian Bureau of Statistics. 2000. 'Australian Social Trends 1998, Population – Population Growth: Growth and distribution of Indigenous people' (accessed at www.abs.gov.au)

—— 2001a. 'Population – Indigenous population' (accessed at www.abs.gov.au)

—— 2001b. 'Population – Aboriginal and Torres Strait Islander Australians: A statistical profile from the 1996 Census (Year Book Australia 1999)' (accessed at www.abs.gov.au)

Badenoch Centennial Committee. 1967. *Badenoch, 1832–1967* [n. pub.]

Barnard, G. W. 2001. 'Diving into the Depths: Reflections on Psychology as a Religion', in D. Jonte-Pace and W. B. Parsons, eds, *Religion and Psychology: Mapping the Terrain*, London: Routledge

Barthes, R. 1990. *S/Z*, Oxford: Blackwell (first published 1973)

Basso, K. H. 1996. 'Wisdom Sits in Places: Notes on a Western Apache Landscape', in S. Feld and K. H. Basso, eds, *Senses of Place*, Santa Fe: School of American Research Press

Basu, P. 1997. 'Narratives in a Landscape: Monuments and Memories of the Sutherland Clearances', unpublished master's thesis, University College London

—— 2000. 'Sites of Memory – Sources of Identity: Landscape-Narratives of the Sutherland Clearances', in J. A. Atkinson, I. Banks and G. MacGregor, eds, *Townships to Farmsteads: Rural Settlement Studies in Scotland, England and Wales*, Oxford: BAR British series 293

—— 2001. 'Hunting Down Home: Reflections on Homeland and the Search for Identity in the Scottish Diaspora', in B. Bender and M. Winer, eds, *Contested Landscapes: Movement, Exile and Place*, Oxford: Berg

—— 2004a. 'My Own Island Home: The Orkney Homecoming', *Journal of Material Culture*, 9 (1): 27–42

—— 2004b. 'Route Metaphors of "Roots-Tourism" in the Scottish Highland Diaspora', in S. Coleman and J. Eade, eds, *Reframing Pilgrimage: Cultures in Motion*, London: Routledge

Baudrillard, J. 1983. *Simulations*, New York: Semiotext(e)

Baumeister, R. F. 1997. 'The Self and Society', in R. D. Ashmore and L. Jussim, eds, *Self and Identity: Fundamental Issues*, Oxford: Oxford University Press

Benjamin, W. 1992. *Illuminations*, London: Fontana (first published 1955)

Bennett, C. 1999. 'Every sperm has a past', *The Guardian*, 29 June

Bennett, M. 1989. *The Last Stronghold: Scottish Gaelic Traditions in Newfoundland*, Edinburgh: Canongate

—— 1998. *Oatmeal and the Catechism: Scottish Gaelic Settlers in Quebec*, Edinburgh: John Donald

Berger, P. L., Berger, B. and Kellner, H. 1973. *The Homeless Mind: Modernization and Consciousness*, New York: Random House

Bigwood, R. 1999. *Tracing Scottish Ancestors*, London: HarperCollins

Birch, T. 1996. 'A Land So Inviting and Still Without Inhabitants: Erasing Koori Culture from (Post-)Colonial Landscapes', in K. Darien-Smith, L. Gunner and S. Nuttall, eds, *Text, Theory, Space: Land, Literature and History in South Africa and Australia*, London: Routledge

Bouquet, M. 1996. 'Family Trees and Their Affinities: The Visual Imperative of the Genealogical Diagram', *Journal of the Royal Anthropological Institute* 2 (1): 43–66

Bourdieu, P. 1977. *Outline of a Theory of Practice*, Cambridge: Cambridge University Press (first published 1972)

—— 1984. *Distinction: A Social Critique of the Judgement of Taste*, London: Routledge and Kegan Paul (first published 1979)

Brooking, T. 1985. 'Tam McCanny and Kitty Clydeside – The Scots in New Zealand', in R. A. Cage, ed., *The Scots Abroad*, London: Croom Helm

Bruce, D. A. 1997. *The Mark of the Scots: Their Astonishing Contributions to History, Science, Democracy, Literature and the Arts*, Secaucus, NJ: Birch Lane

Bruce, I. S. 2000. 'The past masters', *The Scotsman*, 13 March

Bruner, E. M. and Gorfain, P. 1988. 'Dialogic Narration and the Paradoxes of Masada', in E. Bruner, ed., *Text, Play and Story: The Construction and Reconstruction of Self and Society*, Prospect Heights, IL: Waveland (first published 1984)

Bruner, J. 1990. *Acts of Meaning*, Cambridge, MA: Harvard University Press

Buchanan, J. 1996. *The Lewis Land Struggle*, Stornoway, Isle of Lewis: Acair

Bumsted, J. M. 1982. *The People's Clearance: Highland Emigration to British North America, 1770–1815*, Edinburgh: Edinburgh University Press

Burns, J. 1988. *A Celebration of the Light: Zen in the Novels of Neil Gunn*, Edinburgh: Canongate

Cage, R. A., ed., 1985. *The Scots Abroad: Labour, Capital, Enterprise, 1750–1914*, London: Croom Helm

Cameron, V. R. 1930. 'Emigrants from Scotland to America, 1774–75', [n. pub.]

Campbell, A. 1998. 'Braveheart', *SCOTS*, 1: 28–30

Campbell, J. L. 1999. *Songs Remembered in Exile*, Edinburgh: Canongate (first published 1990)

Canadian Broadcasting Company (CBC) 1999. 'The Search for Norquoy', radio documentary produced by Dick Gordon, tx. 21 November

Cannizzo, J. 2000. 'Monumental Images: Scott and the Creation of Scotland', in J. M. Fladmark, ed., *Heritage and Museums: Shaping National Identity*, Shaftesbury: Donhead

Cardell, K. and Cumming, C. 1999. 'Gaelic Voices from Australia', *Scottish Gaelic Studies*, 19: 21–58

Carey, J., ed., 1999. *The Faber Book of Utopias*, London: Faber and Faber

Carter, P. 1987. *The Road to Botany Bay: An Essay in Spatial History*, London: Faber and Faber

—— 1992. *Living in a New Country: History, Travelling and Language*, London: Faber and Faber

Casey, E. S. 1993. *Getting Back into Place: Toward a Renewed Understanding of the Place-World*, Bloomington, Ind.: Indiana University Press

—— 1996. 'How to Get from Space to Place in a Fairly Short Stretch of Time: Phenomenological Prolegomena', in S. Feld and K. H. Basso, eds, *Senses of Place*, Sante Fe: School of American Research Press

Chaliand, G. and Rageau, J.-P. 1997. *The Penguin Atlas of Diasporas*, New York: Penguin (first published 1991)

Chambers, I. 1994. *Migrancy, Culture, Identity*, London: Routledge

Chapman, M. 1992. *The Celts: The Construction of a Myth*, Basingstoke: Macmillan

Chapman, R. W., ed., 1970. *Johnson's Journey to the Western Islands of Scotland and Boswell's Journal of a Tour to the Hebrides with Samuel Johnson*, London: Oxford University Press

Christian, P. 1999. *Web Publishing for Genealogy*, London: Hawgood

Clark, I. D. 1990. *Aboriginal Languages and Clans: An Historical Atlas of Western and Central Victoria, 1800–1900*, Victoria: Monash Publications in Geography No. 37

Clark, M. 1997. *Speaking Out of Turn: Lectures and Speeches, 1940–1991*, Carlton South, Victoria: Melbourne University Press

Clarke, R. ('Rory Mor') 1994. 'In Search of the Black Officer', *Creag Dhubh*, 51: 30–5

Clifford, J. 1997. *Routes: Travel and Translation in the Late Twentieth Century*, Cambridge, MA: Harvard University Press

Clifford, J. and Marcus, G. E., eds, 1986. *Writing Culture: The Poetics and Politics of Ethnography*, Berkeley, CA: University of California Press

Cohen, E. 1992. 'Pilgrimage and Tourism: Convergence and Divergence', in A. Morinis, ed., *Sacred Journeys: The Anthropology of Pilgrimage*, Westport, CT: Greenwood Press

Cohen, R. 1997. *Global Diasporas: An Introduction*, London: UCL Press

Collis, J. 1996. 'Celts and Politics', in P. Graves-Brown, S. Jones and C. Gamble, eds, *Cultural Identity and Archaeology: The Construction of European Communities*, London: Routledge

Connerton, P. 1989. *How Societies Remember*, Cambridge: Cambridge University Press

Conroy, S. 1996. *The Name's the Same: Scottish Placenames Worldwide*, Glendaruel: Argyll

Cornell, S. 1988. *The Return of the Native: American Indian Political Resurgence*, New York: Oxford University Press

Cory, K. B. 1996. *Tracing Your Scottish Ancestry*, Edinburgh: Polygon (first published 1990)

Cousineau, P. 1999. *The Art of Pilgrimage: The Seeker's Guide to Making Travel Sacred*, Shaftesbury: Element

Craig, D. 1990. *On the Crofters' Trail: In Search of the Clearance Highlanders*, London: Jonathan Cape

Crawford, E. M. 1997. *The Hungry Stream: Essays on Emigration and Famine*, Omagh: Centre for Emigration Studies, Ulster-American Folk Park

Cromarty, S. 1998. Editorial, *SCOTS*, 1: 4–5

—— 2001. Editorial, *SCOTS*, 11: 4–5

Crumley, J. 1997. 'Be of This Land', script for audio-visual presentation

Cumming, C. 1996. 'Emigrant Scots and Indigenous Australians – "Comunn na Feinne" Geelong, Australia and the Aboriginies', paper presented at the 'Scots and Aboriginal Cultures' conference, University of Guelph

Curthoys, A. 1999. 'Expulsion, Exodus and Exile in White Australian Historical Mythology', *Journal of Australian Studies*, 61: 1–18

Davis, T., Naidoo, U., Prestney, S. and Wilson, P., 1998. Editors' Note, *Melbourne Journal of Politics*, 25: vii–x

Devine, T. M. 1988. *The Great Highland Famine: Hunger, Emigration and the Scottish Highlands in the Nineteenth Century*, Edinburgh: John Donald

—— ed., 1992. *Scottish Emigration and Scottish Society*, Edinburgh: John Donald

—— 1999. *The Scottish Nation, 1700–2000*, London: Allen Lane

—— 2003. *Scotland's Empire, 1600–1815*, London: Allen Lane

Dodgshon, R. A. 1989. 'Pretense of Blude and Place of Thair Duelling: The Nature of Scottish Clans, 1500–1745', in R. A. Houston and I. D. Whyte, eds, *Scottish Society, 1500–1800*, Cambridge: Cambridge University Press

Dominy, M. D. 1995. 'White Settler Assertions of Native Status', *American Ethnologist*, 22 (2): 358–74

Donath, J. 1999. 'Identity and Deception in the Virtual Community', in P. Kollock and M. A. Smith, eds, *Communities in Cyberspace*, London: Routledge

Donnachie, I. 1992. 'The Enterprising Scot', in I. Donnachie and C. Whatley, eds, *The Manufacture of Scottish History*, Edinburgh: Polygon

Dumont, F. 1993. 'The Region of the Heart', in M. Richardson, ed., *The Dedalus Book of Surrealism: The Identity of Things*, Sawtry: Dedalus (first published 1939)

Dunn, C. W. 1953. *Highland Settler: A Portrait of the Scottish Gael in Cape Breton and Eastern Nova Scotia*, Toronto: University of Toronto Press

Dunn, D., ed., 1992. *The Faber Book of Twentieth-Century Scottish Poetry*, London: Faber and Faber

Durkheim, E. 1995. *The Elementary Forms of Religious Life*, New York: The Free Press (first published 1912)

Durie, A. 1992. 'Tourism and Commercial Photography in Victorian Scotland: The Rise and Fall of G. W. Wilson & Co., 1853–1908', *Northern Studies*, 12: 84–104

Eade, J. and Sallnow, M., eds, 1991. *Contesting the Sacred: The Anthropology of Christian Pilgramage*, London: Routledge

Ebron, P. A. 2002. *Performing Africa*, Princeton, NJ: Princeton University Press

Edensor, T. 1997. 'Reading Braveheart: Representing and Contesting Scottish Identity', *Scottish Affairs*, 21: 135–58

Eliade, M. 1958. *Patterns in Comparative Religion*, London: Sheed and Ward

Elsaesser, T. 1996. 'Subject Positions, Speaking Positions', in V. Sobchack, ed., *The Persistence of History: Cinema, Television and the Modern Event*, New York: Routledge

Fernback, J. 1999. 'There is a There There: Notes Toward a Definition of Cybercommunity', in S. G. Jones, ed., *Doing Internet Research: Critical Issues and Methods for Exploring the Net*, Thousand Oaks, CA: Sage

Fladmark, J. M., ed., 2000. *Heritage and Museums: Shaping National Identity*, Shaftesbury: Donhead

Fortier, A.-M. 1999. 'Re-Membering Places and the Performance of Belonging(s)', in V. Bell, ed., *Performativity and Belonging*, London: Sage

Foster, R. Hosking, R. and Nettelbeck, A. 2001. *Fatal Collisions: The South Australian Frontier and the Violence of Memory*, Kent Town, South Australia: Wakefield Press

Foucault, M. 1988. 'Technologies of the Self', in L. H. Martin, H. Gutman and P. H. Hutton, eds, *Technologies of the Self: A Seminar with Michel Foucault*, London: Tavistock

Francaviglia, R. 2000. 'Selling Heritage Landscapes', in A. R. Alanen and R. Z. Melnick, eds, *Preserving Cultural Landscapes in America*, Baltimore: Johns Hopkins University Press

Fraser-Mackintosh, C. 1877. 'The Depopulation of Aberarder in Badenoch', *Celtic Magazine*, 11: 418–25

Frey, N. L. 1998. *Pilgrim Stories: On and Off the Road to Santiago*, Berkeley, CA: University of California Press

Fry, M. 2002. *The Scottish Empire*. Edinburgh: Birlinn

—— 2004. *How the Scots made America*. New York: St Martins Press

Gabaldon, D. 1991. *Outlander*, New York: Delacorte Press

Gass, W. H. 1982. 'Monumentality/mentality', *Oppositions*, 25: 126–44

Geertz, C. 1988. *Works and Lives: The Anthropologist as Author*, Cambridge: Polity

—— 1993. *The Interpretation of Cultures*, London: Fontana (first published 1973)

Gerber, P. 1997. *Stone of Destiny*, Edinburgh: Canongate
Gibson, R. 1996a. *Highland Clearances Trail*, Evanton: Highland Heritage Books
—— 1996b. *Toppling the Duke: Outrage on Ben Bhraggie?*, Evanton: Highland Heritage Books
Giddens, A. 1991. *Modernity and Self-Identity: Self and Society in the Late Modern Age*, Cambridge: Polity
Goffman, E. 1959. *The Presentation of Self in Everyday Life*, New York: Doubleday Anchor
Gold, J. R. and Gold, M. M. 1995. *Imagining Scotland: Tradition, Representation and Promotion in Scottish Tourism since 1750*, Aldershot: Scolar Press
Gordon, A. 1999. 'Orkney and Manitoba sign friendship treaty', *The Orcadian*, 10 June
Gordon, S. 1995. *Highways and Byways in the Central Highlands*, Edinburgh: Birlinn (first published 1935)
Gouriévidis, L. 1993. 'The Image of the Highland Clearances, *c.*1880–1990', unpublished doctoral thesis, University of St Andrews
Graburn, N. H. H. 1989. 'Tourism: The Sacred Journey', in V. L. Smith, ed., *Hosts and Guests: The Anthropology of Tourism*, Philadelphia, PA: University of Pennsylvania Press
Griggs, R. 2000. 'Scotland in a New Light: Towards a Collective National Image', in J. M. Fladmark, ed., *Heritage and Museums: Shaping National Identity*, Shaftesbury: Donhead
Grimble, I. 1962. *The Trial of Patrick Sellar*, London: Routledge Kegan Paul
—— 1968. Introduction, in D. C. Thomson and I. Grimble, eds, *The Future of the Highlands*, London: Routledge and Kegan Paul
—— 1996. Introduction, in D. MacLeod, *Gloomy Memories: The Highland Clearances of Strathnaver*, Bettyhill: Strathnaver Museum
Gunn, N. M. 1954. *The Other Landscape*, London: Faber and Faber
—— 1972. Foreword, in D. Omand, ed., *The Caithness Book*, Inverness: Highland Printers
—— 1976. *Young Art and Old Hector*, London: Souvenir (first published 1942)
—— 1987. 'Caithness and Sutherland', in A. McCleery, ed., *Landscape and Light: Essays by Neil M. Gunn*, Aberdeen: Aberdeen University Press (first published in 1935)
—— 1991. *Highland River*, Edinburgh: Canongate (first published 1937)
—— 1993. *The Atom of Delight*, Edinburgh: Polygon (first published 1956)
Hague, E. 2002. 'The Scottish Diaspora: Tartan Day and the Appropriation of Scottish Identities in the United States', in D. C. Harvey, R. Jones, N. McInroy and C. Milligan, eds, *Celtic Geographies: Old Culture, New Times*, London: Routledge
Halbwachs, M. 1941. *La Topographie légendaire des évangiles en Terre Sainte*, Paris: Dumont
Haley, A. 1991. *Roots*, London: Vintage (first published 1976)
Hammond, C., ed., 1991. *Creation Spirituality and the Dreamtime*, Newton, New South Wales: Millennium Books
Harper, M. 2003. *Adventurers and Exiles: The Great Scottish Exodus*, London: Profile Books
Harper, M., ed., 2005. *Emigrant Homecomings: The Return Movement of Emigrants, 1600–2000*, Manchester: Manchester University Press
Harper, M. and Vance, M. E., eds, 1999. *Myth, Migration and the Making of Memory: Scotia and Nova Scotia, c.1700–1990*, Halifax, Nova Scotia: Fernwood and Edinburgh: John Donald
Hart, F. R. 1978. *The Scottish Novel: A Critical Survey*, London: Murray
Harvey, D. C., Jones, R., McInroy, N. and Milligan, C., eds, 2002. *Celtic Geographies: Old Cultures, New Times*, London: Routledge
Harvie, C. 1989. 'Scott and the Image of Scotland', in R. Samuel, ed., *Patriotism: The Making and Unmaking of British National Identity: Volume 2: Minorities and Outsiders*, London: Routledge
Havemann, P., ed., 1999. *Indigenous Peoples' Rights in Australia, Canada and New Zealand*, Auckland: Oxford University Press

Heelas, P. 1996. *The New Age Movement: The Celebration of the Self and the Sacralization of Modernity*, Oxford: Blackwell

Henderson, L. and Cowan, E. J. 2001. *Scottish Fairy Belief: A History*, East Linton: Tuckwell

Herman, A. 2002. *How the Scots Invented the Modern World*. New York: Three Rivers Press

Hewitson, J. 1993. *Tam Blake and Co.: The Story of the Scots in America*, Edinburgh: Canongate

Hine, C. 2000. *Virtual Ethnography*, London: Sage

Holton, G. S. and Winch, J. 1997. *My Ain Folk: An Easy Guide to Scottish Family History*, East Linton: Tuckwell

Holy, L. 1996. *Anthropological Perspectives on Kinship*, London: Pluto

Honderich, T., ed., 1995. *The Oxford Companion to Philosophy*, Oxford: Oxford University Press

Hunter, J. 1994. *A Dance Called America: The Scottish Highlands, the United States and Canada*, Edinburgh: Mainstream

—— 1995. *On the Other Side of Sorrow: Nature and People in the Scottish Highlands*, Edinburgh: Mainstream

—— 1996. *Glencoe and the Indians*, Edinburgh: Mainstream

—— 2000. *The Making of the Crofting Community*, Edinburgh: John Donald (first published 1976)

Hutton, P. H. 1993. *History as a Art of Memory*, Hanover, NH: University Press of New England

Irvine, S. 1996. *Your Scottish Ancestry: A Guide for North Americans*, Ancestry Publishing [n.p.]

Ivakhiv, A. J. 2001. *Claiming Sacred Ground: Pilgrims and Politics at Glastonbury and Sedona*, Bloomington, IN: Indiana University Press

James, A. 1995. *Scottish Roots: A Step-by-Step Guide for Ancestor Hunters*, Edinburgh: Saltire Society (first published 1981)

Jedrej, C. and Nuttall, M. 1996. *White Settlers: The Impact of Rural Repopulation in Scotland*, Luxembourg: Harwood Academic

Jones, S. and Graves-Brown, P. 1996. 'Archaeology and Cultural Identity in Europe', in P. Graves-Brown, S. Jones and C. Gamble, eds, *Cultural Identity and Archaeology: The Construction of European Communities*, London: Routledge

Kapferer, B. 1988. *Legends of People, Myths of State: Violence, Intolerance, and Political Culture in Sri Lanka and Australia*, Washington, DC: Smithsonian Institution Press

Kennedy, M. 1999. 'Lochaber No More: A Critical Examination of Highland Emigration Mythology', in M. Harper and M. E. Vance, eds, *Myth, Migration and the Making of Memory: Scotia and Nova Scotia, c.1700–1990*, Halifax, Nova Scotia: Fernwood and Edinburgh: John Donald

Kerby, A. P. 1991. *Narrative and the Self*, Bloomington, IN: Indiana University Press

King, M. 1985. *Being Pakeha: An Encounter with New Zealand and Maori Renaissance*, London: Hodder and Stoughton

Kollock, P. and Smith, M. A. 1999. Introduction, in M. A. Smith and P. Kollock, eds, *Communities in Cyberspace*, London: Routledge

LaCapra, D. 2001. *Writing History, Writing Trauma*, Baltimore, MD: Johns Hopkins University Press

Lakoff, G. and Johnson, M. 1980. *Metaphors We Live By*, Chicago: University of Chicago Press

Lambek, M. 1996. 'The Past Imperfect: Remembering as Moral Practice', in P. Antze and M. Lambek, eds, *Tense Past: Cultural Essays in Trauma and Memory*, New York: Routledge

Lambek, M. and Antze, P. 1996. Introduction, in P. Antze and M. Lambek, eds, *Tense Past: Cultural Essays in Trauma and Memory*, New York: Routledge

Lane, L. N. 1988. 'The Wathaurong, Geelong's Earliest Inhabitants', unpublished address to the Geelong Historical Society

Lasch, C. 1991. *The Culture of Narcissism: American Life in an Age of Diminishing Expectations*, New York: Norton (first published 1979)

Laurence, M. 1989. *The Diviners*, London: Virago (first published 1974)

Lelong, O. and Wood, J. 2000. 'A Township through Time: Excavation and Survey at the Deserted Settlement of Easter Raitts, Badenoch, 1995–99', in J. A. Atkinson, I. Banks and G. MacGregor, eds, *Townships to Farmsteads: Rural Settlement Studies in Scotland, England and Wales*, Oxford: BAR British series 293

Lévi-Strauss, C. 1964. *Totemism*, London: Merlin Press (first published 1962)

—— 1966. *The Savage Mind*, London: Weidenfeld and Nicolson (first published 1962)

—— 1968. *Structural Anthropology 1*, London: Penguin (first published 1958)

Lifton, R. J. 1993. *The Protean Self: Human Resilience in an Age of Fragmentation*, New York: Basic Books

Linklater, M. 1999. 'Scottish history is being vandalised', *Scotland on Sunday*, 24 October

Logan, J. 1867. *The Scottish Gael, or, Celtic Manners as Preserved Among the Highlanders*, Inverness: Mackenzie (first published 1831)

Longmuir, J. 1860. *Speyside: Its Picturesque Scenery and Antiquities*, Aberdeen: Smith

Lorimer, H. 2002. 'Sites of Authenticity: Scotland's New Parliament and Official Representations of the Nation', in D. C. Harvey, R. Jones, N. McInroy and C. Milligan, eds, *Celtic Geographies: Old Culture, New Times*, London: Routledge

Lovell, N., ed., 1998. *Locality and Belonging*, London: Routledge

Lowenthal, D. 1985. *The Past is a Foreign Country*, Cambridge: Cambridge University Press

—— 1997. 'European Landscape Transformations: The Rural Residue', in P. Groth and T. W. Bressi, eds, *Understanding Ordinary Landscapes*, New Haven, CT: Yale University Press

—— 1998. *The Heritage Crusade and the Spoils of History*, Cambridge: Cambridge University Press

Lynch, M. 1992. *Scotland: A New History*, London: Pimlico

McAdams, D. P. 1997. 'The Case for Unity in the (Post)Modern Self', in R. D. Ashmore and L. Jussim, eds, *Self and Identity: Fundamental Issues*, Oxford: Oxford University Press

McArthur, C., ed., 1982. *Scotch Reels: Scotland in Cinema and Television*, London: British Film Institute

McArthur, C. 1994. 'Culloden: A Pre-Emptive Strike', *Scottish Affairs*, 9: 97–126

Macaskill, B. 2000. 'Repellent postures', Letters to the Editor, *The Herald*, 12 May

Macbain, A. 1890. 'Badenoch: Its History, Clans, and Place Names', *Transactions of the Gaelic Society of Inverness*, 16: 148–97

MacCannell, D. 1976. *The Tourist: A New Theory of the Leisure Class*, London: Macmillan

McCrone, D., Morris, A. and Kiely, R. 1995. *Scotland – the Brand: The Making of Scottish Heritage*, Edinburgh: Edinburgh University Press

McDermid, F. 2000. 'Like a skeleton in a cupboard', Letters to the Editor, *The Herald*, 18 May

Macdonald, S. 1997a. 'A People's Story: Heritage, Identity and Authority', in C. Rojek and J. Urry, eds, *Touring Cultures: Transformations of Travel and Theory*, London: Routledge

—— 1997b. *Reimagining Culture: Histories, Identities and the Gaelic Renaissance*, Oxford: Berg

MacDonell, M. 1982. *The Emigrant Experience: Songs of Highland Emigrants in North America*, Toronto: University of Toronto Press

MacEowen, F. 2002. *The Mist-Filled Path: Celtic Wisdom for Exiles, Wanderers, and Seekers*, Novato, CA: New World Library

MacIntyre, A. 1981. *After Virtue: A Study in Moral Theory*, London: Duckworth

Mackenzie, A. 1883. *The History of the Highland Clearances*, Inverness: Mackenzie

MacLennan, M. 1979. *A Pronouncing and Etymological Dictionary of the Gaelic Language*, Stornoway, Lewis: Acair and Edinburgh: Mercat (first published 1925)

MacLeod, D. 2000. 'Trying to heal this Scottish open sore', Letters to the Editor, *The Herald*, 19 May

Macmillan, D. 1990. *Scottish Art, 1460–1990*, Edinburgh: Mainstream

Macpherson, A. 1893. *Glimpses of Church and Social Life in the Highlands in Olden Times*, Edinburgh: William Blackwood

Macpherson, A. G. 1966. 'An Old Highland Genealogy and the Evolution of a Scottish Clan', *Scottish Studies*, 10: 1–42

——— 1993. *The Posterity of the Three Brethren: A Short History of the Clan Macpherson*, Newtonmore, Inverness-shire: Clan Macpherson Association (first published 1966)

——— 2000. 'More World-Wide Macphersons: The Surname as Placename', *Creag Dhubh*, 52: 25–6

Macpherson, E. 1996. 'Address by Euan Macpherson of Glentruim to the Clan on Sunday, 6 August 1995', *Creag Dhubh*, 48: 7–8

Macpherson, R. W. [n.d.] 'The Macphersons and Macknoes in Western Australia', unpublished family history

Malinowski, B. 1953. *Argonauts of the Western Pacific: An Account of Native Enterprise and Adventure in the Archipelagoes of Melanesian New Guinea*, New York: Dutton (first published 1923)

Malkki, L. 1992. 'National Geographic: The Rooting of Peoples and the Territorialization of National Identity among Scholars and Refugees', *Cultural Anthropology* 7 (1): 24–44

Marcus, G. E. 1995. 'Ethnography in/of the World System: The Emergence of Multi-Sited Ethnography', *Annual Review of Anthropology*, 24: 95–117

Marx, K. 1970. *Capital: A Critique of Political Economy, Volume 1*, London: Lawrence & Wishart (first published 1887)

Matheson, A. 1993. *The British Looking Glass*, Dunbeath: Laidhay Preservation Trust (first published 1870)

Meek, D. E. 1995. *Tuath Is Tighearna/Tenants and Landlords: An Anthology of Gaelic Poetry of Social and Political Protest from the Clearances to the Land Agitation, 1800–1890*, Edinburgh: Scottish Academic Press

Miller, D., ed., 2001. *Home Possessions: Material Culture Behind Closed Doors*, Oxford: Berg

Miller, D. and Slater, D. 2000. *The Internet: An Ethnographic Approach*, Oxford: Berg

Miller, H. 1995. 'The Presentation of the Self in Electronic Life: Goffman on the Internet', paper presented at the 'Embodied Knowledge and Virtual Space' conference, Goldsmiths College, University of London

——— 1999. 'The Hypertext Home: Images and Metaphors of Home on World Wide Web Homepages', paper presented at the Design History Society 'Home and Away' conference, Nottingham Trent University; http://ess.ntu.ac.uk/miller/cyberpsych/homeweb.htm

Miller, K. A. 1985. *Emigrants and Exiles: Ireland and the Irish Exodus to North America*, New York: Oxford University Press

Mitchell, J. 1982. *Megalithomania: Artists, Antiquarians and Archaeologists at the Old Stone Monuments*, London: Thames & Hudson

Mitchison, R. 1981. 'The Highland Clearances', *Scottish Economic and Social History*, 1 (1): 4–24

Mitra, A. 1997. 'Virtual Commonality: Looking for India on the Internet', in S. G. Jones, ed., *Virtual Culture: Identity and Communication in Cybersociety*, Thousand Oaks, CA: Sage

Moody, D. 1988. *Scottish Family History*, London: Batsford

Morinis, A. 1992. Introduction, in A. Morinis, ed., *Sacred Journeys: The Anthropology of Pilgrimage*, Westport, CT: Greenwood Press

Morley, D. and Robins, K. 1995. *Spaces of Identity: Global Media, Electronic Landscapes and Cultural Boundaries*, London: Routledge

Murdoch, S. 1999. 'The Search for Northern Allies: Stuart and Cromwellian Propagandists and Protagonists in Scandinavia, 1649–60', in B. Taithe and T. Thornton, eds, *Propaganda: Political Rhetoric and Identity, 1300–2000*, Stroud: Sutton

Nagel, J. 1995. 'American Indian Ethnic Renewal: Politics and the Resurgence of Identity', *American Sociological Review*, 60 (6): 947–65

Nash, C. 2002. 'Genealogical Identities', *Environment and Planning D: Society and Space*, 20 (1): 27–52

—— 2004. 'Genetic Kinship', *Cultural Studies*, 18 (1): 1–33

Newton, M. 2000. *A Handbook of the Scottish Gaelic World*, Dublin: Four Courts Press

—— 2001. *We're Indians Sure Enough: The Legacy of the Scottish Highlanders in the United States*, Saorsa Media [n.p.]

Nicholson, C. 1992. *Poem, Purpose and Place: Shaping Identity in Contemporary Scottish Verse*, Edinburgh: Polygon

Ní Suaird, D. 1999. 'Jacobite Rehetoric and Terminology in the Political Poems of the Fernaig MS (1688–1693)', *Scottish Gaelic Studies*, xix: 93–140

Nora, P. 1989. 'Between Memory and History: Les Lieux de Mémoire', *Representations*, 26: 7–25

Novick, P. 1999. *The Holocaust and Collective Memory: The American Experience*, London: Bloomsbury

O'Donohue, J. 1998. *Eternal Echoes: Exploring Our Hunger to Belong*, London: Bantam

O'Farrell, P. 1976. 'Emigrant Attitudes and Behaviour as a Source for Irish History', *Historical Studies*, 10: 109–31

Olwig, K. F. and Hastrup, K., eds, 1997. *Siting Culture: The Shifting Anthropological Object*, London: Routledge

Ortner, S. 1973. 'On Key Symbols', *American Anthropologist*, 75 (6): 1338–46

Otto, R. 1980. *The Idea of the Holy*, London: Oxford University Press (first published 1923)

Pálsson, H. and Edwards, P., trans., 1981. *Orkneyinga Saga: The History of the Earls of Orkney*, London: Penguin

Paterson, L., ed., 1998. *Understanding Constitutional Change: Special Issue of Scottish Affairs*, Edinburgh: Unit for the Study of Government in Scotland

Petrie, D. 2000. *Screening Scotland*, London: British Film Institute

Pittock, M. G. H. 1991. *The Invention of Scotland: The Stuart Myth and the Scottish Identity, 1638 to the Present*, London: Routledge

Prebble, J. 1961. *Culloden*, London: Martin Secker & Warburg

—— 1968. *Glencoe*, London: Penguin (first published 1966)

—— 1969. *The Highland Clearances*, London: Penguin (first published 1963)

—— 1988. *The King's Jaunt: George IV in Scotland*, London: Collins

Prentis, M. D. 1987. *The Scottish in Australia*, Melbourne: AE Press

Preston, J. J. 1992. 'Spiritual Magnetism: An Organizing Principle for the Study of Pilgrimage', in A. Morinis, ed., *Sacred Journeys: The Anthropology of Pilgrimage*, Westport, CT: Greenwood Press

Pringle, T. R. 1988. 'The Privation of History: Landseer, Victoria and the Highland Myth', in D. Cosgrove and S. Daniels, eds, *The Iconography of Landscape*, Cambridge: Cambridge University Press

Rapport, N. and Dawson, A., eds, 1998, *Migrants of Identity: Perceptions of Home in a World of Movement*, Oxford: Berg

Ray, C. 2001. *Highland Heritage: Scottish Americans in the American South*, Chapel Hill: University of North Carolina Press

—— 2005. 'Bravehearts and Patriarchs: Masculinity on the Pedestal for Southern "Scots"', in C. Ray, ed., *Transatlantic Scots*, Tuscaloosa, AL: University of Alabama Press

Reader, I. and Walter, T., eds, 1993. *Pilgrimage in Popular Culture*, Basingstoke: Macmillan

Reynolds, H. 1996. *Dispossession: Black Australians and White Invaders*, St Leonards, New South Wales: Allen and Unwin

Richards, E. 1982. *A History of the Highland Clearances: Volume 2: Emigration, Protest, Reasons*, London: Croom Helm

—— 1985a. *A History of the Highland Clearances: Volume 2: Agrarian Transformation and the Evictions, 1746–1886*, London: Croom Helm

—— 1985b. 'Australia and the Scottish Connection, 1788–1914', in R. A. Cage, ed., *The Scots Abroad*, London: Croom Helm

—— 2000. *The Highland Clearances: People, Landlords and Rural Turmoil*, Edinburgh: Birlinn

Ricoeur, P. 1992. *Oneself as Another*, Chicago: Chicago University Press

Riegl, A. 1982. 'The Modern Cult of Monuments: Its Character and its Origin', *Oppositions*, 25: 21–51 (first published 1903)

Roberts, J. L. 1999. *Feuds, Forays and Rebellions: History of the Highland Clans, 1475–1625*, Edinburgh: Edinburgh University Press

Rolls, M. 1998. 'The Jungian Quest for the Aborigine Within: A Close Reading of David Tacey's *Edge of the Sacred: Transformation in Australia*', *Melbourne Journal of Politics*, 25: 171–87

Rooks, A. [n.d.] 'The Low Road', self-published family narrative

Rushdie, S. 1992. *Imaginary Homelands: Essays and Criticism, 1981–91*, London: Granta

Safran, W. 1991. 'Diasporas in Modern Societies: Myths of Homeland and Return, *Diaspora* 1 (1): 83–99

Said, E. W. 1978. *Orientalism*, London: Routledge Kegan Paul

Salmond, A. 1982. 'Theoretical Landscapes: On Cross-Cultural Conceptions of Knowledge', in D. Parkin, ed., *Semantic Anthropology*, London: Academic Books

Samuel, R. and Thompson, P., eds, 1990. *The Myths We Live By*, London: Routledge

Scarlett, M. H. 1988. *In the Glens Where I Was Young*, Moy, Inverness-shire: Siskin

Scott, W. 1985. *Waverley*, London: Penguin (first published 1814)

Scottish Executive. 2000. *A New Strategy for Scottish Tourism*, Edinburgh: Scottish Executive

Scottish Parliament. 2000. Scottish Parliament Official Report: Highland Clearances, 8 (7): Col 700–12, 27 September

Scottish Tourist Board (VisitScotland). 2002. 'Key Statistics on Overseas Visitors to Scotland' (accessed at www.scotexchange.net)

Seaton, A. V. and Hay, B. 1998. 'The Marketing of Scotland as a Tourist Destination, 1985–96', in R. MacLellan and R. Smith, eds, *Tourism in Scotland*, London: International Thomson Business Press

Shields, R., ed., 1996. *Cultures of Internet: Virtual Spaces, Real Histories, Living Bodies*, London: Sage

Shoumatoff, A. 1995. *The Mountain of Names: A History of the Human Family*, New York: Kodansha (first published 1985)

Sked, P. 1991. *Glenfinnan*, Edinburgh: National Trust for Scotland

—— 1997. *Culloden*, Edinburgh: National Trust for Scotland

Smith, A. D. 1991. *National Identity*, London: Penguin

Smith, R. 1998. 'Public Policy for Tourism in Scotland', in R. MacLellan and R. Smith, eds, *Tourism in Scotland*, London: International Thomson Business Press

Snelling, J. 1990. *The Sacred Mountain: The Complete Guide to Tibet's Mount Kailas*, London: East-West

Sontag, S. 1983. 'Against Interpretation', in *A Susan Sontag Reader*, London: Penguin (first published 1964)

Spence, D. 1984. *Narrative Truth and Historical Truth: Meaning and Interpretation in Psychoanalysis*, New York: Norton

Stafford, F. 1988. *The Sublime Savage: James Macpherson and The Poems of Ossian*, Edinburgh: Edinburgh University Press

Stanner, W. E. H. 1979. *White Man Got No Dreaming: Essays, 1938–1973*, Canberra: Australian National University Press

Stasiulis, D. and Yuval-Davis, N., eds, 1995. *Unsettling Settler Societies: Articulations of Gender, Race, Ethnicity and Class*, London: Sage

Sterne, J. 1999. 'Thinking the Internet: Cultural Studies Versus the Millennium', in S. G. Jones, ed., *Doing Internet Research: Critical Issues and Methods for Exploring the Net*, Thousand Oaks, CA: Sage

Stewart, K. C. 1996. 'An Occupied Place', in S. Feld and K. H. Basso, eds, *Senses of Place*, Santa Fé, CA: School of American Research Press

Strathern, M. 1992. *After Nature: English Kinship in the Late Twentieth Century*, Cambridge: Cambridge University Press

—— 1995. 'Nostalgia and the New Genetics', in D. Battaglia, ed., *Rhetorics of Self-Making*, Berkeley, CA: University of California Press

Sykes, B. 1999. *The Human Inheritance: Genes, Language and Evolution*, Oxford: Oxford University Press

Tacey, D. 1998. *Edge of the Sacred: Transformation in Australia*, Sydney: HarperCollins

—— 2000. *Re-Enchantment: The New Australian Spirituality*, Sydney: HarperCollins

Tagore, R. 1984. *Some Songs and Poems from Rabindranath Tagore*, London: East-West

Taylor, C. 1985. *Human Agency and Language: Philosophical Papers I*, Cambridge: Cambridge University Press

—— 1989. *Sources of the Self: The Making of the Modern Identity*, Cambridge: Cambridge University Press

Thompson, F. G. 1974. *The Highlands and Islands*, London: Hale

Thomson, D. 1989. *An Introduction to Gaelic Poetry*, Edinburgh: Edinburgh University Press (first published 1974)

Tilley, C. 1994. *A Phenomenology of Landscape: Places, Paths and Monuments*, Oxford: Berg

—— 1999. *Metaphor and Material Culture*, Oxford: Blackwell

Tölölyan, K. 1991. Preface, *Diaspora* 1 (1): 3–7

—— 1996. 'Rethinking Diaspora(s): Stateless Power in the Transnational Moment', *Diaspora* 5 (1): 3–36

Tonkin, E. 1992. *Narrating Our Pasts: The Social Construction of Oral History*, Cambridge: Cambridge University Press

Tranter, N. 1975. *The Wallace*, London: Coronet

—— 1985. *The Bruce Trilogy*, Sevenoaks, Kent: Coronet (first published 1969–71)

Trevor-Roper, H. 1983. 'The Invention of Tradition: The Highland Tradition of Scotland', in E. Hobsbawm and T. Ranger, eds, *The Invention of Tradition*, Cambridge: Cambridge University Press

Turner, V. 1974. *Dramas, Fields, and Metaphors: Symbolic Action in Human Society*, Ithaca, NY: Cornell University Press

—— 1991. *The Forest of Symbols: Aspects of Ndembu Ritual*, Ithaca: Cornell University Press (first published 1969)

Turner, V. and Turner, E. L. B. 1978. *Image and Pilgrimage in Christian Culture: Anthropological Perspectives*, New York: Columbia University Press

Tyler, S. A. 1986. 'Post-Modern Ethnography: From Document of the Occult to Occult Document', in J. Clifford and G. E. Marcus, eds, *Writing Culture: The Poetics and Politics of Ethnography*, Berkeley, CA: University of California Press

Urry, J. 1990. *The Tourist Gaze*, London: Sage

—— 1995. *Consuming Places*, London: Routledge

Warren, P. 1999. 'Can't see the net for the trees – genealogy second only to sex', *Scotland on Sunday*, 28 November

Waters, M. C. 1990. *Ethnic Options: Choosing Identities in America*, Berkeley, CA: University of California Press

Watson, D. 1984. *Caledonia Australis: Scottish Highlanders on the Frontier of Australia*, Sydney: Collins

Watson, W. J. 1916. *The Celtic Placenames of Scotland*, Edinburgh: Royal Celtic Society

Weiner, A. B. 1992. *Inalienable Possessions: The Paradox of Keeping-While-Giving*, Berkeley, CA: University of California Press

White, H. 1981. 'The Value of Narrativity in the Representation of Reality', in W. J. T. Mitchell, ed., *On Narrative*, Chicago: Chicago University Press

White, K. 1999. 'The Nomadic Intellect', paper presented at the 'Scotland Abroad' conference, University of Glasgow

Whyte, D. 2001. *Crossing the Unknown Sea: Work as a Pilgrimage of Identity*, New York: Riverhead Books

Wilson, R. S. 1999. *Publishing Your Family History on the Internet*, Wrightwood, CA: Compuology

Winter, J. 1995. *Sites of Memory, Sites of Mourning: The Great War in European Cultural History*, Cambridge: Cambridge University Press

Withers, C. W. J. 1988. *Gaelic Scotland: The Transformation of a Culture Region*, London: Routledge

—— 1992. 'The Historical Creation of the Scottish Highlands', in I. Donnachie and C. Whatley, eds, *The Manufacture of Scottish History*, Edinburgh: Polygon

—— 1994. 'Picturing Highland Landscapes: George Washington Wilson and the Photography of the Scottish Highlands', *Landscape Research*, 19 (2): 68–79

Womack, P. 1989. *Improvement and Romance: Constructing the Myth of the Highlands*, Basingstoke: Macmillan

Wood, P. [n.d.] *Some Geelong Scots*, Geelong, Victoria: Geelong Historical Society

Wyman, M. 1993. *Round Trip to America: The Immigrants Return to Europe, 1880–1930*, Ithaca, NY: Cornell University Press

Young, J. E. 1993. *The Texture of Memory: Holocaust Memorials and Meaning*, New Haven, CT: Yale University Press

Zukin, S. 1991. *Landscapes of Power: From Detroit to Disney World*, Berkeley, CA: University of California Press

Index

Printed in the USA/Agawam, MA
July 17, 2014

593133.007